COMPANY
ACCOUNTS

COMPANY ACCOUNTS

ANALYSIS, INTERPRETATION AND UNDERSTANDING

Fourth Edition

Maurice Pendlebury and Roger Groves

INTERNATIONAL THOMSON BUSINESS PRESS
I(T)P® An International Thomson Publishing Company

London • Bonn • Boston • Johannesburg • Madrid • Melbourne • Mexico City • New York • Paris
Singapore • Tokyo • Toronto • Albany, NY • Belmont, CA • Cincinnati, OH • Detroit, MI

Company Accounts

Copyright © 1999 Maurice Pendlebury and Roger Groves

 A division of International Thomson Publishing Inc.
The ITP logo is a trademark under licence

British Library Cataloguing-in-Publication Data
A catalogue record for this book is available from the British Library

First published 1994 by Routledge
Simultaneously published in the USA and Canada by Routledge
Reprinted 1994
Reprinted by International Thomson Business Press 1996 and 1997
This edition 1999 by International Thomson Business Press

Typeset by MHL Typesetting Limited, Coventry
Printed in the UK by The Alden Press, Osney Mead, Oxford

ISBN 1-86152-262-2

International Thomson Business Press
Berkshire House
168–173 High Holborn
London WC1V 7AA
UK

http://www.itbp.com

Contents

Preface

This book provides a thorough and analytical discussion of the nature and format of published company annual reports and accounts and a full introduction to the analysis and interpretation of financial statements. It takes notice of the effects and impacts of existing legislation and regulations and all published accounting and financial reporting standards, thereby providing a relevant and up-to-date guide to this important area.

We have designed the book to be most useful for students on MBA or similar advanced-level courses in management and also to undergraduate students specializing in management and business studies who require the ability to comprehend and interpret company financial statements. In addition the book should prove extremely useful to anyone, whether they be investors, lenders, creditors or managers, who require a clear understanding of the information contained in the annual report of a company and of the techniques needed to analyse the information and assess the underlying strengths, weaknesses and potential of the company.

In Part One, we provide a systematic description of the nature and role of the company annual reports and accounts and a detailed discussion of the impact of British legislation and regulation and of professional practices and recommendations. In Part Two, we provide a detailed examination of the principal and subsidiary financial statements of a leading British company, and an explanation of how the information contained in these statements, together with other publicly available data, can be used to provide a structured approach to the interpretation and analysis of that company's performance. In addition, the final chapter of Part Two provides a discussion of the major research findings and practical applications concerning the use of ratio analysis in assessing the performance and financial position of a company. This chapter will be more particularly appropriate for MBA and other management students. The appendices include the complete text of the company's financial statements, together with a glossary of accounting terms and a glossary of ratios.

We are grateful to the directors of The BOC Group plc for permission to reproduce an extensive extract from the company's annual report for the year ended 30 September 1997. It is worth pointing out that The BOC Group and its directors have consistently been at the forefront of progress in information provision and disclosure. The authors of this book are particularly pleased to be able to acknowledge here the very marked contribution that the company and its executives have made to financial reporting in the UK.

As teachers and researchers, we are deeply appreciative of the considerable assistance given by successive generations of students who have permitted us to try out our ideas and refine our teaching practices with their cooperation. Our colleagues at the Cardiff Business School have demonstrated continued support and interest, and we are especially grateful to Julie Roberts for her unfailing goodwill and dedication in the task of turning a number of drafts into a cohesive finished typescript.

Maurice Pendlebury
Roger Groves

1 The purpose, regulation and format of company reports

Many people are affected by and are properly interested in the activities and influences of the modern company: investors (whether equity or preference shareholders), creditors and lenders (whether debenture or mortgage holders, trade suppliers or bank officials), employees and their representatives, government officials and administrators (whether tax collectors or statisticians) and members of the local, regional and national communities within which the corporation operates. Each of these parties has a clear right, in law or otherwise, to have reasonable access to certain levels of information about the company's activities and prospects. This chapter sets the scene by discussing the accountability and stewardship aspects of a company's reporting practices and by outlining some of the legal and professional background for those practices. The considerable increase of legislative demands upon limited companies has led to a widening of the range of information that a company must provide. The even greater increase in the ethical and professional requirements imposed by accountants, stock market administrators and others, and more recently the significant amount of media attention given to the unexpected failure of some major companies, has brought about a burgeoning succession of standards and pronouncements with which a company is obliged to comply, and these will be examined in Part One.

Types of company

Although much business activity in the UK is carried out by sole traders or partnerships, the most important form of business entity is undoubtedly the limited liability company. Limited liability companies have a legal status quite separate and distinct from that of their owners, and the liability of owners is limited to the amount of money they have invested in a company. The ownership of a company is divided into shares of equal value, and every company must have at least two shareholders, but there is no upper limit and some companies have many thousands of shareholders. Companies with such large numbers of shareholders would almost certainly be *public* limited companies and would almost certainly be *quoted*. A public limited company is one in which shares can be owned by the general public, and since 1981 the name of such a company has been followed by the abbreviation plc (public limited company). (Companies registered in Wales have the option of using ccc – cwmni cyfyngedig cyhoeddus.) A 'quoted' or 'listed' company is one whose shares can be bought and sold on a stock exchange. The BOC Group plc, for example, is both a public and a quoted company.

Only public companies can have a stock market quotation, but not all of them choose to do so. There are over 11,000 public companies in existence but less than 3,000 of these are quoted. A company that is not public is known as a private company and is not allowed to sell its shares to the public. The vast majority of limited companies are private companies, with almost 1,100,000 currently in existence, and yet it is the relatively few public companies that contribute most to the economic activity and employment opportunities of the country. The shares in private companies tend to be traded infrequently and are usually held by only a small number of shareholders. Shareholders in private companies also tend to be much more closely involved with company management than is typically the case with a public company. It is in fact the separation of the ownership of a public company (which rests solely with its shareholders) from its day-to-day control (which rests largely with its full-time directors and managers) which underpins the requirement for proper accountability and stewardship, and the need for a framework of regulation and supervision of limited companies generally.

Accountability and stewardship

The separation of ownership from the management of a company, combined with substantial protection afforded to company directors and managers by the concept of limited liability, has meant that those responsible for the financial and trading activities of a company are required to report conscientiously and honestly on the affairs of the company and its current and prospective status.

Shareholders assign to a board of directors the duties and obligations of running their company from year to year, while retaining the legal duties and obligations of owning shares in a company. Some directors act in a part-time or non-executive capacity, which means that in effect the affairs of the company will often be under the routine control of a handful of executive directors. Executives must report on their stewardship of what may be very considerable assets and on their management of very substantial operations.

Without delving too deeply into company law, the legal control and ownership of a limited company resides in the shareholders in a general meeting. For many companies, this may involve nothing more than the directors and their immediate families. For one of the 3,000 or so quoted public companies in the UK, this general meeting could potentially involve some 40,000 or 50,000 separate shareholders. In practice, company general meetings rarely attract more than 100 or 200 actual participants. Nevertheless, as the steward of an estate is responsible to its owner, so the directors of a company are responsible to its shareholders.

The whole question of the direction and control of companies was put into sharp focus following a series of spectacular company failures and in May 1992 the 'Cadbury Committee' was set up to examine the financial aspects of corporate governance. The Committee's report was published in December 1992 and contained a code of best practice which companies are expected to follow and which requires specific actions to be taken by the directors. The report points out (p. 16) that the code of best practice is based on the principles of openness, integrity and accountability. Openness is stated to be the basis for the confidence which needs to exist between business and all those who have a stake in its success. Integrity is defined as 'both straightforward dealing and completeness'. For accountability it is pointed out that

> Boards of directors are accountable to their shareholders and both have to play their part in making that accountability effective. Boards of directors need to do so through the quality of the information which they provide to shareholders, and shareholders through their willingness to exercise their responsibilities as owners.

In general terms, that accountability is served by reporting to the shareholders on the sales and other activities of the company during a stated period (usually a twelve-month fiscal or calendar year, supplemented by half-yearly reports) and on the profits (or losses) generated by those activities. Such reports will take the form of a financial statement (the trading and profit and loss account) reporting the money value of those activities and their results, and a further statement (the balance sheet) reporting the position in money terms of the company at the year end and revealing the impact of the previous year's activities on the company's assets and liabilities. The directors also provide further statements revealing the cash flows of the company (see Chapter 4) and the total recognized gains and losses of the company (see Chapter 5).

Additionally, these financial statements will be accompanied by a review by both the chairman and the chief executive of the important events of the past year and expectations for the future (see Chapter 6) and also supported in Chapter 7 by a qualitative report by the directors and an operating and financial review which amplify the statements and report certain additional information.

Where legally or institutionally necessary, the directors' reports and statements are accompanied by a report from the company's auditors (whose qualifications are prescribed by law) attesting the reasonable reliability and apparent truth and fairness of the company's financial statements. The nature and implications of the auditors' opinion are discussed more fully in Chapter 8; it has to be recognized that an 'unqualified' auditors' report (i.e. one in which no reservations are expressed on the grounds of uncertainty or disagreement) is not the equivalent of a guarantee that the company's affairs are wholly sound and its future secure.

Although the law currently says little about the statutory duties of auditors, the various professional bodies of accountancy have laid down certain minimal standards which must be complied with. All those who rely on financial statements, whether as shareholders, creditors, regulators or similarly interested parties, are closely affected by auditors' work and a proper appreciation of the nature and scope of an audit is essential to a full understanding of the purpose and characteristics of company accounts.

Regulation and supervision

The process of providing the various financial statements, supporting notes and reports is known collectively as financial reporting. If this is to have an important part to play in the accountability of companies, then some form of regulation and supervision is necessary. Although some would argue that financial reporting does not need to be regulated at all, most governments throughout the world ensure that a regulatory framework does exist. However, the regulation of financial reporting is not undertaken solely by governments; often, it is seen as a joint responsibility of government on the one hand and private sector organizations, such as the accountancy profession and the Stock Exchange, on the other. Thus in the UK there are several sources of regulation, including the following.

Parliament is responsible for the legislation which directly affects financial reporting, e.g. the Companies Act 1985.

Government not only initiates the legislative process but also exerts considerable influence through the activities of the Department of Trade and Industry (DTI).

The Financial Reporting Council develops policy on accounting standards and guidance on work programmes and issues of public concern.

The Accounting Standards Board (ASB) issues exposure drafts of proposed accounting standards as part of a process leading to Financial Reporting Standards (FRSs). (Before August 1990 standards were set by the Accounting Standards Committee (ASC) and were known as Statements of Standard Accounting Practice (SSAPs).) The ASB is assisted by an Urgent Issues Task Force (UITF) which attempts to obtain a voluntary and speedy consensus on the accounting treatment that should apply in situations where unsatisfactory or conflicting interpretations have developed.

The Financial Reporting Review Panel examines the accounts of companies which do not appear to comply with the requirement to show a true and fair view.

The Stock Exchange produces rules concerning the financial disclosure of quoted companies. The Stock Exchange expects quoted companies to comply with accounting standards and reasons for noncompliance must be disclosed.

The International Accounting Standards Committee (IASC) has the objective of working generally for the improvement and harmonization of regulations, accounting standards and procedures relating to the presentation of financial statements. The ASB supports the IASC in this and each FRS contains a section explaining how it relates to the International Accounting Standard dealing with the same topic.

Other influences include various pressure groups, organizations and individuals which have some influence on the content of Companies Acts and accounting standards, including government departments, employer organizations (such as the Confederation of British Industry (CBI)) and other professional bodies (such as the Law Society).

A major issue which emerges out of this regulatory partnership between public and private sectors concerns the precise role of each partner. There are different types of regulation and these can be classified as those concerned with:

- disclosure of information;
- the format in which information is to be disclosed;
- the measurement and valuation of information.

In the past it could be said that regulations from the public sector (e.g. Companies Acts) were concerned mainly with disclosure, whereas those from the private sector (e.g. accounting standards) were concerned mainly with format, measurement and valuation. However, there have always been some examples of this distinction being breached and in recent years these have become much more frequent. Thus, for example, the Companies Act 1981 introduced a requirement for specific formats to be used for the profit and loss account and the balance sheet. Similarly, from 1975 until 1992 there was an accounting standards requirement to disclose a source and application of funds statement. This has now been superseded by a requirement to disclose a cash flow statement. The impact of the various sources of regulation on financial reporting practices is described fully and discussed in Part One (Chapters 2–8), but it is useful here to examine in a little more detail the major constituents of the regulatory framework outlined above.

Legal regulation

The legal regulation of accounting can be traced as far back as the Joint Stock Companies Act of 1844, but the statutes which have had the greatest influence on the current state of company financial reporting are the more recent Companies Acts of 1948, 1967 and 1981. The provisions of these Acts (and also the Companies Acts of 1976 and 1980) were consolidated into the Companies Act 1985, which, as amended by the Companies Act 1989, contains the overall legal framework.

The Acts of 1948 and 1967 were very important in laying down the basic disclosure requirements which still apply today. The 1948 Act also introduced the requirement for auditors to report on whether the accounts give a true and fair view of the company's financial position at the end of an accounting period and of its profit or loss for that period. As a result of the 1981 Companies Act, the need for accounts to give a true and fair view became an 'overriding consideration'. This means that information not specifically required by law must be provided in order to give a true and fair view. Similarly, departure from the specific requirements of the law is permitted in situations where compliance with the law would prevent a true and fair view being shown. (Where departure does occur, full particulars must be given, together with reasons for that departure and an explanation of the effect of such a departure.) The 1981 Act was also very much concerned with the need for disclosure, and a notable example of this was a new requirement for cost of sales information to be given in the profit and loss account. However, the most important features of the 1981 Act were that it prescribed the formats that could be used for presenting company financial information and that it required some basic accounting principles to be written into the law. Both of these features are examples of the increasing influence of the European Community (EC) on the regulatory framework of accounting in the UK.

One of the objectives of the EC is to harmonize company law in member states. This is achieved through the development of directives, which, when approved and adopted by the EC Council of Ministers, are meant to be binding on the member states. The EC directive with the greatest impact on accounting has been the Fourth Directive. This was adopted by the EC in 1978 and it contains detailed regulations concerning the format, content, valuation methods and publication of accounts; these regulations were reflected in the requirements of the Companies Act 1981. Because the provisions of the 1981 and earlier Acts are now consolidated into the Companies Act 1985 (as amended by the Companies Act 1989) it is this amended 1985 Act that will be referred to in the chapters that follow.

Regulation by the accountancy profession

Until 1 August 1990, the principal means by which the accountancy profession contributed to the regulation of financial reporting was through the ASC. This was an organization made up of representatives of the six major professional accounting bodies in the UK, together with the preparers and users of accounting information. The objectives of the ASC were to define accounting concepts, to reduce differences in financial accounting and reporting practices and to codify generally accepted best practice in the public interest. One of the ways in which it achieved these objectives was by issuing SSAPs. During its existence the ASC issued twenty-six SSAPs, some of which were subsequently revised. All the SSAPs were preceded by exposure drafts to permit full consultation on proposed standards and a total of fifty-five exposure drafts were issued.

On 1 August 1990 the ASC was replaced by the ASB and the twenty-two SSAPs that were then extant were adopted by the ASB. The ASB, like the ASC before it, embodies a substantial amount of technical expertise, with nine members including a full-time chairman and a Technical Director, and its funding and membership is drawn from the accountancy profession, the financial community and the government.

The ASB is guided on its work programme and on issues of public concern by the Financial Reporting Council, whose chairman is appointed jointly by the Secretary of State for Trade and Industry and the Governor of the Bank of England. The Financial Reporting Council also provides a high level of support for accounting standard setting and operates through a Financial Reporting Review Panel to examine and question examples of material departure from accounting standards. The 1985 Act (as amended) requires companies (other than small or medium-sized companies) to disclose whether their accounts have been prepared in accordance with applicable standards and to give particulars of, and reasons for, material departures from standards. Compliance with accounting standards will normally be required for accounts to show a true and fair view but if in exceptional circumstances compliance with an accounting standard is inconsistent with the need to give a true and fair view then departure from the requirements of the standard is permitted.

Where the accounts of a company do not comply with the requirements of accounting standards the Financial Reporting Review Panel can consider these and decide what action to take. At the time of writing approximately 40 cases that have been considered by the Financial Reporting Review Panel have been publicized. Although these have, for the most part, been limited to obtaining an agreement from the companies concerned that they will amend the practice complained of in subsequent years, the Panel can ask that the accounts of a company be revised and apply to the courts for an order requiring the directors of the company to do so.

The ASB issued its statement of aims in 1991 and these are as follows:

> The aims of the Accounting Standards Board are to establish and improve standards of financial accounting and reporting, for the benefit of users, preparers and auditors of financial information.

The ASB intends to achieve its aims by:

- developing principles to guide it in establishing standards and to provide a framework within which others can exercise judgement in resolving accounting issues;
- issuing new accounting standards or amending existing ones, in response to evolving business practices, new economic developments and deficiencies being identified in current practice;
- addressing urgent issues promptly.

The ASB has approached the development of principles on a piecemeal basis in the form of seven chapters. These were combined and published as a draft *Statement of Principles for Financial Reporting* in November 1995. The seven chapters are as follows:

1 The objectives of financial statements;
2 The qualitative characteristics of financial information;
3 The elements of financial statements;
4 Recognition in financial statements;
5 Measurement in financial statements;
6 Presentation of financial statements;
7 The reporting entity.

An outline of the contents of each of the above chapters is provided in the Appendix to this chapter (see pages 17–18). The *Statement of Principles* attracted considerable criticism when it was published. Much of the criticism surrounded the proposal in Chapter 5 to move from historic cost accounting to current value accounting and the proposal in Chapter 6 to increase the importance of the statement of total recognized gains and losses at the expense of the profit and loss account. The ASB responded by publishing the *Statement of Principles for Financial Reporting: the way ahead*, in 1996, in which it acknowledged that more work was required and that a revised exposure draft would be issued.

The standards issued by the ASB are called Financial Reporting Standards (FRSs). As with the ASC, wide consultation is seen as an important part of the standard setting process. All accounting standards are preceded by the issue of an exposure draft. Those issued by the ASB are called Financial Reporting Exposure Drafts (FREDs). Several FRSs and FREDs have already been issued by the ASB as well as a number of discussion documents, which provide an even earlier stage of consultation than exposure drafts.

The way in which the ASB addresses urgent issues promptly is through the UITF: The authority and scope of the UITF was explained in a 1991 ASB pronouncement to be 'a committee of the Accounting Standards Board comprising a number of people of major standing on the field of financial reporting'. Its main role is to consider situations where unsatisfactory or conflicting interpretations of accounting standards or Companies Act provision have developed or are likely to develop. Where such situations occur a voluntary consensus as to the appropriate accounting treatment is sought and this is then issued as a consensus pronouncement. The ASB in its 1991 pronouncement states that

> Consensus pronouncements should be considered part of the corpus of practices forming the basis for determining what constitutes a true and fair view. Such pronouncements consequently may be taken into consideration by the Financial Reporting Review Panel in deciding whether financial statements call for review.

It is clear therefore that UITF pronouncements, which are issued in the form of abstracts, are intended to be complied with by companies when preparing financial statements. The UITF has already issued several of these abstracts.

Regulation by the Stock Exchange

The Council of the Stock Exchange requires that the published financial statements of listed companies (i.e. those public companies whose shares are quoted and can be traded on the Stock Exchange's markets) contain certain types of information. Although much of this information is already required, either by law or accounting standard, the Stock Exchange also imposes additional disclosure requirements. An example of these is the requirement for UK incorporated listed companies to include in their annual report and accounts a statement as to whether or not they have complied with the Cadbury committee's code of best practice. Listed companies are also expected to comply with the provisions of accounting standards (SSAPs and FRSs) and companies are required to give reasons for any significant departures from standard accounting practice.

The International Accounting Standards Committee (IASC)

The IASC was set up in 1973 with a membership drawn from just nine countries. By 1997 the IASC had 199 member bodies in 88 countries. In its attempt to harmonize international financial reporting, the IASC formulates and publishes international accounting standards (IASs) and promotes their world-wide acceptance and observance.

Initially, the standards produced by the IASC tended to permit alternative ways of measuring or disclosing financial information. Compliance is voluntary and so permitting more than one acceptable way of dealing with a specific accounting issue was a means of ensuring support for the standard. The main impact was therefore the prohibiting of the more undesirable accounting practices rather than achieving real harmonization. Although the IASC has, in recent years, attempted to reduce the number of permitted alternative accounting treatments, the influence of the IASC in the UK has been relatively minor. In the UK each FRS contains a section outlining consistency with the IAS treatment of the topic but the ASB makes it clear in its 1993 'Foreword to Accounting Standards' that where the requirements of an accounting standard and an IAS differ, the accounting standard should be followed.

However, the influence of the IASC might increase significantly following its agreement in 1995 with the International Organisation of Securities Commissions (IOSCO). Under this agreement the IASC will produce a set of core IASs which could then be accepted by IOSCO as representing the accounting rules to be used by multinational companies for the purpose of cross-border security issues and listings. This would permit companies to be listed on a foreign stock exchange, say New York or London, without having to comply with US or UK accounting standards and requirements. Domestic companies listed on those exchanges would presumably then question closely why they should have to comply with their own domestic standards and requirements if foreign companies did not, particularly if the IASs were perceived to be less onerous than the domestic requirements. The IASC is expected to complete the production of the set of core IASs in 1998 and if these are accepted by IOSCO then the role of the IASC in accounting standard setting will strengthen.

Other influences on regulation

With the growth in recent years of pressure groups, such as those concerned with environmental issues, racial and ethnic minorities, disabled or disadvantaged groups and political ideologies, more attention has been paid to companies' published accounts as a source of information on those companies' social and environmental impacts. Equally, many companies have taken the opportunity to include with their financial statements detailed information designed to rebut or forestall criticism or pressure on social and environmental grounds.

Legal requirements on the disclosure of information on matters relating to employment, health and safety at work, training and the employment of disabled people, for example, have been considerably extended in recent years and have forced the wider disclosure of many employee-related matters. In 1975, the Accounting Standards *Steering* Committee (the body which preceded the Accounting Standards Committee) produced a discussion document in which it advocated the production of an increased series of reports and statements. The Committee's proposals received a mixed reception, but some of its more beneficial suggestions have been adopted, as discussed in Chapter 7.

In addition, the activities of chemical companies, mineral-extraction companies and the like have come in for closer scrutiny by lobbyists and campaigners. That increased scrutiny has, almost invariably, resulted in enhanced or widened disclosure of relevant financial and non-financial information.

The suggestion has often been made that companies should move away from the traditional, solely financial, orientation of company reports and introduce a wider degree of disclosure in respect of all the resources used in a company's business, including human and environmental resources. This method of presenting information has been labelled 'social accounting' or 'social reporting', and it has attracted some support from both academic and practising accountants. Nonetheless, it has been eschewed by many companies on the grounds of cost and complexity and by others on the grounds of irrelevance or inapplicability. Some companies have presented so-called social reports but the area of social accounting has been largely ignored by both companies and practitioners.

A further influence on the regulation of financial statements has been the growth in recent years of the use of off-balance-sheet finance and window-dressing schemes by companies. In a statement issued by the Institute of Chartered Accountants in England and Wales (Technical Release 603, December 1985), off-balance-sheet finance was defined as

> The funding or refinancing of a company's operations in such a way that, under legal requirements and existing accounting conventions, some or all of the finance may not be shown on its balance sheet.

Window dressing was defined as

> Transactions, the purpose of which is to arrange affairs so that the financial statements of the concern give a misleading or unrepresentative impression of its financial position.

It is clear from these definitions that off-balance-sheet financing and window-dressing schemes provide the opportunity to mislead the users of financial statements. The problem facing the regulatory process was to decide on the best way to prevent the use of such schemes. One approach would have been to introduce a series of specific requirements aimed at restricting each scheme. However, given the wide range of opportunities for off-balance-sheet financing and window dressing, this would require a significant number of detailed provisions, with no guarantee that they could keep pace with the development of new schemes by imaginative preparers of accounts. An alternative would be to issue a general standard based on the concept of 'substance over form'. This concept would require that the accounts of a company should reflect the economic reality of the underlying transactions, rather than their legal form. Although some would argue that the concept of substance over form must always apply if accounts are to give a true and fair view, not all would agree. The Law Society, for example, in 1986 issued a paper entitled 'Off-balance sheet finance and window-dressing' in which concern was expressed that reliance on substance over form could introduce too much subjectivity into the preparation of accounts. The Law Society argued that the analysis of the legal position in relation to assets and liabilities provides the most objective basis because it gives a clear point of reference, whereas a subjective evaluation of the economic or real effect of a transaction does not.

However, the ASB (and before it the ASC) is very clearly supportive of the concept of substance over form. The ASC issued two exposure drafts (ED 42 in 1988 and ED 49 in 1990) which proposed that transactions should be accounted for in accordance with their substance. The ASB then withdrew ED 42 and ED 49 and replaced them with FRED4, which reiterated the commitment to substance over form. FRS 5 ('Reporting the substance of transactions') was issued in April 1994 and this shows only minor changes from FRED4. Although FRS 5 is drafted in terms of general principles rather than a series of rules it does provide detailed Application Notes to clarify the application of the Standard to the specific topics of: consignment stock; sale and repurchase agreements; factoring of debts; securitized assets; and loan transfers.

These are the most frequently encountered areas where the distinction between the legal ownership of assets and the substantive ownership might give rise to off-balance-sheet financing opportunities. FRS 5 makes it clear that it is the substance and economic reality of transactions that should be reported in financial statements.

Generally Accepted Accounting Practices (GAAP)

All of the influences outlined above on the form and content of the published accounts of a company gave rise to what is often referred to as 'UK GAAP'. In some countries, e.g. USA and Canada, the term GAAP has a very clear meaning and definition. In the UK the term is used much more loosely and includes all practices that are considered to be permissible or legitimate, either through support by statute, accounting standard or official pronouncement, or through consistency with the needs of users and of meeting the fundamental requirement to present a true and fair view, or even simply through authoritative support in the accounting literature. GAAP is therefore more than just the requirements of accounting standards and the law; it is a dynamic concept which changes in response to changing circumstances. The accounting concepts that are discussed below also represent an important part of GAAP.

Accounting concepts

The regulatory framework of accounting that was outlined earlier provides the disclosure and measurement rules that have to be followed by companies. In addition, the financial accounts of business organizations are based on a set of generally accepted assumptions which are known as accounting concepts. Accounting concepts are not a set of rigid rules but are practices which currently have general acceptability but which could change and evolve to reflect changes in accounting development. The accounting concepts that are considered most important are as follows:

- the entity concept;
- the money measurement concept;
- the going concern concept;
- the cost concept;
- the realization concept;
- the accruals concept;
- the matching concept;
- the periodicity concept;
- the consistency concept;
- the prudence concept;
- the materiality concept.

The entity concept

Under company law a company is a separate legal entity which is quite distinct from its owners. For other types of business organizations it is an accepted principle of financial accounting that a business should be regarded as a separate entity. A business has assets and liabilities and the difference between the two is the capital or equity of a business. This belongs to the owners and under the entity concept the capital of a business is regarded (and accounted for) as the amount a business owes to its owners.

The money measurement concept

Under the money measurement concept only those events to which a monetary value can be attached appear in the accounts. Thus the *quality* of a workforce is not usually capable of being expressed as a monetary amount and is therefore not shown in the accounts. However, the amount paid to the workforce is a monetary value and so does appear. Likewise the amounts spent on recruiting and training the workforce are accounted for. Money is an obvious standard of measurement and by restricting accounting information to the monetary value of transactions, the concept limits the type of information that might be recorded and provides a basis for comparisons to be made. However, there are problems associated with the money measurement concept.

In the first place the value of money does not remain constant over time. At times of inflation the value of money declines and so the monetary value of transactions of earlier years are not equivalent to the monetary values of today. Also, limiting information to monetary values only means that the accounts, and particularly the balance sheet of an organization, are unlikely to disclose all of the relevant information about a business. For example, most successful businesses enjoy an element of goodwill, which might be based on reputation or be due to operational efficiencies.

Because of this a business might well be worth more than the value of all of its assets less liabilities that do have monetary values, such as buildings, equipment, vehicles, stock, etc. This 'extra' value is goodwill, but because it is so difficult to attach a monetary value to this goodwill element it is only accounted for when a business is purchased and a market value is then determined. For most of the time that a business exists, therefore, the goodwill is not accounted for because its monetary value is not known.

The money measurement concept provides a good example of how accounting concepts are not rigid rules but are capable of evolving and developing, and another example of this is the treatment of brand names. One obvious reason for goodwill existing in a business is when the products of a company have brand names which contribute significantly to product demand and therefore profitability. Until recently brand names were not thought of as being capable of having a monetary value attached to them and were not included in the balance sheets of businesses. In recent years, however, several major companies have now decided to place a monetary value on brand names and include these as assets in the balance sheet.

The going concern concept

The assumption under the going concern concept is that a business will continue to operate in the foreseeable future and is not about to be closed down. Immediately some types of assets are brought into use their disposal value is very low relative to their acquisition cost. The going concern concept means that the underlying disposal value of an asset can be ignored and the acquisition cost can be spread over the years that benefit from the asset's use.

The cost concept

The cost concept is often referred to as historic cost accounting because of the reliance for accounting purposes on the original acquisition cost of assets. One of the reasons for using the original acquisition cost is that it is an easily verifiable and therefore objective value. However, when prices are not stable the use of historic cost can mean that the asset values used when preparing final accounts might be quite different to current market values and therefore a misleading picture of the business is provided. Proposals for moving away from the cost concept to some form of market valuation basis have been made and experimented with over the years, but the cost concept still predominates. However, many companies periodically revalue certain of their fixed assets so that they then reflect the market value at the time of valuation; this is known as modified historic cost accounting.

The draft Statement of Principles issued by the ASB (see Appendix to this chapter on pages 17–18) reveals a distinct preference for companies to move away from historic cost accounting and make greater use of current value accounting.

The realization concept

There is a very close link between the realization concept and the cost concept. Although the assets of a business may increase in value, there is no certainty that the profit will be realized until the asset is sold. Thus only when the sale is made will the profit be recognized. This is a clear example of the caution that is inherent in accounting. However, it is not deemed necessary to wait for cash to be received before recognizing a profit. Once a sale is made a legally enforceable contract exists and the profit can be recognized at that point.

The accruals concept

The accruals concept is consistent with the realization concept in that revenues and costs are recognized as they are earned or incurred, not as money is received or paid. This distinguishes accruals accounting from cash accounting. Under cash accounting it is the time of payment or receipt of cash that determines in which accounting period a transaction should be accounted for. Under accruals accounting it is the time an expense is incurred or revenue is earned that determines the accounting period in which the transaction is accounted for. The accruals concept, when combined with the matching concept, provides the basis for the determination of profit and loss.

The matching concept

The matching concept requires the revenues earned by a business to be matched with the expenses incurred in earning those revenues. In reality the revenues of a specific transaction are not matched with the expenses of that transaction but the revenues of each accounting period are matched with the expenses of that period. The difference between the two is the profit or loss for the period. The difficulty associated with this is of course identifying which accounting period benefits from certain types of expense. For example, an asset such as plant or machinery that will enable revenues to be earned over several accounting periods should be charged as an expense in the form of depreciation to each period that will benefit. How to do this in a manner that exactly reflects the benefits of each period is probably impossible for many types of asset.

The periodicity concept

Under the periodicity concept accounts are prepared for a specific period. The specific period is usually one year and for companies this is the period required by law. Annual reporting is now firmly established for most organizations. However, not all transactions are conveniently completed within one year and this gives rise to the problems discussed under the matching concept of determining an *accurate* means of allocating expenditure and revenue between different periods. For example, a major civil engineering construction contract may take several years to complete and yet for the purposes of the annual accounts it will be necessary to show the proportion of the expenses, revenues and profit (or loss) that should be recorded each year in the accounts of the construction company.

The consistency concept

In accounting there are often several acceptable ways of determining asset values and the proportion of the cost of assets that should be borne by each accounting period. Examples of different methods of valuing closing stock and determining depreciation expenses are given in Chapter 2. The consistency concept requires there to be consistency of treatment of like items within each accounting period and from one period to the next. In other words once one of the generally accepted methods is chosen this method should usually be used consistently from year to year. However, if there are compelling and justifiable reasons for changing the method of valuing a particular item, e.g. closing stock, then this is permitted under the consistency concept, but the impact of the change on current year profit and the impact the change would have had on the accounts of the previous year should be reported to provide comparability.

An important qualitative characteristic of financial information that has been identified in the ASB's *Statement of Principles* is that of comparability (see Appendix to this chapter on pages 17–18). The consistent application of accounting methods throughout an enterprise and through time is a key requirement for comparability.

The prudence concept

The prudence concept is often referred to as the conservatism concept. The preparation of accounts requires judgements to be made about the future and because of the uncertainties associated with this a prudent or cautious approach is required for profit determination. Under this concept all expected losses should be taken into account immediately they are known about, whereas expected gains are not recognized until actually realized. An example of the widespread use of the prudence concept is in closing stock valuation. The normal rule is that closing stock should be valued at cost, but if the market value of the stock falls below cost then the market value should be used. This is the 'lower of cost or net realizable value' that is generally applied to all stock valuations. The prudence concept is clearly useful in terms of preventing over-optimistic calculations of profit to be reported. Overstatement of profit might lead to excessive dividend payments being made or to incorrect investment decisions being taken. However, the concept of prudence should not be taken to excess because the understatement of profit which would result might be just as misleading as the overstatement and might discourage investment unnecessarily.

The materiality concept

Under the materiality concept only information that is essential to the decisions being taken by the users of accounting reports is required to be included. In other words information is material if its omission or misstatement would affect the economic decisions taken by users of financial statements. If too much detail is provided in financial statements the ability to reveal a true and fair view might well be impaired. On the other hand if too little information is given then this would create difficulties. Materiality requires a judgement to be exercised on striking the appropriate balance. Materiality can only be considered in relation to context. In a small business a transaction of £100 might be material whereas in a large company £1 million might not be material. Those responsible for preparing accounts have to make a professional judgement on which items and amounts are likely to influence the decisions of users of accounting information.

Summary

The accounting concepts outlined above do not ensure uniformity in the preparation of accounts. There are still a wide range of generally accepted valuation and measurement bases that companies might choose to use and the concepts of accounting do not eliminate or restrict such a choice. Accounting concepts are simply the main assumptions underpinning accounts preparation and it is important to the understanding and interpretation of financial statements that users are aware of these assumptions. The concepts tend to emphasize the reliability of information rather than usefulness and many would argue that reliability should be the overriding characteristic of financial accounting. However, because the concepts are not rigid rules they are capable of evolving and changing to reflect changes in the requirements and needs of the day.

Format

There are two related considerations in respect of the format of published accounts and reports: the actual format of the accounts themselves (i.e. their content and structure as ordained by law or best practice) and the format of the document in which they are published (i.e. its characteristics and usual form). In broad terms, the first of these considerations applies to virtually all companies, while the second varies markedly from company to company.

Content and structure of financial statements

In accordance with the Companies Act 1985, balance sheets and profit and loss accounts must be presented in conformity with one of the prescribed formats. Two alternative formats are permitted for the balance sheet, allowing either a horizontal or a vertical presentation of specific minimum levels of information. Four alternative formats are permitted for the profit and loss account, allowing for either a horizontal or a vertical presentation and for either an 'operational' or an 'expenditure' basis of calculation. These alternative formats are described and discussed more fully in Chapters 2 and 3, and pro forma examples are presented in illustration.

Once a particular format has been selected, it should be adopted consistently in subsequent periods unless there are special reasons for not doing so. In each case, comparative figures for preceding periods must be in a compatible format.

For any given format, the order in which the items are listed, and the headings and subheadings describing them, are strictly delineated. Subject to those statutory requirements, items may be shown in greater detail than is laid down, new headings may be introduced, items may be combined where they are not individually material, certain items may be shown in the notes rather than on the face of the account and arrangements and headings may be adapted where the special nature of a company's business requires it.

The discussion in the following chapters draws on the published report and accounts of The BOC Group plc for the year to 30 September 1997. The full text of the company's financial review is reproduced in Appendix A and many examples from its reports and accounts appear throughout the book,

Published reports and accounts

Leaving aside the statutory definition of the 'publication' of company accounts (which covers the delivery of certified copies of the financial statements and auditor's report to the Registrar of Companies and the transmission of copies to the shareholders of limited companies), the conventional view of a company annual report and set of accounts is a glossy booklet, generally of A4 size, illustrated with photographs of the company's directors and some of its activities, containing a chairman's statement and other promotional or publicity material and supplemented by a closely printed section carrying complex and detailed financial data.

The annual report and accounts offers a unique opportunity of providing not only the statutory legal and financial information and notices but also important corporate reports, statements and background information. Against that has to be weighed the very considerable costs of designing, printing, producing and distributing each annual report to very large numbers of shareholders.

For the majority of companies, the annual report and accounts document is little more than the bare provision of statutory information and a brief statement from the chairman or the directors. For the 3,000 or so companies listed on the Stock Exchange, the yearly document is generally more informative.

Faced with the ever-increasing costs of reproducing and then mailing the very many items of information now required to be included in company accounts and reports it has often been argued that companies should be permitted to send a simplified version to shareholders. The Companies Act 1985 made provision for regulations to be made which would permit companies to send summarized financial statements to shareholders. Such regulations now exist (The Companies [Summary Financial Statement] Regulations 1990), and companies are now permitted to send summarized financial statements, the form and content of which are specified in the regulations, to their shareholders, but with the full version of the annual report and accounts being available to those shareholders who request it.

Equally, simplified or extracted financial statements are often made available to employees and their representatives. In most cases, those employee reports consist of highlighted paragraphs or inserted pages in the normal employee newspaper or bulletin. In some instances, employee reports are prepared specifically and issued separately.

Both these areas of reporting, to shareholders and to employees, are crucially important. Of their nature, both those sets of readers are relatively unsophisticated in the interpretation and manipulation of accounting and financial data, and might therefore prefer to receive a simplified set of accounts. However, it is clear that the safeguards embodied in various statutes and professional recommendations cannot lightly be abandoned in the pursuit of 'readability' or 'relevance' and full, detailed and wide-ranging statements must continue to be available.

Conclusion

As W. T. Baxter has said (Lee 1981), the original purpose of company reports is still fundamental and

> even if reports help decision making in only an indirect way, we have no cause to feel apologetic about them. They are important. Their original task . . . was to provide evidence that the accounting records have been kept properly, and to show what has happened to the owners' wealth. This they still do. They are the culmination of complex and exacting work. Much of it may have become routine, yet it is essential for business survival.

What accounting reports and financial statements give, then, are items of background information. They provide a framework against which may be judged the stewardship of a company's directors and managers and the viability and health of the company.

Appendix

The development of principles has been addressed by the ASB in its *Statement of Principles for Financial Reporting*, which was issued in Exposure Draft form in November 1995. The *Statement of Principles* consists of the following seven chapters.

1 *The objective of financial statements*   This is defined as the provision of 'information about the financial position, performance and financial adaptability of an enterprise that is useful to a wide range of users for assessing the stewardship of management and for making economic decisions.'

2 *The qualitative characteristics of financial information*   *Relevance* and *reliability* are the two primary characteristics of accounting information. *Relevant* information helps users to evaluate past, present or future events or to confirm or correct their past evaluations, and *reliable* information is 'free from material errors or bias and can be depended upon by users to represent faithfully what it purports to represent or could reasonably be expected to represent'. These primary characteristics are supported by the secondary characteristics of *comparability* and *understandability*. *Comparability* points to the need for the consistent use of accounting methods through time and adequate disclosure of accounting policies, and *understandability* requires the clear presentation of information. A further characteristic is that of *materiality*. Information whose omission or misstatement could influence the economic decisions of users taken on the basis of the financial statements is material. *Materiality* is in fact the first characteristic to consider because if information is not material then the other characteristics do not have to be considered.

3 *The elements of financial statements*   The following seven elements are defined: *assets* – these are 'rights or other access to future economic benefits controlled by an entity as a result of past transactions or events'; *liabilities* – 'obligations of an entity to transfer economic benefits as a result of past transactions or events'; *ownership interest* – 'the residual amount found by deducting all the entity's liabilities from all the entity's assets', this is the equivalent of the equation: assets − liabilities = equity; *gains* – 'increases in ownership interest, other than those relating to contributions by owners'; *losses* – 'decreases in ownership interest, other than those relating to distribution to owners'; *contributions from owners* – 'increases in ownership interest resulting from investments made by owners in their capacity as owners'; *distribution to owners* – 'decreases in ownership interest resulting from transfers made to owners in their capacity as owners'.

4 *Recognition in financial statements*   Assets and liabilities are to be included in financial statements if there is sufficient evidence that rights or access to future economic benefits or obligations to transfer economic benefits have occurred and that a monetary amount can be established with sufficient reliability. If there is sufficient evidence that the amount of an asset or liability has subsequently changed and the new amount can be measured with sufficient reliability then the asset or liability should be recorded at the changed amount.

5 *Measurement in financial statements*   This is the most controversial part of the *Statement of Principles*. A review of the features of historic cost accounting and current value accounting is provided and this leads to the conclusions by the ASB that 'practices should develop by evolving in the direction of greater use of current values to the extent that this is consistent with the constraints of reliability and cost'.

6 *Presentation of financial information*   The profit and loss account, the statement of total recognized gains and losses, the balance sheet and the cash flow statement are identified as the four primary financial statements. The ASB argue that the profit and loss account should report only gains and losses from operating activities, with the statement of total recognized gains and losses having the more important role of reporting both the gains and losses from operating activities and the gains and losses (realized and unrealized) 'that result from changes in the value of those assets and liabilities that are held on a continuing basis for use in the entity's business'.

7 *The reporting entity*   Where one entity owns the shares of one or more other entities and can therefore exert an influence on those other entities then the effect of that influence has to be properly reflected in financial statements. The ASB confirms that where an investor controls an investee then consolidated financial statements are required and confirms that the entity approach to consolidation (consolidate subsidiaries in full and adjust for minority interests) is preferred to the proprietary approach (proportional consolidation line by line).

Part One

Published financial statements

2 The profit and loss account

In essence the profit and loss account (often known as the income statement) summarizes the results of the company's activities during the financial period under review. It reports sales or turnover, operating expenses, exceptional items, interest payments, taxation charges and dividends paid and proposed. It has a particular attraction for most users of accounts, in that it reports a 'bottom line' figure – the profit or loss for the financial year – which can be used as a shorthand performance measure.

This chapter examines the alternative formats for the profit and loss account that are permitted by the 1985 Act, as amended, and describes and discusses the various items to be included on the face of the account or in the notes thereto. In addition, the provisions and requirements of accounting standards, and in particular the requirements of FRS 3 ('Reporting financial performance'), will be linked with the legal requirements.

Formats

Schedule 4 to the 1985 Act, as amended, sets out the permitted formats for financial statements. These formats were first prescribed by the 1981 Act and, although the use of standardized formats had been common practice in European countries for a number of years, their introduction into the UK was a significant departure from previous practice. There are advantages and disadvantages in standardizing format. On the one hand, it encourages greater consistency of treatment between one financial period and another, and facilitates comparison between the results of one year and another. It also ensures that different companies follow much the same disclosure practices, in terms of the nature of the items and the extent of the information disclosed. On the other hand, the prescription of standard formats removes some of the otherwise welcome flexibility that companies had adopted in presenting their results, allowing them to present their individual accounts in what they considered the most appropriate way. By and large, however, such considerations applied with more force to balance sheets than to profit and loss accounts. On the whole, the introduction of standardized formats and enhanced minimum levels of disclosure is to be welcomed.

Four alternative formats are now permitted for a company's profit and loss account. Tables 2.1–2.4 reproduce the four alternative profit and loss account formats. Formats

Table 2.1 Profit and loss account – format 1

1 Turnover
2 Cost of sales
3 Gross profit or loss
4 Distribution costs
5 Administrative expenses
6 Other operating income
7 Income from shares in group undertakings
8 Income from participating interests[a]
9 Income from other fixed asset investments
10 Other interest receivable and similar income
11 Amounts written off investments
12 Interest payable and similar charges
13 Tax on profit or loss on ordinary activities
14 Profit or loss on ordinary activities after taxation
– Minority interests[b]
15 Extraordinary income
16 Extraordinary charges
17 Extraordinary profit or loss
18 Tax on extraordinary profit or loss
– Minority interests[b]
19 Other taxes not shown under the above items
20 Profit or loss for the financial year

Notes: [a]In group accounts, this item is replaced by
             Interests in associated undertakings
             Other participating interests
           [b]Group accounts only.

1 and 2 are vertical arrangements, while formats 3 and 4 are double-sided or horizontal arrangements. The essential difference between the alternative formats is in their classification of the presented information. Formats 1 and 3 classify income and operating expenses by function, whereas formats 2 and 4 classify information by type of income and expense.

This essential difference can be shown summarily as follows. Formats 1 and 3 require operating expenses to be separated into:

■ cost of sales;
■ distribution costs;
■ administrative expenses;

leading to the identification of operating profit perhaps more easily than other alternative arrangements. Formats 2 and 4 require operating expenses to be separated into:

■ change in stocks of finished goods and in work in progress;
■ own work capitalized;
■ raw materials and consumables;
■ other external charges;
■ staff costs;
■ depreciation and other amounts written off tangible and intangible fixed assets;
■ exceptional amounts written off current assets;
■ other operating charges.

Table 2.2 Profit and loss account – format 2

---

1 Turnover
2 Change in stocks of finished goods and in work in progress
3 Own work capitalized
4 Other operating income
5 (a) Raw materials and consumables
    (b) Other external charges
6 Staff costs:
    (a) wages and salaries
    (b) social security costs
    (c) other pension costs
7 (a) Depreciation and other amounts written off tangible and intangible fixed assets
    (b) Exceptional amounts written off current assets
8 Other operating charges
9 Income from shares in group undertakings
10 Income from participating interests[a]
11 Income from other fixed asset investments
12 Other interest receivable and similar income
13 Amounts written off investments
14 Interest payable and similar charges
15 Tax on profit or loss on ordinary activities
16 Profit or loss on ordinary activities after taxation
– Minority interests[b]
17 Extraordinary income
18 Extraordinary charges
19 Extraordinary profit or loss
20 Tax on extraordinary profit or loss
– Minority interests[b]
21 Other taxes not shown under the above items
22 Profit or loss for the financial year.

Notes: See Table 2.1.

Formats 2 and 4 make the calculation of cost of sales and gross profit less easy than under alternative formats. In the case of many companies, gross profit is a significant performance measure and its calculation under formats 2 and 4 is possible only if substantial further information is provided in respect of such items as depreciation, employment costs and other operating charges.

Companies and their advisers are able to adopt the format that they consider most appropriate, but it is considered that the vertical formats have rather more to commend them than do their horizontal counterparts. The range of permitted formats reflects the differences in the practices followed in different European countries. In the UK most of the larger companies tend to follow format 1.

Before turning to an examination of the various permitted components of the alternative formats, it is necessary to set out the rules by which modification or extension of the permitted formats is allowed. Items to appear in statutory balance sheets and profit and loss accounts are denoted by either letters (A, B, C etc.), Roman numerals (I, II etc.) or arabic numbers (1, 2, 3 etc.). Every balance sheet and profit and loss account must show the items denoted by letters or Roman numerals in the respective formats. As can be seen from Tables 3.1 and 3.2 (in Chapter 3) the standard formats for balance sheets include items that are prefixed by letters, Roman numerals and arabic numerals and items prefixed by the letters and Roman numerals must be

Table 2.3 Profit and loss account – format 3

A	*Charges*	*B*	*Income*
1	Cost of sales	1	Turnover
2	Distribution costs	2	Other operating income
3	Administrative expenses	3	Income from shares in group undertakings
4	Amounts written off investments	4	Income from participating interests[a]
5	Interest payable and similar charges	5	Income from other fixed asset investments
6	Tax on profit or loss on ordinary activities	6	Other interest receivable and similar income
7	Profit or loss on ordinary activities after taxation	7	Profit or loss on ordinary activities after taxation
–	Minority interests[b]	–	Minority interests[b]
8	Extraordinary charges	8	Extraordinary income
		–	Minority interests[b]
9	Tax on extraordinary profit or loss	9	Profit or loss for the financial year
–	Minority interests[b]		
10	Other taxes not shown under the above items		
11	Profit or loss for the financial year		

Notes: See Table 2.1.

shown in the order and under the headings and sub-headings given (unless the amounts are nil for both this financial year and the preceding financial year). However, the profit and loss accounts formats 1 and 2 contain only arabic number items and these can therefore be combined on the face of the accounts if the amounts involved are not material to an assessment of the company's profit or loss for the relevant period, or if such a combination would facilitate that assessment. In the latter circumstances, the individual amounts must be disclosed separately in the notes to the account.

The Act specifically requires only three items to be shown on the face of the profit and loss account:

1 the amount of the company's profit or loss on ordinary activities, before taxation;
2 the amount of any transfers to or withdrawals from the company's reserves, both completed and proposed;
3 the aggregate amount of any dividends paid and proposed.

As all items listed in the prescribed formats are prefixed by arabic numbers, this allows a company's directors to adapt the arrangement and headings of those items in the manner most appropriate to the company's affairs. There is also the flexibility mentioned earlier – that of combining the items on the face of the account.

This flexibility must be used sensibly. It is unlikely that directors would be justified in combining all the items making up profit or loss on ordinary activities before taxation and showing just one amount on the face of the account, with the individual items making up that amount relegated to the notes. In fact greater detail than is prescribed by the permitted formats can be given and new items or headings can be introduced for matters not otherwise covered. A significant development in this respect has been the introduction of FRS 3 ('Reporting financial performance'). FRS 3 has taken advantage of the permitted flexibility to bring about a major reshaping of the profit and loss account. The standard requires all profit and loss items from turnover down to operating profit to be analysed between continuing operations (sub-divided into acquisitions and other) and discontinued operations. As a minimum the analysis in

Table 2.4   Profit and loss account – format 4

A	Charges	B	Income
1	Reduction in stocks of finished goods and in work in progress	1	Turnover
2	(a) Raw materials and consumables	2	Increase in stocks of finished goods and in work in progress
	(b) Other external charges	3	Own work capitalized
3	Staff costs:	4	Other operating income
	(a) wages and salaries	5	Income from shares in group undertakings
	(b) social security costs	6	Income from participating interests[a]
	(c) other pension costs	7	Income from other fixed asset investments
4	(a) Depreciation and other amounts written off tangible and intangible fixed assets	8	Other interest receivable and similar income
	(b) Exceptional amounts written off current assets	9	Profit or loss on ordinary activities after taxation
5	Other operating charges	–	Minority interests[b]
6	Amounts written off investments	10	Extraordinary income[b]
7	Interest payable and similar charges	–	Minority interests[b]
8	Tax on profit or loss on ordinary activities	11	Profit or loss for the financial year
9	Profit or loss on ordinary activities after taxation		
–	Minority interests[b]		
10	Extraordinary charges		
11	Tax on extraordinary profit or loss		
–	Minority interests[b]		
12	Other taxes not shown under the above items		
13	Profit or loss for the financial year		

Notes: See Table 2.1

respect of turnover and operating profit must be reported on the face of the profit and loss account. Information on three specific categories of exceptional items must also be disclosed on the face of the profit and loss account. One consequence of this is that many of the items that would often have been disclosed on the face of the profit and loss account prior to the issue of FRS 3 now appear in the notes so as to make space for the new required format.

The logic behind the distinction between continuing and discontinued operations is that where financial statements are used to assess the likely future performance of a company then the results from those operations that the company no longer owns or runs need to be excluded because it is only the continuing operations that will affect the future. Similarly, if the actual results of a period are to be sensibly compared with forecasts made for that period, then the contributions from any operations acquired during the year need to be eliminated so that like can be compared with like.

The consolidated profit and loss account for The BOC Group plc for the year ended 30 September 1997 (see Table 2.5) provides an example of the disclosure requirements of FRS 3. As can be seen the Companies Act format 1 has been followed, but not all of the items denoted by arabic numbers have been included. This extracted account will form the basis for the following discussion of the usual profit and loss account components.

Table 2.5   The BOC Group plc – consolidated profit and loss account (year ended 30 September 1997)

	1997 (£ million)	1996 (£ million)
Turnover:		
Continuing operations	3,929.9	4,014.4
Acquisitions	33.7	5.1
Turnover including share of associated undertakings	**3963.6**	**4019.5**
Less associated undertakings' turnover	285.9	267.4
Turnover of subsidiary undertakings	3,677.7	3,752.1
Cost of sales	(2,105.5)	(2,115.5)
Gross profit	1,572.2	1,636.6
Net operating expenses	(1,093.4)	(1,154.7)
Operating profit:		
Continuing operations	478.5	481.7
Acquisitions	0.3	0.2
Profit of subsidiary undertakings	478.8	481.9
Share of profit of associated undertakings	61.6	57.5
Operating profit	**540.4**	**539.4**
Interest (net)	(95.2)	(94.5)
Profit on ordinary activities before tax	**445.2**	**444.9**
Tax on profit on ordinary activities	(129.1)	(137.0)
Profit on ordinary activities after tax	**316.1**	**307.0**
Minority interests	(28.5)	(28.7)
Profit for the financial year	**287.6**	**278.3**
Dividends including non equity	(140.4)	(130.1)
Surplus for the financial year	147.2	148.2
Earnings per 25p Ordinary share, net basis, undiluted	59.31p	57.74p

Contents

The following sections describe and discuss the various items to be included either on the face of the profit and loss account or in the notes thereto. Reference is made to three complementary sets of requirements: the statutory requirements contained in the Companies Acts; the professional requirements contained in accounting standards and accountancy bodies' recommendations; the supervisory requirements imposed on public listed companies by the Council of the Stock Exchange.

Turnover

All formats given in the fourth schedule to the 1985 Act, as amended, require the disclosure of turnover. In the case of consolidated financial statements, turnover should exclude intra-group transactions.

FRS 3 requires turnover to be analysed between continuing operations, acquisitions and discontinued operations, with acquisitions being presented as a component of continuing operations. Discontinued operations are defined as operations of the reporting entity that are sold or terminated either in the reporting period or before the earlier of three months after the commencement of the subsequent period and the date on which the financial statements are approved. Terminated operations must have ceased permanently to be treated as discontinued. Also sales or terminations must be material and any assets, liabilities, results of operations and activities must be clearly distinguishable, physically, operationally and for financial reporting purposes, if they are to be categorized as discontinued.

Acquisitions are defined in the FRS as operations of the reporting entity that are acquired in the period. In effect this means operations that are purchased rather than operations that a company builds up itself. Thus, for example, if a company decides to move into a new product line by purchasing another entity this would be an acquisition, whereas building up the new product line by itself would not. The BOC Group's disclosure of its turnover is shown in Table 2.5.

In addition, the Companies Act 1985 requires turnover to be reported (by way of a note to the accounts) in respect of each substantially different class of business carried on by the company and each geographical area in which the company operates. If a class of business or geographical segment is significant to the company as a whole its turnover should be reported. SSAP 25 ('Segmental reporting') states that a segment will normally be regarded as significant if its turnover to third parties is 10 per cent or more of total turnover to third parties. SSAP 25 also requires geographical segmental disclosure to distinguish between turnover by origin (i.e. the geographical area from which products or services are supplied) and turnover by destination (i.e. the geographical area to which goods or services are supplied).

The reasons for requiring companies to disclose segmental information of this nature is that users of financial statements are able to assess the contribution of each segment to overall turnover, and can then employ judgements about the relative risk and growth potential of each segment. BOC provides information on turnover by class of business and by geographical area and also by country of origin and country of destination in note 1 to its accounts (see Appendix A). The analysis of BOC's 1997 turnover is as follows:

	Gases and related products (£ million)	Vacuum technology (£ million)	Distribution services (£ million)	Health care (£ million)	Total by origin (£ million)	Total by destination (£ million)
Europe	659.3	109.4	287.9	161.3	1,217.9	1,058.7
Americas	805.0	202.6	–	262.9	1,270.5	1,484.0
Africa	341.0	–	–	–	341.0	341.0
Asia/Pacific	1,024.6	55.0	1.4	53.2	1,134.2	1,079.9
	2,829.9	367.0	289.3	477.4	3,963.6	3,963.6

Cost of sales

Formats 1 and 3 of the Companies Act require the disclosure of cost of sales as a separate item. It was pointed out earlier that, following the introduction of FRS 3, all items from turnover down to operating profit must be analysed between continuing operations, acquisitions and discontinued operations. The analysis for cost of sales is shown in note 2 to the profit and loss account (see Appendix A, page 217). Cost of sales will normally include all direct elements of the cost of ordinary activities, and will typically include:

- opening stocks and work in progress;
- direct materials;
- other external charges;
- direct labour;
- fixed and variable production overheads;
- depreciation or diminution in value of productive assets;
- research and development costs;

and adjustments will be made for closing stocks and work in progress.

In a retail business the most important element of the total cost of sales figure will probably be the cost of direct materials purchased for resale. In a manufacturing organization, where raw materials are turned into finished goods, the expenditure on manufacturing wages and the depreciation of manufacturing equipment will also be significant elements. Although it is not the intention of this book to explain the techniques and rules of accounting, it is useful at this stage to provide a brief illustration of how the permitted variety in accounting measurement method might affect the calculation of the cost of direct materials and the charge for depreciation.

Direct materials

When materials are purchased, either for resale or as raw material input to a manufacturing process, they become an asset known as stock. This stock will eventually be sold and then replaced by a further purchase of materials which will in turn be sold, and so on throughout the accounting period. At the end of the accounting period it will then be necessary to determine the cost of direct materials sold. This is usually calculated as the cost of stock at the beginning of the period, plus the purchases made during the period, less the cost of stock held at the end of the period. Because stock is constantly being depleted and then replaced, it is often impossible to identify particular items of stock as belonging to a specific batch purchased, and there is usually no attempt to do so. Where the cost of materials purchased does not change throughout the accounting period, then this practice presents few problems. However, where price changes do occur, and it is not possible to identify which items in stock were bought at which price, then the only way in which a value can be placed on closing stock is by making an assumption about the pattern of stock flows into and out of the business. The three most widely recognized methods of accounting for stock are FIFO (first in first out), LIFO (last in first out) and weighted average.

FIFO assumes that the items carried at the oldest prices will be the first to be sold. LIFO assumes that the items acquired at the most recent prices will be the first to be sold. Weighted average calculates the cost of each stock item sold as the average of all items of that type held in stock at the time of sale. The following simple example illustrates the use of each of these three methods.

Example 2.1

The Plastic Products company started business on 1 January 19X1. It purchases one particular type of plastic valve which it shapes and polishes and then sells. The

Table 2.6 Purchases and sales for the Plastic Products company

Date	Purchases		Sales	
	Units	Price per unit (£)	Units	Price per unit (£)
1 January	3,000	12		
31 January			2,000	21
1 March	4,000	13		
31 March			3,000	22
1 July	4,000	14		
31 July			5,000	23
1 November	5,000	15		
30 November			3,000	25

purchases and sales that took place during the year were as shown in Table 2.6. The cost of direct materials sold under each of three alternative methods would be calculated as shown in Tables 2.7–2.9. Under all three methods there is a different closing stock figure. Every time issues are made under the FIFO system, the earliest prices are used up first. For example, on the 31 March 3,000 units were issued. Of these, 1,000 are assumed to be the units remaining in stock after the 31 January issue and are therefore priced at £12 per unit. This is the earliest price available. The balance of 2,000 units are assumed to come from the units received on 1 March priced at £13, i.e. the next earliest price available. At 31 December there are 3,000 units remaining in stock and these are assumed to be from the 5,000 purchased on 1 November at £15 each.

Under the LIFO system, issues are made first from the most recent prices available. Thus, for example, the issue of 5,000 units on 31 July is priced on the assumption that

Table 2.7 FIFO method of accounting for stock

Date	Received	Issued		Value (£)
1/1	3,000 @ £12			
31/1		2,000	@ £12	24,000
1/3	4,000 @ £13			
31/3		3,000	1,000 @ £12	38,000
			2,000 @ £13	
1/7	4,000 @ £14			
31/7		5,000	2,000 @ £13	68,000
			3,000 @ £14	
1/11	5,000 @ £15			
30/11		3,000	1,000 @ £14	44,000
			2,000 @ £15	
31/12	Cost of sales			£174,000
31/12	Closing stock	3,000	@ £15	£45,000

Table 2.8 LIFO method of accounting for stock

Date	Received	Issued		Value (£)
1/1	3,000 @ £12			
31/1		2,000	@ £12	24,000
1/3	4,000 @ £13			
31/3		3,000	@ £13	39,000
1/7	4,000 @ £14			
			1,000 @ £13	
31/7		5,000		69,000
			4,000 @ £14	
1/11	5,000 @ £15			
30/11		3,000	@ £15	45,000
31/12	Cost of sales			£177,000
		1,000	@ £12	
31/12	Closing stock			£42,000
		2,000	@ £15	

Table 2.9 Weighted-average method of accounting for stock

Date		Units	Cost (£)	Average cost per unit (£)	Value (£)	Cost of sales (£)
1/1	Received	3,000	12	12	36,000	
31/1	Issued	2,000		12	24,000	24,000
	Balance	1,000		12	12,000	
1/3	Received	4,000	13		52,000	
	Balance	5,000		12.8[a]	64,000	
31/3	Issued	3,000		12.8	38,400	38,400
	Balance	2,000		12.8	25,600	
1/7	Received	4,000	14		56,000	
	Balance	6,000		13.6[b]	81,600	
31/7	Issued	5,000		13.6	68,000	68,000
	Balance	1,000		13.6	13,600	
1/11	Received	5,000	15		75,000	
	Balance	6,000		14.77[c]	88,600	
30/11	Issued	3,000		14.77	44,310	44,310
1/12	Balance	3,000		14.77	44,290	
31/12	Cost of sales					174,710

Notes: [a]Weighted average = 64,000/5,000 = £12.8.
[b]Weighted average = 81,600/6,000 = £13.6.
[c]Weighted average = 88,600/6,000 = £14.77.

4,000 of them were the units received on 1 July at £14: this is the latest price available. The balance of 1,000 were the units remaining unsold after the issue on 31 March; these had cost £13 each. The closing stock of 3,000 units is therefore made up of the 2,000 remaining out of the 5,000 received on 1 November at £15 each, and for the balance of 1,000 units it is necessary to go right back to the 1 January purchases at £12 per unit to find the most recent price still available.

Under the weighted-average approach, a new price is calculated every time new stock is received. For example, after the 31 January issue there are 1,000 units in stock at £12 each. Then on 1 March, 4,000 more units are received at a cost of £13 each. The new weighted-average price at 1 March is therefore calculated as (1,000 × £12 + 4,000 × £13)/5,000 = £12.8. The closing stock at 31 December is simply the weighted average of £14.77 per unit that was calculated after the 1 November receipt of 5,000 units, multiplied by the 3,000 units remaining in stock.

This example shows that when the three different approaches are applied to an identical set of data it is possible to obtain three different figures for closing stock and therefore three different figures for the cost of materials sold. The Companies Act permits the use of any of the above methods, but the appendix to SSAP 9 ('Stocks and long-term contracts') points out that LIFO is unlikely to provide a sufficiently close approximation to actual cost to be permissible. It can be seen from this example that, at times of rising prices, LIFO will result in a higher cost of sales and therefore a lower reported profit figure.

The use of FIFO produces the opposite effect, and this perhaps explains why FIFO is permitted as a basis for calculating taxable profit, whereas LIFO is not. Although weighted average appears to offer a useful compromise, it does require more calculations to be made, because a new weighted-average figure is required each time new stock is received.

Depreciation

Fixed assets, such as buildings, plant and machinery, vehicles etc., are usually expected to be used by a business for several years, and yet it has to be recognized that they will eventually wear out or become obsolete. Some method of spreading the cost of such assets over their useful economic life is therefore needed, and this is what depreciation is intended to do. The four profit and loss account formats require the disclosure of depreciation provisions, either in a note to the financial statements (under formats 1 and 3) or on the face of the account (under formats 2 and 4). The provisions of schedule 4 to the 1985 Act are fully consistent with the requirements of SSAP 12 ('Accounting for depreciation'), stating that the historical cost or revalued book cost of fixed assets, less any estimated residual value, should be written off systematically over the 'useful economic life' of the assets. (The 'useful economic life' of an asset is defined as the period over which the present owner will derive benefit from its use.)

The assessment of depreciation calls for the estimation of at least three factors:

1 the cost or valuation of the asset;
2 the probable realizable value on disposal at the end of the asset's working life (the residual value) in the business of the company;
3 the expected length of the asset's working life (or useful economic life) to the business of the company.

Thus, even before different measurement methods are considered, any calculation of depreciation demands a considerable amount of judgement, particularly in respect of the likely residual value and the estimated working life. There are then several methods that might be used to determine a depreciation charge for each accounting period. Two of the most widely used of these are the *straight-line* method and the *reducing-balance* method. The straight-line method assumes that an asset will be used up evenly throughout its useful life and therefore allocates a uniform amount of depreciation to each accounting period. The reducing-balance method assumes that the loss in value is heaviest in the early years of an asset's life and therefore allocates a high proportion of the depreciation expense to those years. Example 2.2 illustrates the use of both these methods.

Example 2.2

Suppose that the Plastic Products company of Example 2.1 also purchased special shaping and polishing equipment on 1 January 19X1. The equipment cost £30,000 and it was estimated that it would last for five years, with an expected trade-in value after that time of approximately £5,000.

Straight-line method   The annual charge is calculated as

$$\frac{\text{Cost} - \text{Residual value}}{\text{Number of years' life}}$$

Therefore,

$$\text{Annual charge} = \frac{£30,000 - £5,000}{5} = £5,000$$

The depreciation charge would therefore be £5,000 for each of the five years' life.

Reducing-balance method   What is required here is a percentage rate which, when applied to the balance at the end of each period, will reduce the book value of the equipment to approximately £5,000. This rate can be found by trial and error, or from the following formula:

$$\text{Percentage rate} = 1 - \sqrt[n]{\left(\frac{\text{Salvage value}}{\text{Cost}}\right)}$$

where n is the number of years of expected useful life. Applying this formula to the data from the Plastic Products company gives

$$\text{Percentage rate} = 1 - \sqrt[5]{\left(\frac{5,000}{30,000}\right)} = \text{approximately 30 per cent}$$

The annual depreciation charge for each of the five years is then as shown in Table 2.10.

At the end of the five-year period the net book value of the equipment will be more or less the same under both methods (i.e. £5,000 with the straight-line method and £5,042 with the reducing-balance method) but the pattern of annual charges for each of the five years will be quite different.

Table 2.10 Annual depreciation charges for the Plastic Products company

Year	Book value at beginning of year (£)		Percentage rate		Annual depreciation charge (£)	Book value at end of year (£)
19X1	30,000	×	30%	=	9,000	21,000
19X2	21,000	×	30%	=	6,300	14,700
19X3	14,700	×	30%	=	4,410	10,290
19X4	10,290	×	30%	=	3,087	7,203
19X5	7,203	×	30%	=	2,161	5,042

If the different cost-of-materials-sold figures obtained in Example 2.1 and the different depreciation charges calculated in Example 2.2 are considered together, then the impact these differences have on gross profit can be determined, and this is illustrated in Example 2.3 below. For the purpose of this example, the sales revenue for the year 19X1 has been calculated from the data given in Example 2.1 to be £298,000 (2,000 × £21 + 3,000 × £22 + 5,000 × £23 + 3,000 × £25), and it has also been assumed that the other cost of sales expenses on such items as 'direct labour' and 'other external charges' amounted to £50,000 for the year to 31 December 19X1.

Example 2.3

The gross profit of Plastic Products for the year to 31 December 19X1 is given in Table 2.11. As can be seen from this table, by applying just three different accounting methods for stock valuation and two different methods for depreciation to the same basic set of data, it is possible to obtain six different gross profit figures. All of these figures could be justified as being the appropriate one to report for Plastic Products, because they are all based on permitted methods of accounting measurement. However, there are methods of calculating depreciation in addition to the two illustrated here, and there are many

Table 2.11 Gross profit of the Plastic Products company

Accounting method	Turnover (£)	Cost of direct materials (£)	Depreciation (£)	Other expenses (£)	Gross profit (£)
FIFO/straight line	298,000	174,000	5,000	50,000	69,000
LIFO/straight line	298,000	177,000	5,000	50,000	66,000
Weighted average/ straight line	298,000	174,710	5,000	50,000	68,290
FIFO/reducing balance	298,000	174,000	9,000	50,000	65,000
LIFO/reducing balance	298,000	177,000	9,000	50,000	62,000
Weighted average/ reducing balance	298,000	174,710	9,000	50,000	64,290

other areas where a choice of measurement method is permitted, so the accounting process could derive many different profit figures from a single set of data, and all of these could be thought of as 'correct'. The facility to choose from a range of permitted measurement methods is both a strength and a weakness of financial reporting. It is argued that without some degree of flexibility it would be difficult to select the methods that are most likely to reflect a true and fair view. On the other hand, such flexibility can lead to difficulties in interpreting accounting information and in obtaining an accurate picture of a company's financial performance. It can also lead to difficulties when comparing one company with another, and an essential part of any examination of company accounts is the careful scrutiny of information disclosed concerning the accounting policies used by a company.

Distribution costs

Distribution costs are required to be shown separately and to be analysed between continuing operations, acquisitions and discontinued operations. Note 2 to the BOC accounts provides this analysis. Broadly, such costs include all costs of holding goods for sale, promotional, advertising and selling costs and costs of transferring goods to customers. The following elements of cost will be included:

- sales salaries, commissions and bonuses and related employment costs (including social security and pension costs);
- advertising and promotion costs;
- warehousing costs;
- transportation costs (including depreciation on vehicles);
- sales outlet costs (including depreciation and maintenance costs);
- sales discounts.

Administrative expenses

Similarly required to be disclosed separately and analysed in accordance with FRS 3, administrative expenses include operational costs other than those associated with the production and distribution of goods and services (which are required to be shown separately, as mentioned earlier). Typically, administrative expenses will include the following:

- administrative staff salaries, bonuses, etc. and related employment costs (including social security and pensions costs), also included are directors' executive salaries and related employment costs;
- administration buildings costs (including depreciation and maintenance);
- professional fees;
- amounts written off in respect of bad debts.

Note 2 to the BOC financial statements shows that administrative expenses were £705.6 million from continuing operations and £7.8 million from acquisitions, making a total of £713.4 million, but only a small number of the individual expense items making up that total are separately identifiable. Thus, for example, directors' emoluments, which include salaries, bonuses, pension contributions and provision for share incentive schemes, are disclosed in the report of the management resources committee (see page 201) and total £5,936 million. Similarly, that part of professional fees that relates to the fees paid to auditors has to be disclosed separately, distinguishing between fees for audit work and fees for non-audit work. Note 2(b) to the accounts (page 217) reveals that the fees paid to auditors were as follows:

	£ million
Audit fees	1.9
Other fees – UK	0.6
– rest of world	0.4
	2.9

However, most of the items of expenditure that make up the total of administrative expenses (and also the total of cost of sales and the total of distribution costs) are only reported as aggregated expenditure items. For example, BOC reports its employee costs as follows (note 6(c) page 225).

	£ million
Wages and salaries	799.9
Social security costs	95.4
Other pension costs	13.9
	909.2

Part of this total of £909.2 million will relate to cost of sales, part to distribution costs, part to administrative expenses and part to research and development but an analysis along these lines is not provided. Similarly, depreciation expenses (see note 7(a), page 230) are analysed by class of fixed asset but not by the category of expenditure to which they relate.

Research and development

Many companies are active in researching, designing and developing new products and SSAP 13 ('Accounting for research and development') requires public companies to disclose the total amount of research and development expenditure charged to the profit and loss account. Note 2 to the BOC Group's 1997 accounts reports that the expenditure on research and development charged to the profit and loss account was £80.6 million.

Other operating income

Other operating income is required to be disclosed separately under all four formats. Included in this category are all other income sources associated with a company's ordinary activities – with the exception of interest receivable and investment income, which are required to be disclosed separately. However, if income from investments or interest receivable is not material, it is permissible for it to be included under this heading. Examples of such other operating income might be:

- rental income from surplus premises or facilities;
- sales income from canteen or recreational facilities.

For most companies, such income is unlikely to be significant, and BOC do not report any income under this heading.

Income from shares in group companies

Companies can and frequently do hold shares in other companies. If this results in one company having effective control over the activities of one or more other companies, then a group relationship exists. The company that exercises control is known as a parent company, with the companies over which control is exercised being known as subsidiaries. A key requirement for determining whether a group exists or not is therefore that of control, and there are two quite distinctly different approaches to this question. The first is the 'legal control' approach, which defines control as being the ownership of more than 50 per cent of the voting rights of a company. The second approach places more emphasis on the 'economic reality' of the relationship between one company and another. Thus if one company has the power to exert a 'dominant influence' over another company and exercises that power, even though it owns less than 50 per cent of the voting rights, then there is effective control. A 'dominant influence' is defined in FRS 2 ('Accounting for subsidiary undertakings') as 'influence that can be exercised to achieve the operating and financial policies desired by the holder of the influence, notwithstanding the rights or influence of any other party'.

The Companies Act 1989 recognises both of these approaches to determining whether control exists. The right to exercise a dominant influence, either through the existence of written control contracts or through provisions in the subsidiary's memorandum of association, creates a parent–subsidiary relationship. Similarly, if an investing company has a 'participating interest' in another company and actually exercises a dominant influence over the investee company or if the two companies are managed on a unified basis, then a parent–subsidiary relationship exists. A participating interest occurs where a company invests in the shares of another company with the intention of exercising influence or control as a result of that investment. A holding of 20 per cent or more of the shares of another company can be presumed to be a participating interest.

Where a group relationship exists, then group accounts must be prepared. In other words, the group has to be accounted for as though it were a single economic entity. A group relationship is nowadays very common and the annual reports of a large number of companies are group accounts. The 1989 Companies Act provides that group accounts will normally consist of a single set of consolidated accounts. Consolidation is simply a process of aggregation whereby the financial statements of the holding company and all of the subsidiary companies of a group are combined into a single set of financial statements. This means that corresponding items of assets, liabilities, revenues and expenses are added together on a line by line basis so as to show the *total* amounts that are under the control of the group as a separate legal entity. If any of these items are in fact not 100 per cent owned by the group, then the amounts not owned are reported separately as minority interest.

Because the consolidated profit and loss account of a group of companies will show the total turnover, the total expenses and the total profit or loss of the group (after eliminating any intra-group transactions), then there will be no need to report separately the 'income from shares in group undertakings'. In fact the only time this item would appear in *group* accounts would be on the relatively rare occasions when subsidiaries had not been consolidated. This item would appear in the separate profit and loss account of the parent company, but it is rare for this to be published in addition to a consolidated profit and loss account. This is because the Companies Act permits its omission provided the consolidated profit and loss account reveals certain minimum information about the profit that is dealt with in the separate accounts of the parent company.

Income from interests in associated undertakings

Income from interests in associated undertakings is required to be shown separately in group accounts under all four formats. An associated undertaking is defined as one in which an investing company has a participating interest (normally taken to be as a holding of 20% or more of the voting rights) and over which the investing company exercises a *significant* influence. The exercise of a *significant* influence does not presume a parent-subsidiary relationship (as was pointed out above this would require a *dominant* influence to be exercised). The accounts of the investing company are therefore not consolidated with the accounts of the investing company but are included under the 'equity method of accounting'. FRS 2 ('Accounting for subsidiary undertakings') defines the equity method as

> A method of accounting for an investment that brings into the consolidated profit and loss account the investor's share of the investment undertaking's results and that records the investment in the consolidated balance sheet at the investor's share of the investment undertaking's net assets including any goodwill arising to the extent that it has not previously been written off.

SSAP 1 ('Accounting for associated companies') requires disclosure in the consolidated profit and loss account of the total of the group's share of associated undertakings' profit less losses before taxation, the group's share of taxation, and the group's share of net profits or losses retained. This is equity accounting. It differs from normal consolidation by requiring disclosure of only the group's *share* of profits, etc., of the associated undertakings. Under normal consolidation it is the *total* amount of the subsidiaries, turnover, profit, assets, etc., that is included in the consolidated accounts, with the interests of minority shareholders shown as a separate item.

BOC provides information on the subsidiary and associated undertakings of the group showing the country of domicile and the percentage of the ordinary shares held by the group (see pages 241–2).

Other investment income

All formats call for the separate disclosure of income from other fixed asset investments and other interest receivable and similar income. Income from listed securities must be reported. Listed companies are those that are quoted on a recognized stock exchange and note 9(c) to the BOC accounts (page 232) shows the income from listed and unlisted securities (including associated undertakings) and, after deducting the dividends received from associated undertakings, reveals that the income from other fixed asset investments was £5.8 million.

Operating profit

FRS 3 requires the operating profit of a company to be analysed between continuing operations (sub-divided into acquisitions and other) and discontinued operations. The term operating profit is not used in the Companies Acts and although it is not *defined* in FRS 3, the standard does state that the normal meaning of operating profit is profit before income from shares in group undertakings. However, the explanation section of FRS 3 does concede that income from associated undertakings can, in certain cases, be considered to be part of operating profit. BOC takes advantage of this concession and includes its profit from associated undertakings as part of its overall operating profit.

SSAP 25 ('Segmental reporting') requires the operating results for each class of business and geographical segment to be reported. BOC analyses its operating profit of £540.4 million by class of business and by region (see notes 1(b) and 1(c) to the financial statements.

Exceptional items

FRS 3 defines exceptional items as

> Material items which derive from events or transactions that fall within the ordinary activities of the reporting entity and which individually or, if of a similar type, in aggregate, need to be disclosed by virtue of their size or incidence if the financial statements are to give a true and fair view.

Following from FRS 3 there are in effect two categories of exceptional items as follows:

1 those that are included under the relevant heading of the profit and loss account to which they relate (cost of sales, distribution costs etc.) and disclosed either on the face of the account or in the notes;

2 those that are required to be disclosed on the face of the profit and loss account *after operating profit and before interest*. These are as follows:
(a) profits or losses on the sale or termination of an operation;
(b) costs of a fundamental reorganization or restructuring having a material effect on the nature and focus of the reporting entity's operations; and
(c) profits or losses on the disposal of fixed assets.

These items have to be analysed between continuing and discontinued operations.

Interest payable and similar charges

Interest payable, and similar charges, are also required to be disclosed separately under all four formats. This heading should include:

- interest charged and payable on borrowings;
- imputed interest element of financing leases and cognate obligations;
- amounts amortized on discounts or premiums on bills, debentures, etc.;
- commitment and procurement fees on loan arrangements and credit facilities;

and the Companies Act requires an analysis of other interest and similar charges to show separately the aggregate interest on bank loans, overdrafts and loans wholly repayable within five years (whether by instalments or not) and on any other loans. In that way, interest on short-term loans is separated from that on medium- and long-term loans.

The capitalization of interest on borrowings to finance assets in the course of their construction is a permitted accounting treatment but one over which there is much controversy. On the one hand it could be argued that interest costs incurred during the period of construction of an asset are just as much a part of the total cost as any other item of expenditure incurred on that asset and therefore spreading these costs over the useful life of the asset is perfectly consistent with the matching concept. On the other hand it could be argued that it is illogical to distinguish interest costs in this way and that identical assets could be valued at different amounts simply because of the way they were financed. There is, as yet, no accounting standard in the UK but it is interesting to note that the IASC in its revised version of IAS 23 ('Borrowing costs') issued in 1993 opted for a 'benchmark treatment' of recognizing all borrowing costs as an expense of the period in which they are incurred but did allow the alternative of capitalization of interest for certain types of qualifying assets. A qualifying asset was defined as an 'asset which necessarily takes a substantial period of time to get ready for its intended use or sale'. BOC discloses in note 3(a) to its accounts that 'interest of £11.2 million was capitalized in 1997'.

Many companies net off against interest payable any interest receivable. This is the practice of BOC and note 3 reveals that the interest payable by BOC and its subsidiaries was £112.9 million, from which is deducted the interest receivable of £13.7 million to arrive at a net amount payable of £99.2 million. The share of the interest payable by associated undertakings of £7.2 million is added to this giving an amount of £106.8 million. Of this amount, £11.2 million is capitalized and added to the value of the assets and the balance of £95.2 million is charged as an expense to the 1997 profit and loss account.

Profit or loss on ordinary activities before taxation

A company's profit or loss on ordinary activities before taxation must be shown on the face of the profit and loss account. The figure reported must represent the balance of all the previously mentioned items, including exceptional items, that relate to the ordinary activities of the company, but excluding taxation and extraordinary items (see later).

Taxation

The treatment of taxation in the profit and loss account is governed both by the provisions of the 1985 Act (as amended) and by the requirements of SSAP 8 ('The treatment of taxation under the imputation system in the accounts of companies') and SSAP 15 ('Accounting for deferred taxation'). In addition, other standards contain matters pertinent to the treatment of taxation in the course of their statements on other topics.

The profit and loss account formats prescribed under the 1985 Act (as amended) require the disclosure of three essential taxation items:

1 tax on profit or loss on ordinary activities;
2 tax on extraordinary profit or loss;
3 other taxes not shown under the above items.

Tax on profit or loss on ordinary activities
The disclosure of charges or provisions under this heading should take account of the following items:

- UK corporation tax on the profit for the period;
- double taxation relief;
- deferred taxation;
- overseas taxation;
- irrecoverable advance corporation tax;
- income tax;
- related companies' corporation tax and deferred taxation;
- changes to taxation provisions for prior periods.

These items would not include taxation relating to extraordinary items, which would be shown separately in the category 'tax on extraordinary profit or loss' (discussed later).

The basis on which corporation tax has been computed and the amount of tax charge have to be disclosed. The BOC accounts (note 4(a) to the financial statements) report a charge of £89.8 million at the rate of 31 per cent on taxable profit in respect of corporation tax for the year ended 30 September 1997.

Double taxation relief is gained on the part of the income that originated overseas and on which foreign tax has been paid.

Deferred taxation is defined variously by different authorities. In terms of SSAP 15, deferred taxation is taxation attributable to 'timing differences'. These are the differences between profits calculated for financial statement purposes and those calculated for taxation purposes. Items of income and expenditure are included in taxation computations in periods different from those in which they were or will be included in financial statements. These timing differences are created in four major ways:

1 timing differences arising from the use of different bases for taxation and reporting statements (i.e. receipts and payments basis for taxation and accruals basis for financial accounts);
2 accelerated capital allowances arising from the initial excess of capital allowances over the corresponding depreciation charges;
3 fixed asset revaluation arising from differences between asset values and original costs;
4 fixed asset disposal arising from taxation liability on 'profits' from fixed asset disposal.

Adjustments to the deferred taxation balance can arise also from changes in the rate of tax.

Overseas taxation should be disclosed separately and the amount reported should include all overseas taxation charged in the financial statements of the overseas branch or company, whether relieved or not.

When a company pays a dividend to shareholders, it currently has to pay to the Inland Revenue an amount of taxation on the dividend. This is called advance corporation tax (ACT), which can usually be set off against the total liability to corporation tax on profits. However, from April 1999 ACT will be abolished.

For a more detailed treatment of company taxation readers are recommended to consult a specialist text, such as *Tolley's Corporation Tax*.

As an example of the reported tax on ordinary activities BOC discloses, on the face of its profit and loss account, a 1997 taxation charge of £129.1 million. A summary of the analysis that is provided in note 4(a) to the accounts (page 222) is as follows:

Tax on profit on ordinary activities

	£ million	£ million
Payable in the UK:	89.8	
Advance corporation tax	(4.0)	
Double tax relief	(30.0)	55.8
Payable overseas:		
US	4.4	
Australia	14.6	
South Africa	9.2	
Other countries	36.3	64.5
Provision for deferred tax overseas		(0.1)
Tax charge arising in associated undertakings		8.9
		129.1

Note that double taxation relief occurs because BOC has overseas subsidiaries which pay tax in the overseas countries on profits earned there. If tax was also charged in the UK on those profits then there would have been double taxation. The UK government has agreements with many countries that effectively provide relief against double taxation by permitting the total UK tax liability to be partially reduced by tax paid overseas.

Tax on extraordinary profit or loss

As a consequence of FRS 3 extraordinary items (see later) have now been virtually eliminated and so this item should appear relatively rarely. However, if there are extraordinary items the tax on these should be shown separately. FRS 3 requires that the taxation attributable to extraordinary items should be calculated by computing the tax charge on the profit or loss for the period as if the extraordinary items did not exist. This notional tax charge can then be compared with the total tax charge, with the difference being attributed to extraordinary items.

Tax on exceptional items

FRS 3 requires the notes to the financial statements to show the effect on tax of the three forms of exceptional item that have to be disclosed on the face of the profit and loss account (see the discussion on exceptional items on page 38).

Extraordinary items and prior period adjustments

There is no statutory definition of what constitutes an 'extraordinary item', but FRS 3 provides the following definition:

> Extraordinary items are material items possessing a high degree of abnormality which arise from events or transactions that fall outside the ordinary activities of the reporting entity and which are not expected to recur. They do not include exceptional items nor do they include prior period items merely because they relate to a prior period.

FRS 3 goes on to provide a very wide definition of 'ordinary activities' and the effect of this is that extraordinary items should almost disappear from the accounts of companies. Prior to the introduction of FRS 3, many of the items that are now categorized as exceptional might have been categorized as extraordinary. The all-important 'bottom-line' performance indicator of profit after taxation would therefore have included exceptional items (i.e. they appeared 'above the line') and excluded extraordinary items (i.e. they appeared 'below the line'). The reason for this was that it enabled the reported after-tax profit figure to include only those items that were expected to occur regularly or frequently. Items that were expected to occur infrequently were reported 'below the line' as extraordinary items so as to avoid the distortions and wide fluctuations in after-tax profit that might result from the inclusion of these unusual items. However, the distinction between exceptional items and extraordinary items lacked precision and this permitted the opportunity for other distortions of reported after-tax profit. For example, if, at the extreme, a company chose to classify all of its unusual items of profit as exceptional (i.e. above the line) and all of its unusual losses as extraordinary (i.e. below the line), then this would boost reported profit and thereby give a misleading signal about the company's financial performance. FRS 3 now significantly restricts such opportunities, with virtually all items being required to be included above the line.

One consequence of removing extraordinary items from the profit and loss account is that there is now a tendency for attention to shift to the profit from continuing operations *before exceptional items* (see page 38). This is particularly so in the case of the items that have to be disclosed on the face of the profit and loss account and could lead to these being thought of as something that should be set aside when considering performance. This is precisely the problem that used to occur with extraordinary items and that FRS 3 aimed to remove.

Prior period adjustments are required where it is necessary to correct a fundamental error in the accounts of a prior period or because of changes in accounting policies. A fundamental error is one which is so significant that it would destroy the true and fair view and hence the validity of the financial statements. It does not include the normal recurring corrections and adjustments of estimates made in previous years. FRS 3 requires prior period adjustments to be accounted for by restating the comparative figures for the preceding period in the accounts and notes and adjusting the opening balance of reserves for the cumulative effect.

Minority interests

Where a parent company holds less than 100 per cent of the shares of a subsidiary, then the shares not held by the parent represent a minority interest in that subsidiary. Thus, for example, if a parent company holds 80 per cent of the shares of a subsidiary, then the holders of the remaining 20 per cent are minority shareholders in that subsidiary. Even though the subsidiary is not 100 per cent owned by the parent, the consolidated accounts include 100 per cent of the subsidiary's turnover, expenses and profit. The part of the consolidated profit that belongs to the minority shareholders in subsidiary companies is reported as minority interests. The Companies Act 1989 requires the amount of any profit or loss on ordinary activities attributable to minority interests to be shown separately in the consolidated profit and loss account after group profit or loss on ordinary activities after tax. If a company reports any extraordinary items then any minority interest in these must also be reported.

Dividends

Although the item 'dividends' is not included in any of the four prescribed formats, the 1985 Act (as amended) does require the aggregate amount of any dividends, paid and proposed, to be disclosed on the face of a company's profit and loss account. This straightforward requirement disguises an area of considerable confusion and complexity – the determination of 'distributable profits'. There are also the difficulties of calculating a company's 'realized' and 'unrealized' profits and losses.

Realized profits are those determined in accordance with generally accepted accounting principles at the time of preparation of the financial statements in question. Generally, this has been interpreted to mean that, where a specific accounting standard requires an item of profit to be recognized in the profit and loss account, then this should normally be treated as a realized profit. Also, profits determined in accordance with the two concepts of accruals and prudence, set out in both SSAP 2 ('Disclosure of accounting policies') and the 1985 Act (as amended), would normally be 'realized'. Under the accruals concept, the financial statements must reflect all items of income and expenditure that relate to the financial year in question: in other words, as these items are earned or incurred and not as money is received or paid. Under the prudence concept, profits should not be anticipated and should only be recognized in the profit and loss account when realized in the form of cash or other assets (including a commitment to pay, or other obligation). Losses are provided when an amount is known with certainty or is a best estimate in the light of the circumstances and available information.

Basically, any company that wishes to make a distribution must have profits available for that purpose. They are the accumulated realized profits that have not previously been either distributed or capitalized, less any accumulated realized losses that have not been previously written off. In addition, a public company must satisfy the further condition that the amount of its assets, after making a distribution, must be at least equal to the aggregate of its called-up share capital and undistributable reserves. Undistributable reserves are:

- the share premium account;
- the capital redemption reserve;
- the excess of accumulated unrealized profits over accumulated unrealized losses;
- any other reserve which is not distributable (e.g. because of provision in the memorandum or articles of association of a company).

The situation is complicated further when revalued assets and associated depreciation charges play a part in the net asset position of a company. Readers are referred to a text-book on advanced financial accounting for a fuller treatment (see, for example, Lewis and Pendrill 1996: 62–70).

Employee information

In respect of employees, the total average number of employees must be disclosed and that total should be broken down on the same basis as the organization of the company's activities. Staff costs must be disclosed under the following separate headings:

- wages and salaries paid or payable for the year;
- social security costs that the company has incurred on behalf of its employees (e.g. employer's national insurance contribution);
- other pension costs that the company has incurred on behalf of its employees (this will include contribution to any pension scheme other than the state scheme).

The Act permits considerable flexibility in the manner in which categories of staff should be reported. This can be by function (sales, production, distribution, administration and so on) or by activity (motor assembly, construction, oil exploration etc.) or by a geographical region. The BOC Group provide both an activity-based classification and a regional classification (see note 6 to the financial statements).

SSAP 24 ('Accounting for pension costs') requires the disclosure of additional information in respect of the pension costs of non-state pension schemes. Pension schemes are classified as either defined contribution schemes or defined benefit schemes. In a defined contribution scheme, the employer makes an agreed contribution to a pension scheme, and the benefits paid out of the scheme will depend on the funds available from these contributions plus any investment earnings thereon. The cost to the company can therefore be measured with reasonable certainty. In a defined benefit scheme, the benefits to be paid will typically depend upon the final pay of the employee. This means it is impossible to be certain in advance that the contributions to the scheme, plus any investment earnings, will be sufficient to cover the benefits that will have to be paid. The final cost of a defined benefit scheme is subject to considerable uncertainty and, because of the very long-term nature of pension commitments, it is necessary to make use of actuarial calculations to help determine the pension cost charge.

For defined contribution schemes, SSAP 24 requires simply the disclosure of the accounting policy followed, the pension cost charge for the period and any outstanding or prepaid contribution at balance sheet date. For a defined benefit scheme, the disclosure requirement is much wider. Examples of the disclosures that have to be made include the following:

- whether the scheme is funded or unfunded;
- the accounting policy;
- whether the pension cost and provision are assessed in accordance with the advice of a professionally qualified actuary;
- the date of the most recent actuarial valuation;
- the pension cost charge for the period;
- an explanation of significant changes from the previous period;
- the amount of any deficiency on a current funding level basis;
- an outline of the results of the most recent formal actuarial valuation;
- any commitment to make additional payments over a limited number of years;
- details of the expected effects on future costs of any material changes in pension arrangements.

Note 6 to the BOC accounts (pages 225–9) reports the net cost of its principal schemes and reveals that they were of the defined benefit type. BOC also reports in note 6e (iii) the cost of other post-retirement benefits to former employees in the US. These might, for example, include post-retirement health care benefits. UITF Abstract 6 ('Accounting for post-retirement benefits other than pensions') extends the requirement of SSAP 24 to include these additional kinds of post-retirement benefit.

Directors' emoluments

The Companies Act requirements relating to the disclosure of directors' emoluments have been amended significantly following The Company Accounts (Disclosure of Directors' Emoluments) Regulations 1997 (SI 1997/570). For accounting periods ending on or after 31 March 1997 disclosure is no longer required of the emoluments of the Chairman or of the number of directors whose remuneration falls into bands of £5,000. However, if the aggregate emoluments of all directors exceed £200,000 per year then the emolument of the highest paid director must be disclosed.

The information that is required to be disclosed in aggregate in respect of directors' remuneration is as follows:

■ emoluments – these include salary, 'golden hellos', fees, bonuses, taxable expense allowances and the estimated monetary value of non-cash benefits (for example company cars, subsidized accommodation, etc.);
■ gains made on exercise of share options – this is the difference between the option price and the market price of the shares at the date of exercise of the option (does not apply to unlisted companies);
■ long-term investment plans – this is any agreement under which money or other assets may become receivable by a director depending on service or performance which cannot be fulfilled within a single year;
■ pension contributions in respect of money purchase benefits – for money purchase schemes (in effect defined contribution schemes), the contributions for the highest paid director and the aggregate for all directors must be shown, also the accrued pension benefit on a defined benefit scheme for the highest paid director and the number of directors in money purchase and defined benefit schemes must be disclosed;
■ excess retirement benefits – the intention of this requirement is to ensure disclosure of pension payments that are in excess of the retirement benefits to which directors were entitled when the benefits first become payable;
■ compensation for loss of office – the aggregate amount of any compensation (including cash benefits and the monetary value of non-cash benefits) to directors or past directors in respect of loss of office must be shown;
■ sums paid to third parties in respect of directors' services – payment to an unconnected organization, such as a bank for persons on secondment as a director, are required to be disclosed.

BOC provides comprehensive information on directors' emoluments in the report of the management resources committee (pages 198–206).

Comparative amounts

The corresponding amounts for the previous year of items in the profit and loss account, balance sheet, cash flow statement, statement of total recognized gains and losses and notes to the accounts are required to be reported. In the profit and loss account the comparative figures have to be analysed into continuing and discontinued activities in the same way as the current year's results. The continuing activities category of the comparative figures should include only the results of activities continuing in the *current* year. The discontinued activities category of the comparative figures will include the results of the activities that were discontinued in both the current and previous year. There will not normally be an acquisitions category in the comparative figures because the acquisitions of the previous year will be the continuing activities of the current year and so to help comparison between the two years will be included as continuing activities in the comparative figures.

Earnings per share

SSAP 3 ('Earnings per share') requires listed companies quoted on a recognized stock exchange to report on the face of the profit and loss account a figure for earnings per share. The basis of the calculation must be shown and details of both the earnings figure used and the number of shares issued must be given. FRS 3 has amended the definition of earnings per share (EPS) as follows:

> *Earnings per share* The profit in pence attributable to each equity share, based on the profits of the period after tax, minority interests and extraordinary items and after deducting preference dividends and other appropriations in respect of preference shares, divided by the number of equity shares in issue and ranking for dividend in respect of the period.

In other words, the profit figure used in the EPS calculation is after exceptional and extraordinary items (if any). Many of the items that prior to FRS 3 would have been classified as extraordinary, and thereby omitted from the calculation of EPS, are now classified as exceptional and are therefore included in the calculation. In any event even if there still are any items that could be classified as extraordinary, the above definition requires that EPS is calculated *after* taking them into account. One likely consequence of the FRS 3 requirement is that the EPS measure will be volatile and could fluctuate quite widely from period to period. FRS 3 therefore permits companies to calculate a further EPS figure which could, for example, be based on 'normal' or 'maintainable' profit, i.e. a profit figure which excludes the distortions caused by abnormal items in a particular year. This additional EPS should not be presented more prominently than the EPS required by FRS 3. An explanation of the reasons for calculating the additional EPS and a reconciliation of this with the EPS required by FRS 3 must be disclosed. Some companies base their additional EPS figure on the 'headline earnings' measure proposed by the Institute of Investment Management and Research (IIMR). This involves adjusting the profit after interest and tax for the effects of profit/losses on the sale or termination of an operation; profits/losses on disposal of and permanent diminution of fixed assets; and any goodwill charged in the profit and loss account. BOC follows the FRS 3 requirement for calculating EPS. The information is provided on the face of the profit and loss account and an explanation of the calculation is given in note 2(c) to the financial statements (see page 218). The calculation of EPS is discussed further in Chapter 10.

Exemptions and modifications

The Companies Act of 1967 abolished the status of 'exempt private company' and for a number of years all limited companies were required to conform to the same basic auditing, disclosure and filing provisions, although differences in status (between 'public' and 'private', or 'parent' and 'subsidiary') led to differences in additional disclosure requirements. The 1985 Act, however, permits reduced disclosure in the documents to be filed with the Registrar of Companies. Two points need to be emphasized: first, the implementation of reduced disclosure is permitted without being demanded; second, the permission extends only to those documents to be delivered to the Registrar and does not cover the documents to be delivered to members of the company in question. Members must receive full accounts, prepared wholly in accordance with the act's requirements.

Two categories of limited company may opt to apply the exemptions from full public disclosure:

1 medium-sized companies;
2 small companies;

and the Act that lays down certain criteria for determining the category into which a company falls. It is perhaps best to consider first those companies that cannot be classified as either medium-sized or small. They are:

- public companies;
- member companies of a group of companies containing a public company;
- banking or insurance companies;
- member companies of a group of companies containing a banking or insurance company;
- member companies of a group of companies containing a non-British corporate body that may lawfully offer its securities to the public;
- member companies of a group of companies containing a non-British corporate body that is a recognized bank or insurance company.

If a company does not fall into any of those categories, it may be eligible to be considered as either medium-sized or small, and those classifications depend entirely on size, as follows. Medium-sized companies are those that fulfil at least two of the following three conditions in respect of the current financial period:

1 turnover did not exceed £11.2 million;
2 total assets did not exceed £5.6 million;
3 average weekly number of employees did not exceed 250.

Similarly, the conditions for being considered a small company are that two or more of the following conditions are satisfied:

- turnover did not exceed £2.8 million;
- total assets did not exceed £1.4 million;
- average weekly number of employees did not exceed 50.

'Total assets' refers to the balance sheet total of fixed and current assets, as specified in the prescribed balance sheet formats, without deduction of any liabilities.

The exemptions for a medium-sized company are limited. It is permitted to omit only the following: turnover; cost of sales information; other operating income; analyses of turnover and profit amongst different classes of business; and analyses of turnover amongst different markets. The whole of the balance sheet and supporting notes, together with the rest of the notes to the profit and loss account, have to be given in full.

The exemptions for a small company are extensive. It is permitted to omit the following: the whole profit and loss account; the directors' report; particulars of the emoluments of directors and higher-paid employees; all of those items in the balance sheet that are not identified with Roman numerals (see Chapter 3); and considerable portions of the notes to the financial statements.

However, these are disclosure exemptions. Given that a smaller company, like any company, has to prepare financial statements that give a true and fair view then it could be argued that they must also follow the requirements of accounting standards. It has been argued that this requirement places a considerable burden on smaller companies and the ASB has responded by issuing in November 1997 a Financial Reporting Standard for Smaller Entities (FRSSE). This may be applied to all companies that meet the conditions outlined above for being considered a small company. The FRSSE consists of a simplified summary of the whole body of existing accounting standards. If companies choose to comply with the requirements of FRSSE then they are exempt from complying with other SSAPs or FRSs or UITF abstracts (unless they are preparing consolidated financial statements in which case a limited number of other standards will still apply).

3 The balance sheet

Perhaps best described as a 'position' statement, the balance sheet reports the position at the close of business on a given day, detailing the values of assets and liabilities at the balance sheet date and offering considerable scope for the analysis of the relationship between the different classes of assets and liabilities. The bases on which assets and liabilities are valued are, of course, of crucial importance.

This chapter examines the alternative formats permitted under the 1985 Act (as amended) by describing and discussing the various items to be included on the balance sheet or in the related notes, and by examining certain wider-ranging topics associated with particular balance sheet entries.

Formats

There are two permitted formats for a company's balance sheet; these are reproduced in Tables 3.1 and 3.2. The first format arranges the balance sheet items vertically (the practice most prevalent amongst UK companies), while the second format arranges those items horizontally (although the presentation does not necessarily have to be side by side).

Headings given Roman letters or numerals must be shown in the order, and under the headings and sub-headings, set out in the prescribed formats; no flexibility is permitted. The prescribed formats do, however, include a number of additional sub-headings, labelled with arabic numerals, which enjoy greater flexibility. These additional sub-headings will be described in the appropriate sections below, and their arrangement and description are adaptable to meet the particular needs or nature of a company's business. They may be combined to facilitate the better assessment of a company's affairs, but the fact of such combination must be stated and the details of such combined items must be disclosed in the notes to the financial statements.

Before turning to the detailed examination of the individual categories and their components, it is useful to consider two actual examples of balance sheets prepared under the provisions of the Act. Table 3.3 presents a modified extract from the balance sheet of The BOC Group plc, as at 30 September 1997; the full version may be seen in Appendix A to this book.

The descriptions and discussions following will deal with the various items in this order:

Table 3.1   Balance sheet – format 1

A	Called-up share capital not paid
B	Fixed assets
	I Intangible assets
	II Tangible assets
	III Investments
C	Current assets
	I Stocks
	II Debtors
	III Investments
	IV Cash at bank and in hand
D	Prepayments and accrued income
E	Creditors: amounts falling due within one year
F	Net current assets (liabilities)
G	Total assets less current liabilities
H	Creditors: amounts falling due after more than one year
I	Provisions for liabilities and charges
J	Accruals and deferred income
–	Minority interests[a]
K	Capital and reserves
	I Called-up share capital
	II Share premium account
	III Revaluation reserve
	IV Other reserves
	V Profit and loss account
–	Minority interests[a]

Note: [a]Group accounts only. This item to be treated as one to which a letter is assigned. Under this format the minority interests are normally shown after 'capital and reserves' rather than after 'accruals and deferred income'.

Table 3.2   Balance sheet – format 2

Assets		*Liabilities*[a]	
A	Called-up share capital not paid	A	Capital and reserves
			I Called-up share capital
B	Fixed assets		II Share premium account
	I Intangible assets		III Revaluation reserve
	II Tangible assets		IV Other reserves
	III Investments		V Profit and loss account
			— Minority interests[b]
C	Current assets		
	I Stocks	B	Provisions for liabilities and charges
	II Debtors		
	III Investments	C	Creditors
	IV Cash at bank and in hand		
		D	Accruals and deferred income
D	Prepayments and accrued income		

Notes: [a] 'Liabilities' may alternatively be shown below 'Assets' or be shown on a separate page.
[b] Group accounts only. This item to be treated as one to which a letter is assigned.

Table 3.3 The BOC Group plc – consolidated balance sheet (at 30 September 1997)

	1997 (£ million)	1996 (£ million)
Fixed assets		
Tangible assets	2,953.7	2,747.6
Intangible assets	28.8	33.4
Investment in own shares	24.0	22.6
Other investments	295.5	263.7
	3,302.0	**3,067.3**
Current assets		
Stocks	354.3	403.4
Debtors due within one year	901.7	906.1
Investments	16.7	7.7
Deposits and cash due within one year	222.2	155.8
Assets due beyond one year	101.9	95.7
Current assets	**1,596.8**	**1,568.7**
Current liabilities		
Creditors: amounts due within one year		
Borrowings and finance leases	(620.4)	(623.1)
Other creditors	(886.2)	(911.9)
Current liabilities	**(1,506.2)**	**(1,535.0)**
Net current assets	**90.2**	**33.7**
Total assets *less* current liabilities	**3,392.2**	**3,101.0**
Long-term liabilities		
Creditors: amounts due beyond one year		
Borrowings and finance leases	(1,001.2)	(767.4)
Other creditors	(23.5)	(26.3)
Provisions for liabilities and charges	(229.7)	(245.8)
	(1,254.4)	**(1,039.5)**
Total net assets	**2,137.8**	**2,061.5**
Capital and reserves		
Called up share capital		
equity capital	121.8	120.8
non-equity capital	2.5	2.5
Share premium account	272.4	259.4
Revaluation reserve	63.8	71.9
Profit and loss account	1,320.7	1,252.5
Related undertakings' reserves	111.6	111.6
Shareholders' funds	**1,892.8**	**1,818.7**
Minority shareholders' interests	245.0	242.8
Total capital and reserves	**2,137.8**	**2,061.5**

- fixed assets;
- current assets;
- creditors;
- provisions for liabilities and charges;
- capital and reserves;
- minority shareholders.

Valuation rules

The fourth schedule to the 1985 Act (as amended) lays down certain rules for the valuation of balance sheet items. These general valuation rules are discussed here, and the rules applicable to specific assets are discussed in the sections that follow. Broadly, the rules permit companies to draw up their financial statements under either the pure historical cost convention or the alternative conventions of historical cost modified to include certain assets at a revalued amount, or current cost. The BOC Group's accounts are based on the historical cost accounting convention, but include the revaluation of certain land and buildings.

The general rules may be summarized as follows. Under the historical cost convention, gross value shall be purchase price or production cost. Under the alternative conventions, gross value shall be either market value determined at the most recent valuation date or current cost. For example, tangible fixed assets shall be valued at market value or at current cost, stocks shall be valued at current cost, investments included in fixed assets shall be valued at market value or at a value determined by the directors on any basis considered appropriate in the circumstances, and investments included in current assets shall be valued at current cost.

Provisions for reduction in value shall be made in respect of all fixed assets where the reduction is expected to be permanent. Where investments are concerned, a provision for diminution in value may be made even where the reduction in value is not expected to be permanent. Fixed assets with finite economic lives shall be subject to depreciation charges as discussed in Chapter 2. Current assets shall be written down to a net realization value where that value is lower than cost or alternative valuation. Conversely, where a provision for reduction in value is no longer necessary, the provision shall be written back (via the profit and loss account) to the extent that it is no longer necessary.

Current cost accounting

The requirement to prepare and publish current cost accounting statements was contained in SSAP 16 ('Current cost accounting'), which was issued in March 1980. In June 1985 the mandatory status of SSAP 16 was suspended and in April 1988 it was formally withdrawn. In 1986 the ASC issued 'Accounting for the effects of changing prices: a handbook', and this is an authoritative reference work on current cost accounting. The 1985 Act does not define current cost and, therefore, where a company chooses to adopt the alternative accounting rules and value some assets at their current costs, then the principles set out in the ASC's handbook would normally be followed.

The basic requirement of current cost accounting is to ensure that the net operating assets of a company, and the calculation of profit, reflect the impact of price changes on the input prices of goods and services used and financed by a company.

When prices are rising, for example, the historical cost accounting profit will need to be adjusted to reflect the additional depreciation, cost of sales and monetary working capital that will be required to maintain the operating capability of a company. These are the basic current cost accounting adjustments. Also, when prices are rising, a company that is partly financed by loans, overdrafts or other fixed monetary liabilities will benefit from the fact that these will be repaid out of a depreciated currency. A gearing adjustment that reduces the total of the basic current cost accounting adjustments by the proportion that is effectively being financed by net monetary liabilities is therefore required. This leads to asset valuations that reflect the 'value to the business' or 'current cost' of an asset. The ASC's definition of *current cost* in its 1986 handbook on accounting for the effect of changing prices and the ASB's definition of *value to the business* in its 1995 statement of principles are identical. Both the *value to the business* of an asset and the *current cost* of an asset are defined as the lower of the replacement cost and the recoverable amount, with the recoverable amount being the higher of value in use and net realizable value. The mechanics of calculating the actual adjustments of current cost accounting are not described here in detail; readers are referred to a textbook on advanced financial accounting. Lewis and Pendrill (1996 chapters 15–18) for example, provides a comprehensive coverage of this topic.

Revaluation of assets

When assets are revalued a gain or loss on revaluation will arise. The Act requires a separate reserve called a valuation reserve to be used to account for such gains or losses and for these to be disclosed separately in the accounts. Thus, for example, if land which cost £400,000 is revalued at £600,000, then the unrealized gain of £200,000 cannot be taken to the profit and loss account but would be credited to a revaluation reserve. Also, following the introduction of FRS 3 ('Reporting financial performance') the unrealized gain of £200,000 would be disclosed in a statement of total recognized gains and losses for the period (see Chapter 5). If in a subsequent period the land is sold for £650,000 then the unrealized gain has become a realized gain and would be transferred out of the revaluation reserve and into the profit and loss reserve. The profit or loss on disposal is the difference between the sales proceeds and the carrying value. In this case the sales proceeds are £650,000, the carrying value is £600,000 and so the profit is £50,000. This can be included in the profit and loss account for the year. The carrying value for an asset is its revalued amount less any depreciation. If the land had been sold for £550,000 then a loss on disposal of £50,000 would be included in the profit and loss account. Prior to the introduction of FRS 3, the entry in the revaluation reserve of £200,000 could have been reversed and the profit would then have been based on the land's original cost of £400,000. Assuming that the land sold for £550,000, then this would have enabled a profit of £150,000 to be included in the profit and loss account.

In reality very few companies in the UK use a pure form of historical cost accounting when preparing financial statements. Even fewer use current cost accounting. The practice that has grown up is to use a modified historical cost approach, which is a mixture of historic cost for some assets and market values or current cost for others. However, there is little consistency in revaluation practices, with companies not obliged to revalue all assets or update previous revaluations. This clearly leads to a lack of comparability of the financial statements of different companies and because of this companies are required under FRS 3 ('Reporting financial performance') to publish a note of the profits or losses on an unmodified historical cost basis. Such a note is intended to enable a fair comparison to be made between companies' profits.

The ASB has also responded to this muddle of valuation approaches by issuing two related discussion papers. The first, in 1993, was on the role of valuation in financial reporting and the second, in 1996, examined the measurement of tangible fixed assets. The ASB argues that a return to pure historical cost accounting would be inappropriate because it is clearly important for many companies to show revaluations. Any attempt to prohibit revaluations would reverse a welcome trend to the provision of more relevant information. The ASB reiterates its preference for current cost or value to the business but also proposes to continue with the present system of modified historical cost. In the 1996 discussion paper the proposal is made that out-of-date valuations should be banned and where assets are revalued then the revaluations should be applied to all assets of a particular class and not just selected assets.

Contents

The prescribed contents of balance sheets under the alternative formats are summarized below in the order outlined earlier.

Fixed assets

The 1985 Act (as amended) defines fixed assets as those intended for use on a continuing basis in the company's activities. Other assets must be taken to be current assets. In each of the prescribed formats, fixed assets must be subdivided into three groups:

1 intangible assets;
2 tangible assets;
3 investments.

In addition, the notes to the financial statements are required to disclose information in the standard format about the cost (or revaluation or current cost) at the beginning and end of the financial year of each item shown as a fixed asset and also the effect on that item of:

■ acquisitions during the year;
■ disposals during the year;
■ transfers during the year;
■ any revision of the amount due to the application of the alternative accounting bases.

Details must also be disclosed for each fixed asset category of the accumulated provision for depreciation and diminution in value at the beginning and end of the financial year, any provisions made in the financial year and any adjustments to the provisions resulting from either the disposal of fixed assets or for any other reason, during the year.

The calculation of depreciation was discussed briefly in Chapter 2 and it was shown how different methods could affect the annual charge for depreciation. SSAP 12 ('Accounting for depreciation') requires companies to disclose the depreciation method used for each major class of depreciable asset and also the useful economic lives or depreciation rates used. The BOC accounting policies in respect of depreciation are shown on page 215. Also, in note 7 to the financial statements (see pages 230–1) information is provided on the tangible assets and related depreciation.

Intangible assets

Intangible assets must be included on the face of the balance sheet under a main heading, with the following sub-headings included either on the face of the balance sheet or in the notes to the financial statements:

- development costs;
- concessions, patents, licences, trade marks and similar rights and assets;
- goodwill;
- payments on account.

The Act lays down that only in special circumstances may an amount be included in the balance sheet in respect of 'development costs', although it does not define those circumstances. In general, research and development costs may not be capitalized; where they are, a reason must be stated. In most respects, the provisions of the schedule are closely similar to those presented in SSAP 13 ('Accounting for research and development'). SSAP 13 provides certain criteria for the capitalization of development costs and those criteria may be considered analogous to the Act's 'special circumstances'. They include: the clear identification of a project; the related expenditure is separately identifiable; the outcome of the project has been assessed with reasonable certainty as to technical feasibility and commercial viability; the future revenues can be reasonably expected to exceed the aggregate costs; and adequate resources exist to complete the project.

'Goodwill' is not defined in the 1985 Act (as amended) but SSAP 22 ('Accounting for goodwill') states that it is the difference between the value of a business as a whole and the aggregate of the fair values of its separable net assets. Goodwill may appear in a balance sheet only where it has been obtained for a valuable consideration (generally either cash or shares); this means that companies cannot capitalize internally generated goodwill. SSAP 22 permitted purchased goodwill arising on an acquisition to be either written off immediately against reserves or amortized (depreciated) through the profit and loss account over its useful economic life. Of these, SSAP 22 preferred the immediate write-off against reserves because this achieves consistency of treatment between purchased and non-purchased (internally generated) goodwill. In other words goodwill exists in most businesses but because it is volatile, difficult to identify and difficult to value it is not accounted for as an intangible asset and does not appear in the balance sheet. However, when one company acquires another a value for goodwill emerges and this has to be accounted for. Writing this goodwill off immediately to reserves means that it would then no longer be reported as an asset and this would be consistent with the accounting treatment of non-purchased goodwill.

The dominant practice in the UK since SSAP 22 was issued in 1984 has been for purchased goodwill to be written-off immediately against reserves; a situation that is out of line with practice in other countries. In the US, for example, positive goodwill has to be amortized on a straight-line basis over its estimated useful life. International Accounting Standard 22 ('Business Combinations') also requires goodwill to be capitalized and amortized. However, following the publication in December 1997 of

FRS 10 ('Goodwill and intangible assets'), accounting practice in the UK will, for accounting periods ending on or after 23 December 1998, follow that of other countries, with purchased goodwill being capitalized and amortized over its useful economic life. It is recommended that useful economic life should not normally exceed 20 years.

One difficulty with the immediate write-off of goodwill against reserves is that the balance sheets of some companies show a very low net worth or even an excess of liabilities over assets, with the result that balance sheets often give a misleading picture. Also it was possible for the calculation of the profit or loss on disposal of a previously acquired business to be overstated if the goodwill relating to the acquisition had already been written-off. This latter possibility was dealt with by UITF pronouncement 3 ('Treatment of goodwill on disposal of a business') which requires that when a previously acquired business is disposed of any goodwill that was written-off to reserves on acquisition should be included as a cost when determining the profit or loss on disposal of the business. BOC indicates in note 15(b) (see page 240) that its accounting policy is to write-off any goodwill paid on acquisition as part of the profit or loss on disposal. No goodwill was written-off on disposals in 1997 but £20.9 million was written off in 1996.

When preparing its accounts BOC currently follows the permitted UK accounting practice of writing-off goodwill immediately against reserves. The amount of goodwill acquired in 1997 is reported in note 15(a) to have been £9.2 million and the write-off to reserves is shown in note 12(c) (see page 236), with £8.9 million being written-off against the accumulated profit and loss account of the group and £0.3 million being written-off against the reserves of associated undertakings. BOC also provides information by way of note on the differences between UK GAAP and US GAAP. As pointed out above, in the US goodwill is capitalized and amortized and so the note on GAAP differences reveals that unamortized goodwill of £135.8 million would appear in the balance sheet as an asset and an £18.6 million amortization expense would have been charged against profit if US GAAP had been followed.

An issue that is closely related to the question of accounting for goodwill is that of accounting for other intangibles, such as brand names. Very often the goodwill figure written-off to reserves or amortized is simply taken to be the excess value of a business over and above the fair value of the net *tangible* assets. This means that intangibles such as brand names are written-off with the goodwill. However, brand names can add significant value to a company and many companies began to include the brand names element of purchased goodwill as separately identifiable intangible assets in their balance sheets. The practice of including brand names in balance sheets then spread to internally generated brands. One of the reasons that is often put forward in support of the inclusion of brand names is that balance sheets will then provide a more realistic picture of the underlying financial strength of a company, and therefore a more realistic picture of shareholders' funds.

FRS 10 will have the effect of significantly limiting the opportunities for recognizing internally generated brand names. Also, where a business combination occurs which leads to purchased goodwill then any brand names that are acquired will form part of the goodwill. As this will, under the requirements of FRS 10, be carried in the balance sheet as an asset then this will presumably remove much of the pressure that first led to the inclusion of the value of brand names in the balance sheet.

BOC's policy with regard to other types of intangible asset, such as patents and trademarks is to capitalize them and write them off over their effective economic lives.

These intangible assets are included on the face of the balance sheet at £28.8 million and note 8 to the accounts reveals the acquisition cost and the amortization charge for the year.

Tangible assets

The amounts of the following fixed assets must be shown either on the face of the balance sheet or in the notes thereto:

- land and buildings;
- plant and machinery;
- fixtures, fittings, tools and equipment;
- payments on account and assets in course of construction.

The category 'land and buildings' must be further divided into freeholds, long leaseholds (more than fifty years unexpired life remaining) and short leaseholds.

It is appropriate here to consider the question of the capitalization of the cost of fixed assets, and to mention items of cost that should be capitalized. In the case of land, capitalized cost should include the purchase price, agents' commissions, legal and surveying fees, draining, clearing, landscaping and demolition costs. If a building is purchased, the capitalized cost should include the purchase price and all repair, alteration and improvement costs. If a building is constructed, the balance sheet cost should include the cost of all work subcontracted, the cost of materials, labour and other direct production overheads and all other incidental costs (excavation, obtaining permits and licences, temporary buildings used as construction offices, and professional fees).

The cost in the balance sheet of other fixed assets should include the purchase price plus any freight, duty and installation charges. Own-built plant and machinery costs will also include the costs of materials, labour and production overheads. In all other cases, the balance sheet total should represent the total cost of relatively permanent items of furniture or fixtures and fittings.

Interest charges on capital borrowed to finance the production of an asset may be capitalized and this was discussed in Chapter 2. Where interest is included in the cost of an asset, that interest must be disclosed in a note to the financial statements.

Leased assets

SSAP 21 ('Accounting for leases and hire purchase contracts') requires the financial statements of a company to reflect the full impact of leasing transactions. The accounting treatment adopted for a leased asset depends on whether the lease is a finance lease or an operating lease. SSAP 21 defines a finance lease as one that transfers to the lessee substantially all of the risks and rewards of owning an asset, with all other leases being classed as operating leases. Assets leased to a company under a finance lease must be accounted for in a way similar to owned assets. Thus a finance lease will appear in a lessee's balance sheet as both an asset and an obligation to pay future rentals, and the asset should be depreciated over the shorter of the lease term and its useful life. At the inception of the lease the amount to be regarded both as the asset and the obligation should be the present value of the minimum lease payments (calculated by discounting at the interest rate implicit in the lease).

In Chapter 1 the concept of substance over form was discussed (see page 10). SSAP 21, which was issued in 1984, was the first accounting standard to apply this concept.

Assets obtained under a finance lease are not legally owned and yet they are required to be accounted for as though they are. Prior to the introduction of SSAP 21 companies could avoid disclosing assets and the associated liabilities on their balance sheets by simply obtaining them under a lease agreement rather than buying them. SSAP 21 prevented this for assets leased to a company under a finance lease agreement.

The precise rules for accounting for finance leases are complex and somewhat outside the scope of this book. Readers who wish to obtain a fuller understanding of the accounting techniques are referred to a textbook on advanced financial accounting (see, for example, Lewis and Pendrill, 1996: chapter 6).

SSAP 21 requires disclosure for each major class of fixed asset held under a finance lease of the gross amount, the related accumulated depreciation and the depreciation allocated for the period. Alternatively, this information may be included within the totals disclosed by each major class of asset for owned assets, provided that the total of the net amount of assets held under finance leases and the total amount of depreciation allocated for the period in respect of finance leases are disclosed separately. The BOC Group adopts the latter approach as can be seen from notes 7(a) and 7(b) on page 230.

Investments

Under the two alternative formats, investments appear in either fixed or current assets. Under the heading 'fixed assets', the following must be shown either on the balance sheet or in the notes to the financial statements:

■ shares in group companies;
■ loans to group companies;
■ participating interests;
■ loans to undertakings in which the company has a participating interest;
■ other investments *other* than loans;
■ other loans;
■ own shares.

In group accounts, participating interests are to be replaced by two items: interests in associated undertakings and other participating interests. Under the heading 'current assets', the following must be disclosed on the face of the balance sheet or in the notes:

■ shares in group undertakings;
■ own shares;
■ other investments.

In general terms, the distinction between the two headings relates to the basis on which investments are held. Those held on a relatively short-term basis would be included under 'current assets'.

As mentioned earlier in this chapter, there are alternative valuation bases for these assets – cost, market value or determined value. Listed investments must be distinguished, sub-divided between those listed on a recognized stock exchange and those listed elsewhere.

Where an investment in shares exceeds 10 per cent of the allotted share capital of the subject company or of the nominal value of any class of equity share capital, or where the value of the investment exceeds 10 per cent of the assets of the investing company, the notes must give additional information:

- the name of the subject company;
- its country of incorporation and/or registration;
- the identity and proportion of the nominal value of each class of shares held.

Companies listed on the Stock Exchange must give additional information, including the principal country of operation of the subject company and the percentage of each class of loan capital attributable to the investing company's interest (direct or indirect).

In its financial statements, the BOC group presents information that reveals the total value of investments in associated undertakings, other investments and own shares, net of provisions to be £319.5 million (see note 9(b) on page 232). That net value is analysed as:

	£ million
Listed: overseas stock exchange	37.2
Unlisted: directors' valuation	282.3
	319.5

The item 'own shares' in note 9(b) refers to BOC's own shares held for satisfying options under the company's share-based incentive schemes. Many companies have taken advantage of the tax incentives available for employee share ownership and have established schemes that enable employees to be allocated free shares under a profit-sharing scheme or give employees the option to buy shares at a favourable price. The shares that are needed for this can be either new shares or existing shares acquired by a trust and held for the employees. The shares acquired in this way are usually financed by a loan from the company or through a bank loan guaranteed by the company. BOC discloses the shares held for share-based incentive schemes as a fixed asset investment costing £24.0 million.

Current assets

Stock

Stocks are required to be disclosed as a main heading in the balance sheet. The word 'stocks' must be used; alternatives are not permitted. The category will require the following sub-headings:

- raw materials and consumables;
- work in progress;
- finished goods and goods for resale;
- payments on account.

A company should normally follow the above categorization, but the directors may adapt the format where the special nature of a company's business makes such an adaptation appropriate. SSAP 9 ('Stocks and long-term contracts') requires that the accounting policies adopted with respect to stocks and work in progress must be disclosed. The value to be used in respect of stocks is their purchase price or production cost, unless their net realizable value is lower, in which case that lower amount is used.

The 1985 Act (as amended) permits several methods of determining the cost of stock to be used, i.e. FIFO, LIFO, weighted average or any other similar method. An example of the use of these methods was considered in Chapter 2. Detailed consideration of the valuation of work in progress and long-term contracts is not appropriate here, and readers are referred to SSAP 9 and a relevant accounting textbook, such as Lewis and Pendrill (1996: 92–101).

The BOC balance sheet (see Table 3.3) shows a value for stocks of £354.3 million and an analysis of that total is provided in note 10a (see page 233) as follows:

	£ million
Raw materials	92.3
Work in progress	73.0
Gases and other finished goods	193.9
Payments on account	(4.9)
	354.3

Note 10 also provides similarly detailed information about the other categories of current assets and liabilities referred to below.

Debtors

Debtors must be disclosed as a main heading on the balance sheet and the following items must be disclosed either on the face of the balance sheet or in the notes thereto:

- trade debtors;
- amounts owed by group undertakings;
- amounts owed by undertakings in which the company has a participating interest;
- other debtors;
- called-up share capital not paid;
- prepayments and accrued income.

While shown under separate main headings on the alternative formats, the two final items above ('called-up share capital not paid' and 'prepayments and accrued income') may be included under 'debtors' when the amounts are not material.

'Trade debtors' will include amounts owed by customers, suppliers' debit balances, contract retentions etc., less any provision for bad and doubtful debts, credits for returns, allowances, cash discounts and rebates.

'Other debtors' will include amounts in respect of debts arising from non-trading or lending activities – amounts due from the sale of fixed assets, insurance claims, refundable deposits and the like. Additionally, the Companies Acts require disclosure under this heading of the following:

- loans to finance share purchases, where such loans are lawful;
- loans to directors;
- loans to officers other than directors.

Cash at bank and in hand

Cash at bank and in hand should not include deposits with building societies or time deposits with banks and the like, which should be shown as current asset investments. However, all other cash and near-cash items should be shown in this category: legal tender, cheques, postal orders, credit card vouchers, demand deposits and the like.

Creditors

Format 1 requires that creditors must be separated into those falling due within one year and those falling due after more than one year. Format 2 provides only one heading for creditors, but the amounts must be shown separately – within one year and after more than one year – and in aggregate. The Act lays down that 'creditors' must be shown under the following sub-headings either on the face of the balance sheet or in the notes to the balance sheet:

■ debenture loans;
■ bank loans and overdrafts;
■ payments received on account;
■ trade creditors;
■ bills of exchange payable;
■ amounts owed to group undertakings;
■ amounts owed to undertakings in which the company has a participating interest;
■ other creditors including taxation and social security;
■ accruals and deferred income.

The last heading is shown separately on the alternative formats, but may be included under creditors where not material.

In general terms, the categories above are straightforward and the calculation of the amounts to be reported is fairly easy. However, care should be taken not to confuse the item 'other creditors including taxation and social security' with the item 'taxation, including deferred taxation' which appears under the heading of 'provisions for liabilities and charges' (see later). UK corporation tax, and tax on profits that is payable to overseas governments, should appear under creditors. This is because these liabilities are certain as to the amount and date when payable and therefore do not fall within the definition of a 'provision'.

Also, there are some general disclosure requirements, in respect of amounts falling due after more than one year, that can usefully be mentioned here. For example, for each item that is payable wholly or in part after five years from the balance sheet date, there must be disclosed:

■ the aggregate amount wholly repayable;
■ the aggregate amount repayable by instalments, and the aggregate amounts of instalments that fall due after more than five years;
■ the terms of payment and the applicable interest rates.

Where large numbers of debts are involved, the disclosure of the last item may be given in general terms.

Certain types of debt liabilities have also given rise to inconsistency in accounting treatment. For example, convertible debt (i.e. debt which can be converted into equity) has the characteristics of both debt and equity. Some companies have chosen to include convertible debt as a liability in their balance sheets (i.e. it will be included as a creditor due within one year or after one year, whichever is appropriate), whereas others have argued that as conversion into equity is highly probable it should appear as part of share capital. The issue in December 1993 of FRS 4 ('Capital instruments') removes the latter option. All convertible debt is now required to be classified in the balance sheet as a liability and disclosed separately from other liabilities.

FRS 4 also requires the disclosure of an analysis of the maturity of all debt showing amounts falling due:

- in one year or less, or on demand;
- between one and two years;
- between two and five years; and
- in five years or more.

For convertible debt the disclosure requirement is for:

- the dates of redemption and the amounts payable on redemption;
- the number and class of shares into which the debt may be converted, and the dates or periods within which conversion may take place; and
- whether conversion is at the option of the issuer or the holder.

Provisions for liabilities and charges

Provisions for liabilities and charges must be shown on the face of the balance sheet as a main heading; the following sub-headings must be disclosed either on the face of the balance sheet or in the notes thereto:

- pensions and similar obligations;
- taxation, including deferred taxation;
- other provisions.

Provisions for liabilities or charges is defined in the Act as 'Any amount retained as reasonably necessary for the purpose of providing for any liability or loss which is either likely to be incurred, or certain to be incurred but uncertain as to amount or as to the date on which it will arise'.

The ASB in FRED 14 ('Provisions and contingencies') proposes a slightly simpler definition as follows: 'Liabilities in respect of which the amount or timing of the expenditure that will be undertaken is uncertain'.

Capital and reserves

Share capital and share premium

The 1985 Act (as amended) and its schedule require the disclosure of the following items:

- the amount of the authorized share capital;
- the amount of the allotted share capital;
- the amount of the called-up share capital that has been paid;
- the number and aggregate value of each class of allotted shares;
- the earliest and latest redemption dates of any redeemable shares and associated details;
- the reasons for and details of any allotment of shares during the period in question;
- the number, description and amount of any share options;
- the amount and period of any arrears in respect of fixed cumulative dividends;
- details of any holdings of the company's securities by subsidiaries or their nominees.

Where companies issue shares for a consideration in excess of their par or face value, the excess is to be placed in a share premium account. For example, if a company issues 400,000 £1 shares at £3 each, then it must credit £800,000 to a share premium account. Once a share premium account has been established it may be used only for purposes laid down in the Act: the issue of fully paid bonus shares, the writing-off of any preliminary or formation expenses, the writing-off of any expenses, commissions or discounts in connection with the issue of shares or debentures, or the provision of any premium payable on the redemption of debentures. Apart from those specific uses, the share premium account has to be treated as if it were part of the paid-up share capital of a company.

Certain types of shares have features which make them economically similar to debt. The basis distinction between debt and equity is that debt carries an obligation to pay interest, whereas there is no obligation to pay anything to equity. The holders of equity may receive a dividend if there are sufficient profits but there is no *entitlement*. The share capital of a company will consist of equity but might also consist of other types of shares (such as preference shares) which have an *entitlement* to a dividend and therefore are more akin to debt. However, company law requires these types of non-equity shares to be included as part of the share capital of a company rather than as a liability. FRS 4 ('Capital instruments') requires the shareholders' funds of a company to be analysed between the amounts attributable to equity interests and the amount attributable to non-equity interests. Disclosure of each class of non-equity share is required together with a summary of the rights to dividends, the date of and amount due on redemption, priority on the winding up of the company and voting rights.

The BOC Group balance sheet (see Table 3.3) reveals that the nominal value of the equity share capital is £121.8 million and the non-equity capital is £2.5 million. The non-equity capital is made up of preference shares and the details of these are reported in note 12(b) (see page 235).

Other reserves and profit and loss account

'Other reserves' will generally be capital redemption reserves or own share redemption reserves. Additionally, a company's articles of association may stipulate the creation of other reserves for specific purposes.

The 1985 Act (as amended) formats require that the retained balance on profit and loss account should be shown on the face of the balance sheet, and movements on profit and loss account must be disclosed.

Minority interests

Minority interests are required to be disclosed on the face of the balance sheet. Minority interest, as a balance sheet item, is defined as the amount of capital and reserves attributable to shares in subsidiary undertakings included in the consolidation and held by or on behalf of persons other than the parent company and its subsidiaries. The consolidation process requires 100 per cent of a subsidiary's assets and liabilities to be aggregated with those of the parent company, even though only, say, 60 per cent of the shares of the subsidiary might be held by the parent. The remaining 40 per cent of the shares are held by minority shareholders and it is the value of their share of the subsidiary undertakings, assets and liabilities that is represented by the item minority interests. FRS 2 ('Accounting for subsidiary undertakings') requires the assets and liabilities of a subsidiary undertaking to be attributed to minority interests on the same basis as those attributed to group interests. Dividends due to minority interests should be shown as liabilities under the heading of 'other creditors including taxation and social security'. FRS 4 ('Capital instruments') requires minority interests to be analysed between equity interests and non-equity interests.

Contingencies and commitments

Contingencies

It is appropriate here to mention the matter of contingent liabilities and assets. Contingencies are conditions that exist at a balance sheet date, but of which the future outcome is uncertain and only confirmed on the outcome of one or more uncertain future events – law suits, guarantees, taxation and the like. The Act requires that, for any contingent liability which has not been provided for in the financial statements, the notes must disclose the amount or estimated amount of that liability, its legal nature and the particulars of any security given. In addition SSAP 18 ('Accounting for contingencies') requires all contingent losses that are *probable* (i.e. that can be estimated with reasonable accuracy at the date on which the directors approve the financial statements) to be accrued in the normal way. Other contingent losses are merely required to be disclosed in the notes, except where the possibility of loss is remote, in which case disclosure is not required.

Note 13b to the BOC accounts (see page 237) reveals that 'other guarantees and contingent liabilities' amount to £34.9 million. The note goes on to report that:

> Various group undertakings are parties to legal actions and claims which arise in the ordinary course of business, some of which are for substantial amounts. While the outcome of some of these matters cannot be foreseen, the directors believe that they will be disposed of without material effect on the net asset position as shown in these financial statements.

Commitments

The Act requires disclosure of the following financial commitments:

- capital commitments (expenditure contracted for or authorized at the balance sheet date);
- pension commitments (those that are provided for in the balance sheet and those that are not provided for);
- other financial commitments (purchase commitments in excess of normal requirement, exposed foreign currency positions, lending or guarantee commitments).

In broad terms, these details are given in respect of any financial commitments that have not been provided for and are relevant to an assessment of the company's affairs. The impact of SSAP 24 on the disclosure of pension commitments was discussed in Chapter 2.

Post balance sheet events

There is now a requirement to report post balance sheet events, generally defined as events that become apparent only between the balance sheet date and the date of the signing of the balance sheet on behalf of the board of directors. Both the Act and SSAP

17 ('Accounting for post balance sheet events') contain requirements in this respect. SSAP 17 makes a distinction between events that require adjustment of the financial statements ('adjusting events') and those that require disclosure but do not require adjustment to the financial statements ('non-adjusting events'). Examples of adjusting events would include the bankruptcy of a debtor after the year-end; a fall in the selling price of a product, causing net realizable value of stocks to fall below cost; changes in the rate of taxation on profits taken up in the financial statements; or the discovery of errors or fraud showing the financial statements to be incorrect. Non-adjusting events might include a fall in the value of property or investments, a change in foreign exchange rates, the issue of shares or the acquisition or disposal of a business.

An example of the disclosure of a non-adjusting event is found in this extract from the notes to the 1997 accounts by Amersham International plc.

> *Merger of Amersham Life Science and Pharmacia Biotech*. Subsequent to the balance sheet date, Amersham has entered into a conditional agreement with Pharmacia and Upjohn Inc ('P&U') to merge Amersham Life Science with Pharmacia Biotech, the biotechnology supply business of P&U forming a new company, proposed to be named Amersham Pharmacia Biotech Limited.

The note then goes on to provide an unaudited pro forma statement showing the effect of the merger on the net assets and equity shareholders' funds of the Amersham Group.

The Act requires disclosure in the directors' report of particulars of important events affecting the company and its subsidiaries that have occurred after the year end. An example of this kind of disclosure can be found in the following extract from the Directors' Report in the 1997 accounts of Powell Duffryn plc.

> Following the year end, Andrews Weatherfoil Limited, was sold in May 1997. In the same month the Group entered into an agreement for the sale of its remaining terminal at Lemont, Chicago, for US$8.0m, and the Group's 50% interest in Corrall Montenay Ltd was sold for £9.6m. In June 1997 the Group acquired the business of Air Compressors Products USA Inc for US$1.5m.

It is clearly a matter of very fine judgement as to whether a post balance sheet event is a 'non-adjusting event', which SSAP 17 requires to be disclosed in the notes as in the Amersham example), or as an 'important event' which the Companies Act requires to be disclosed in the directors' report (as in the Powell Duffryn example).

It is useful in this context to mention the requirements in respect of the signing of the balance sheet. Under the Companies Acts provisions, every balance sheet of a company shall be signed by two directors on behalf of the board of directors. Additionally, SSAP 17 requires that each set of accounts should indicate the date on which the financial statements were approved by the board of directors. That date is important, in that it establishes the date up to which the directors are responsible for disclosing material post balance sheet events. The date will either be shown on the face of the balance sheet, above the signatures of the directors, or as the first item in the notes to the financial statements. Failing that, the date should be stated in the course of the auditors' report. These latter suggestions are not mandatory, but are considered representative of best practice.

The date of approval of the financial statements of the BOC Group is shown on the face of the balance sheet to have been 28 November 1997.

4 The cash flow statement

In September 1991 the ASB issued FRS 1 ('Cash flow statements') requiring all companies (except for small companies, wholly owned subsidiaries, building societies and mutual life assurance companies) to publish a cash flow statement. Prior to the introduction of FRS 1, companies had been required by SSAP 10 to provide a statement of source and application of funds.

The basic purpose of a cash flow statement is simply to report the cash receipts and the cash payments of an accounting period. As such it is claimed to be objective and understandable and to avoid many of the allocations that are needed for conventional profit determination. The matching concept requires the matching of the income of a period with the expenses of a period, with the difference between the two being profit or loss. Because many income and expense items do not conveniently fall into a particular period but have an impact on several periods it is necessary to allocate such items over the periods that are affected. As was seen in Chapter 2 there are a range of permitted methods for determining closing stock values and periodic depreciation charges and each method produced different costs for each accounting period. These are just two of the very many examples where items have to be allocated on an arbitrary basis to specific accounting periods. Cash flow statements avoid the need to make such periodic allocations.

However, a cash flow statement that simply reported the aggregate of cash receipts and the aggregate of cash payments would probably not be particularly useful. The original FRS 1 therefore required cash flows to be classified under the standard headings of: operating activities; returns on investment and servicing of finance; taxation; investing activities; and financing.

The requirements of FRS 1 were undoubtedly a major development in financial reporting and although it generally worked quite well there were some criticisms, particularly in relation to the requirement for cash flow statements to report the 'inflows and outflows of cash and cash equivalents'. The definition of cash as cash in hand and deposits repayable on demand with any bank or other financial institution was relatively straightforward. However, the definition of cash equivalents did cause problems. The inclusion of cash equivalents was an attempt to recognize that cash over and above that immediately needed would not be held in the form of cash but would be invested in short-term investments. Providing these investments were highly liquid, could be converted into known amounts of cash and were not subject to significant changes in value because of interest rate changes then they were accountable for as cash equivalents. To ensure that changes in interest rates would not bring about a significant change in the value of an investment, a cut-off date of not more than three months to maturity was imposed. This arbitrary cut-off date was difficult to defend and in October 1996 the ASB published a revised version of FRS 1 that contained a much tighter and much purer definition of cash. Cash is now defined as:

> Cash-in-hand and deposits repayable on demand with any qualifying financial institution, less overdrafts from any qualifying financial institution repayable on demand. Deposits are repayable on demand if they can be withdrawn at any time without notice and without penalty or if a maturity or period of notice of not more than 24 hours or one working day has been agreed.

The revised FRS 1 requires the cash flow statement to be classified under eight standard headings as follows:

1 operating activities;
2 returns on investment and servicing of finance;
3 taxation;
4 capital expenditure and financial investment;
5 acquisitions and disposals;
6 equity dividends paid;
7 management of liquid resources; and
8 financing.

The first six headings should follow the above sequence but the last two can be combined under a single heading providing that the cash flows that relate to each are shown separately and that separate sub-totals are given.

The BOC Group's cash flow statement for 1997 is reported in Table 4.1. This provides the classification of cash flows for 1997, together with the comparatives for the previous year, in the format required by the revised FRS1, and will form the basis for the discussion of the components of the cash flow statement.

Cash flow statement components

Operating activities

The net cash flow from operating activities is the cash surplus or deficit for the period that results from the items that normally make up the operating profit of the profit and loss account. It will therefore include the cash receipts from sales; the cash payments to suppliers, employees, providers of services, etc. It will be different from the operating profit because it will not include non-cash transactions such as credit sales, credit purchases and depreciation.

FRS 1 requires operating cash flows to be reported by using the indirect method but permits the information required by the direct method to be reported as well. Under the direct method the cash book is analysed into the various types of cash receipts and payments of the period and these are reported in the statements of operating cash flows. Under the indirect method it is only the net cash flow from operating activities

Table 4.1 The BOC Group plc – cash flow statement (year ended 30 September 1997)

	1997 (£ million)	1996 (£ million)
Net cash inflow from operating activities	**733.8**	**625.1**
Returns on investments and servicing of finance		
Interest paid	(113.3)	(108.9)
Interest received	15.9	23.5
Dividends paid to minorities in subsidiaries	(6.3)	(5.9)
Interest element of finance lease rental payments	(0.2)	(0.4)
Preference dividends paid	(0.1)	(0.1)
Returns on investments and servicing of finance	**(104.0)**	**(91.8)**
Tax paid	**(109.5)**	**(115.8)**
Capital expenditure and financial investment		
Purchases of tangible fixed assets	(650.8)	(533.6)
Sales of tangible fixed assets	34.5	47.1
Purchases of current asset investments	(9.0)	(4.7)
Capital expenditure and financial investment	**(625.3)**	**(491.2)**
Acquisitions and disposals		
Acquisitions of businesses	(31.7)	(25.8)
Net cash/(overdrafts) acquired with subsidiaries	0.5	0.2
Disposals of businesses	23.8	13.8
Net overdrafts disposed of with subsidiaries	—	2.0
Investments in associated undertakings	(26.3)	(12.1)
Acquisitions of intangibles	(1.2)	(3.9)
Purchases of trade investments	(13.4)	(4.9)
Sales of other investments	9.7	17.0
Acquisitions and disposals	**(38.6)**	**(13.7)**
Equity dividends paid	**(121.5)**	**(121.1)**
Net cash outflow before use of liquid resources and financing	**(265.1)**	**(208.5)**
Management of liquid resources		
Net (purchase)/sale of short-term investments	**(62.3)**	**(19.8)**
Financing		
Issue of shares	22.1	20.7
Increase in debt	342.1	182.2
Net cash inflow from financing	**364.2**	**202.9**
Increase/(decrease) in cash	**36.8**	**(25.4)**

that is reported and this is arrived at by starting with the operating profit and then adjusting this for all non-cash items.

As can be seen from Table 4.1, BOC uses the indirect method and reports simply the net cash flow from operations of £733.8 million. However, FRS 1 requires a note showing the reconciliation of this figure to the operating profit. This is provided in note 14(a) (see page 238) as follows:

	1997
Net cash inflows from operating activities	*£ million*
Operating profit	540.4
Depreciation and amortization	276.5
Operating profit of associated undertakings	(61.6)
Dividends from associated undertakings	19.5
Change in stocks	29.0
Change in debtors	(60.3)
Change in creditors	23.5
Exceptional cash flows	(11.4)
Other	(21.8)
Net cash inflow from operating activities	733.8

Even if the direct method is used to report cash flows from operations, a statement showing the reconciliation with operating profit is still required.

Returns on investment and servicing of finance

The purpose of this category is to capture all of the cash flows that result from payments to the providers of finance and from ownership of investment. In Table 4.1 BOC report interest paid; interest received; dividends paid to minority shareholders; dividends paid to preference shareholders; and the interest element of finance lease payments. Dividends relating to equity shares appear under a separate heading in the cash flow statement. If the returns on investment and servicing of finance classification were not provided, these types of cash flows would have to be categorized as relating to either operating activities or financing activities or capital expenditure and financial investment activities or acquisitions and disposals activities. At times such a distinction might be difficult to make. Also, by categorizing interest payments under this heading the cash flows from operating activities are not affected by the way in which a company is financed and this should improve comparability. Any interest paid in the year that has been capitalized should be reported under this heading (rather than part of capital expenditure and financial investments).

Taxation

The use of this category avoids the need for arbitrary allocations of taxation to other categories such as cash flows from operating activities. Cash flows in respect of taxation on profits tend to arise because of the activities of previous periods rather than the current period and so this provides a further rationale for a separate category for taxation. It follows from this that it is only tax flows relating to payments (or refunds) of tax on profits that is reported here. Cash flows in respect of VAT, property tax (business rates) or other taxes not assessed on profits should not be reported under this heading. VAT and property tax, for example, will normally form part of the cash flows from operating activities. The usual accounting treatment is for cash flows to be reported net of VAT with only the net amount of cash due to or from the VAT authorities included as an operating cash flow.

Capital expenditure and financial investment

This category includes all cash flows relating to the acquisition or disposal of fixed assets (including investments). The following cash inflows should be separately disclosed:

- receipts from sales of property, plant and equipment;
- receipts from the repayment of loans made to other entities (other than receipts forming part of a disposal or a movement in liquid resources (see below);
- receipts from the sale of debt instruments of other entities (other than receipts forming part of a disposal or movement in net liquid resources).

The cash outflows that are required to be disclosed are as follows:

- payments to acquire property, plant and equipment;
- loans made by the reporting entity to other entities (other than payments forming part of acquisition or a movement in liquid resources);
- payments to acquire debt instruments of other entities (other than payments forming part of an acquisition or a movement in net liquid resources).

Table 4.1 shows that BOC's net cash outflow from capital expenditure and financial investment for the year to 30 September 1997 was £625.3 million.

The purchase of fixed assets on credit can complicate the classification of the associated cash flows. If a fixed asset is paid for in cash or a down payment of part of the total acquisition cost is made in cash, then these are clearly capital expenditure and financial investment flows. Subsequent repayments of what is essentially a loan from the seller of the fixed asset are financing cash flows. The treatment would also apply to the acquisition of assets under hire purchase contracts or where assets are obtained under a finance lease, with the payments of principal being classified as financing cash flows rather than capital expenditure and financial investment cash flows. (A short-term difference between the time when an asset is acquired and the subsequent payment would not of course change the cash flow classification from capital expenditure and financial investment to financing.

Acquisition and disposals

This heading covers cash receipts from the disposal of any trade or business or from the sale of investments in an entity that as a result of the sale ceases to be either an associate, a joint venture or a subsidiary. Likewise any payments to acquire any trade or business or for investing in an entity that would result in the entity becoming an associate, joint venture or subsidiary is also covered by this heading.

The revised version of FRS 1 requires any balances of cash and overdrafts acquired on the purchase of subsidiaries or any balances of cash and overdrafts transferred as part of the sale of subsidiaries to be disclosed separately.

The complication caused by the purchase of fixed assets on credit as discussed above also applies when the payment to acquire a subsidiary is deferred. When the deferred payment is eventually made the question that then arises is whether this should be treated as a financing cash flow or as an acquisition and disposal. The revised FRS 1 is silent on this point.

BOC reports several items under the heading acquisitions and disposals and also shows separately the cash balances and overdrafts on the acquisition and disposal of subsidiaries. The amount of £31.7 million for acquisition of businesses is analysed further in note 15(a) to the financial statements (see page 240).

Equity dividends paid

The amounts to be included under this heading are the dividends paid on the company's equity shares, excluding any related tax credit.

Management of liquid resources

The cash flows included under this heading are defined in FRS 1 (para. 2) as those related to 'current asset investments held as readily disposable stores of value'. The standard makes it clear that 'readily disposable' means an investment that could be disposed of without curtailing or disrupting the business of the entity. This in turn means investments that are either readily convertible into known amounts of cash at, or close to, their carrying amounts (which would tend to exclude any that are more than one year from maturity at acquisition), or traded in an active market.

FRS 1 requires the separate disclosure of:

■ cash inflows from withdrawals from short-term deposits not qualifying as cash;
■ cash inflows from the disposal or redemption of other investments held as liquid resources;
■ cash outflows for payments into short-term deposits not counting as cash;
■ cash outflows to acquire any other investments held as liquid resources.

The items can however be netted off for presentation purposes if the cash inflows and outflows are due to the high turnover occurring from the rollover or reissue of short maturity items. BOC has obviously taken advantage of this netting-off provision and reports simply the net purchase of short-term investments as £62.3 million.

Financing

Included in this category are the receipts from and payments to providers of finance. Only the principal amounts involved are included, with interest, dividends, etc. appearing under returns on investments and servicing of finance. The cash inflows that are required to be disclosed under this heading are:

■ receipts from issuing shares or other equity instruments; and
■ receipts from issuing debentures, loans, notes and bonds and from other long- and short-term borrowings (other than overdrafts).

The financing cash outflows include the following and these also are required to be separately disclosed:

■ repayments of amounts borrowed (other than overdrafts);
■ the capital element of finance lease rental payments;
■ payments to re-acquire or redeem the entity's shares; and
■ payments of expenses or commissions on any issue of shares.

One complication arises with the premium payable on redemption of loans or shares. Where a premium payable on redemption is in the nature of interest then presumably this should be classified under the returns on investments and servicing of finance heading.

Usefulness of cash flow statements

The requirement to include a cash flow statement in the annual report of a company is a relatively recent one and the extent to which users of financial statements find it useful still has to be established. The statement which it replaces, the funds flow statement, was generally perceived to be helpful in answering questions concerning the resources that a company had available to it and the use it made of those resources. However, funds flow statements were based on movements in working capital rather than cash and this could obscure movements relevant to the liquidity and viability of an entity. An example of this provided by FRS 1 is where a significant decrease in cash is masked by an increase in stocks or debtors. Companies might therefore run out of cash while reporting increases in working capital. Similarly a decrease in working capital does not necessarily indicate a cash shortage. Also a wide variety of funds flow statements were presented, with some companies reporting movements in net liquid funds and others reporting movements in working capital, net borrowings or total external financing.

The ASB feels that by concentrating on cash flows only, the cash flow statement will, in conjunction with the balance sheet, provide information on liquidity, viability and financial adaptability and the information will be easier to understand than are changes in working capital. Also, the cash flow statement and its associated notes do not simply reorganize existing opening and closing balance sheet information (as was the case with the source and application of funds statements) but provides new data.

In addition cash flows have the advantages mentioned earlier in this chapter of being more objective and less dependent on arbitrary allocations than conventional accruals-based financial statements. The cash flow statement might be expected therefore to become one of the prime sources of information about the financial performance and financial position of a company.

In an attempt to bring out the distinction between cash flow statements and the conventional accruals based profit and loss statements an illustration drawn from the following simple set of information has been provided.

Example 4.1

Suppose that New Company Limited was formed on 1 January 19X0 and commenced in business on that date as manufacturers of central heating thermostats. Because they were a new start-up company they were offered brand new factory premises by the local industrial development agency for a low start rent of £15,000 per year payable quarterly in advance. On 1 January 19X0 the four owners of the company each invested £25,000 of their own money to provide a total of £100,000 of equity share capital. Also on that date New Company Limited obtained a medium term loan of £100,000 at an interest rate of 11½ per cent per annum from the local industrial development agency. During the year to 31 December 19X0, the following nine transactions took place:

1 Purchased manufacturing plant and equipment for £175,000. All of this had been paid for by the end of the year but none of the installation costs of £17,500 had been paid.
2 The rent for the year had been paid and in addition the rent for the first quarter of 19X1 had been paid early in December 19X0.
3 Six months interest on the loan had been paid by 31 December 19X0.
4 Wages and salaries expenses totalling £220,000 were incurred and paid for during the year.
5 Raw materials amounting to £217,000 had been purchased during the year but only £193,000 of this had been paid for by 31 December 19X0.
6 The stock of raw materials that had not been used by 31 December 19X0 was valued at £21,500 and the stock of finished goods was valued at £36,200. There was no work in progress.
7 Heating, lighting and miscellaneous expenses totalling £92,450 were paid for during the year.
8 It was decided that no dividend would be paid to the shareholders for the first year of business and no taxation was due.
9 The sales value of central heating thermostats sold during the year was £560,020. This amount includes £33,400 that had not been received from customers by 31 December 19X0.

Shortly after the end of the financial year it was noted that an invoice amounting to £11,207 for electricity that had been consumed in December 19X0 for heating and lighting the factory had not been paid. It was estimated that the plant and machinery would have a useful life of seven years and no residual value. It was also estimated that approximately 20 per cent of the amounts due from debtors at 31 December 19X0 might never be recovered.

From this data the cash flow statement shown in Table 4.2 has been prepared by simply classifying the data for actual cash outflows or inflows under the appropriate standard heading. The direct method of determining the operating cash flow has been used, and the format follows the revised version of FRS 1.

The statement in Table 4.2 does, of course, make no adjustment for non-cash items. For example the value of central heating thermostats sold was £560,020 but only £526,620 of this was received from customers in the form of a cash receipt. The remaining £33,400 is the amount due from debtors, i.e. customers who have bought the thermostats on credit terms but not yet paid the amount they owe. The cash flow statement only recognizes the cash received from customers. Similarly, the total expenditure on heating, lighting and miscellaneous expenses was not simply the cash paid during the year on these items of £92,450 but also included the amount of £11,207 in respect of electricity consumed during the year but not paid for by the end of the year. However, the cash flow statement simply focuses on the cash payment of £92,450. The cash flow statement therefore ignores the accruals concept discussed in Chapter 1.

An alternative way to examine the performance of New Company Limited is to prepare a conventional profit and loss account that does follow the accruals (and also the matching) concepts. Under this approach all income from the sale of thermostats, irrespective of whether the cash has been received, will be recorded and all expenditure that relates to the year will be included, even though some of the items have not been paid for by the end of the financial year.

Table 4.2   Cash flow statement – New Company Limited

Cash Flow Statement – Year ended 31 December 19X0	£	£
Operating cash flows		
Cash received from customers		526,620
Less		
Wages	220,000	
Raw materials	193,000	
Rent	18,750	
Heating, lighting, miscellaneous	92,450	524,200
Cash flow from operating activities		2,420
Returns on investments and servicing of finance – interest paid		(5,750)
Taxation		—
Capital expenditure and financial investments		
Manufacturing plant and equipment		(175,000)
Acquisitions and disposals		—
Equity dividends paid		—
Net cash outflow before use of liquid resources and financing		(178,330)
Financing		
Issue of shares	100,000	
Issue of debt	100,000	200,000
Increase in cash		21,670

This does, however, bring into play the need to consider other concepts. It has to be recognized that not all of the amounts due from customers, which in the case of New Company Limited total £33,400, might be received and therefore the concept of prudence or conservatism would require an adjustment to be made. In this case it is estimated that 20 per cent of the total debtors of £33,400, i.e. £6,680 might never be recovered. Recognizing the possibility of bad debts is also consistent with the matching concept. If no adjustment were made in 19X0, then the period in which it became certain that the amounts were irrecoverable, which might be 19X1 or 19X2, would have to bear the cost of bad debts that relate to the 19X0 accounting year. This would be in conflict with the matching concept which requires expenses to be charged to the period that gave rise to the expenses, which in this case is clearly 19X0, the year in which the sales were made.

If these concepts of accruals and matching are followed then the closing stocks of raw materials and finished goods should not be an expense of 19X0 because they have not been sold in 19X0 and the cost of plant and equipment will be spread over the years that benefit from its use through an annual depreciation charge. This was discussed in Chapter 2.

Table 4.3   Profit and loss account – New Company Limited

Profit and Loss Account – Year Ended 31 December 19X0

	£	£
Sales		560,020
Cost of sales – purchases	217,000	
Less closing stock	57,700	159,300
Gross profit		400,720
Heating and lighting	103,657	
Wages and salaries	220,000	
Interest (£100,000 × 11½%)	11,500	
Rent	15,000	
Depreciation (175,000 + 17,500) ÷ 7	27,500	
Bad debts provision (33,400 × 20%)	6,680	384,337
Profit for year		16,383

Note

(i)   The closing stock of £57,700 is made up of raw materials valued at £21,500 and finished goods valued at £36,200.

(ii) The purchase price of the plant and equipment was £175,000 to which has been added the installation costs of £17,500 to give a total cost of £192,500. The plant and machinery has an estimated useful life of seven years with no residual value and so a straight line depreciation charge of £192,500 ÷ 7, i.e. £27,500 has been made.

A 'conventional' profit and loss account, which is based on the accounting concepts outlined in Chapter 1, for New Company Limited is shown in Table 4.3.

If the cash flow statement and the profit and loss account for New Company Limited are now compared it can be seen that they both provide different kinds of information about the performance of the company. The cash flow statement is based on information that is entirely objective. It makes no assumptions about whether debtors will or will not pay or how the costs of long-lived assets should be spread over their useful life. It simply works on the basis that if cash is received or paid it will be recorded in the cash flow statement. The operating cash flow surplus of £2,420 might therefore be thought of as an objective and reliable measure of the ability of the company to generate cash from its ongoing day-to-day activities. The cash flow statement also provides very clear information concerning the liquidity of the company and about the sources and uses of cash.

However, as a performance measure the cash flow statement is flawed because it does not tell the whole story. It does not show the total of the benefits or revenues earned by the company in 19X0, or the expenses incurred by the company in 19X0 to achieve those revenues. This is the role of the profit and loss account. The profit of £16,383 for New Company Limited for 19X0 might therefore represent a more relevant measure of performance because it is the balance that remains after taking into account all of the revenues and all of the expenses for 19X0. But is it reliable? Had the depreciation expense been allocated over a different period, say 6 or 8 years, or had a reducing balance method of calculating the annual charge been used, then a different amount to £27,500 would have been charged. Similarly, the closing stock might have been valued differently and the bad debts provision might have been estimated at higher or lower than 20%. All of these adjustments are based on estimates or judgements about uncertain future events. Providing the methods used comply with generally accepted accounting practices, then the different amounts would be defensible and the different profit or loss amounts that would result would be equally defensible. The example of depreciation charges and inventory valuation for the Plastic Products company, that was included in Chapter 2, showed that choice in accounting measurement can produce different measures of profit or loss for the same underlying economic events. This is the dilemma of conventional accruals-based accounting. Conceptually, profit or loss is a very sound measure of performance. In reality, it suffers from the fact that it is based on a series of estimates and judgements and had different but equally valid estimates and judgements been made then the resultant profit or loss would have been different. On the other hand the cash flow statement, which avoids the estimates and judgements and therefore is more reliable, fails to take into account the full range of events that affected performance. The obvious answer is to use both statements together to obtain as clear a picture as possible of the underlying strengths and weaknesses of a company.

5 Other reports and statements

The impact of FRS 3 ('Reporting financial performance') on the profit and loss account of a company has already been discussed in Chapter 2. FRS 3 also introduced a requirement for further reports and statements as follows:

- a statement of total recognized gains and losses;
- a note of historical cost profit or losses; and
- a reconciliation of movements in shareholders' funds.

Statement of total recognized gains and losses

This statement is effectively a fourth primary statement and must appear alongside the profit and loss account, balance sheet and cash flow statement. This statement recognizes that the profit and loss account of a company is primarily concerned with the *realized* profit or losses of a period. In addition there are unrealized gains and losses, such as an increase in the value of assets, which do not form part of the calculation of profit. The FRS points out that it is necessary to consider all gains or losses recognized in a period when assessing the financial performance of a company and it is this that has led to the requirement for the statement of total recognized gains and losses. The purpose of this statement, therefore, is to report the total of all gains and losses of the reporting entity that are recognized in a period and are attributable to shareholders. The ASB defines gains as increases in equity, other than those relating to contributions from owners, and losses as decreases in equity, other than those relating to distributions to owners.

The statement of total recognized gains and losses for The BOC Group plc is reported in Table 5.1.

Where an unrealized but recognized gain or loss is realized in a subsequent period, then it cannot be included as profit for that period, otherwise this would be tantamount to reporting the gain or loss twice – once through the statement of total recognized gains and losses when the gain or loss was first recognized and once through the profit and loss account when the gain or loss was subsequently realized. Thus, for example, the BOC statement of total recognized gains and losses shows that there was no unrealized surplus or deficit on revaluations in 1997, but there was an unrealized

Table 5.1   The BOC Group plc – statement of total recognized gains and losses (year ended 30 September 1997)

	1997 (£ million)	1996 (£ million)
Profit for the financial year	**287.6**	**278.3**
Unrealized surplus/(deficit) on revaluations	—	(0.7)
Exchange translation effect on		
results for the year	(4.0)	(3.2)
foreign currency net investments	(89.8)	(13.7)
Total recognized gains and losses for the year	**193.8**	**260.7**

deficit of £0.7 million in 1996. If the assets that gave rise to this deficit are subsequently sold, any profit or loss on sales that goes to the profit and loss account will be the difference between the sales proceeds and the original acquisition cost. Prior to the introduction of FRS 3, as was pointed out in Chapter 3, it was possible for earlier revaluation surplus or deficit adjustments to be reversed so that the profit or loss on sale could be based on the depreciated historical cost of the asset.

It was also explained in Chapter 3 that any goodwill that was written-off to reserves on acquisition of a business, is now required by UITF 3 ('Treatment of goodwill on disposal of a business') to be reinstated as a cost when determining the profit or loss on the sale of the business. Any goodwill that has been written-off to reserves, or any that is subsequently reinstated, is not to be included in the statement of total recognized gains and losses. This is because items included in this statement are not permitted to be reversed out and included in the profit and loss account and yet goodwill written-off to reserves has to be reinstated in the profit and loss account to satisfy the requirements of UITF 3. The solution therefore has been to exclude goodwill write-offs from the statement of total recognized gains and losses.

Any capital contributed to a company by shareholders or any dividends or capital repayments to shareholders or movements in reserves do not represent gains or losses and are not included in the statement.

Note of historical profit or loss

It was pointed out in Chapter 3 that companies are allowed to draw up their accounts on either a pure historical cost basis or on one of the alternative bases. An alternative basis that is widely used is that of historic cost modified by the revaluation of certain assets. Where a company uses this basis and this results in a profit or loss that is materially different to the profit or loss that would have resulted from the use of unmodified historical cost, then a note of the historical cost profits and losses is required. The note of historical cost profit or loss must be reported immediately after either the profit and loss account or the statement of total recognized gains and losses.

The FRS offers two reasons for requiring disclosure of profit or loss on the unmodified historical cost basis. The first of these is that as long as there is discretion over the timing or scale of revaluations included in financial statements then the unmodified historical cost basis will give a profit or loss figure that is more comparable with that of other companies. The second reason is the wish of some users to assess the

Table 5.2 The Albert Fisher Group – note of historical cost profit for the year ended 31 August 1997

	£ million
Reported profit on ordinary activities before taxation	41.5
Difference between historical cost depreciation charge and actual charge for the year calculated on revalued amounts	0.1
Historical cost profit on ordinary activities before taxation	41.6

profit or loss on the sale of assets that is based on the historical cost of the assets sold rather than the revalued amount.

The note of historical cost profits and losses will therefore typically include such items as:

■ the difference between an historical cost depreciation charge and the depreciation charge actually used in the profit and loss account that was based on the revalued amount; and

■ gains reported in the statement of total recognized gains and losses of previous periods and realized in the current period. In this case the note would show the difference between the profit on disposal of an asset calculated using the depreciated historical cost of the asset and the profit based on the revalued amount of the asset.

BOC do not provide a note of historical cost profit or loss for the year to 30 September 1997, which presumably means that this was not materially different from the reported profit. For the purposes of illustrating the note an example taken from the accounts of the Albert Fisher Group plc for the year ended 31 August 1997 is shown in Table 5.2.

Reconciliation of movements in shareholders' funds

FRS 3 requires the presentation of a note which reconciles the opening amount of shareholders' funds with the closing amount for the period. This reconciliation can be presented either as a primary statement or as a note to the accounts. BOC have reported it in the form of a primary statement and this is reproduced in Table 5.3. The profit or loss for the period and the other recognized gains or losses are two of the items that will bring about a change in the shareholders' funds and these are included in the reconciliation. In addition the reconciliation will include other items as follows:

■ dividends for the period;

■ capital contributions from shareholders or repaid to shareholders during the period, e.g. the amount received in respect of new shares;

■ goodwill eliminated against reserves during the period or goodwill reinstated because of the disposal of a previously acquired business.

Goodwill arising on the acquisition of a business and written-off to reserves is not included in the statement of total recognized gains or losses but has to be included in the reconciliation of movements in shareholders' funds because it has the effect of reducing these. Any goodwill that is reinstated on the subsequent disposal of a business

Table 5.3 The BOC Group plc – reconciliation of movements in shareholders' funds (year ended 30 September 1997)

	1997 (£ million)	1996 (£ million)
Profit for the financial year	**287.6**	**278.3**
Dividends	(140.4)	(130.1)
	147.2	148.2
Other recognized gains and losses	(93.8)	(17.6)
Goodwill		
taken to reserves on acquisitions	(9.2)	(6.8)
reversal of write-off through profit and loss		
account on disposals	—	20.9
Shares issued	11.1	9.6
Scrip dividends	18.8	8.8
Net increase in shareholders' funds for the year	**74.1**	**163.1**
Shareholders' funds at 1 October	1818.7	1655.6
Shareholders' funds at 30 September	1892.8	1818.7

is added to the reserves on reinstatement and deducted from the profit and therefore has no effect on the *total* of shareholders' funds.

The Companies Act 1985 (as amended) requires a note showing the movements on reserves and although it is not clear from FRS 3 whether this could be combined with the reconciliation of movements in shareholders' funds, the implication from the explanatory section of the FRS is that the two notes should be shown separately.

6 The chairman's statement and the chief executive's review

The chairman's statement

The statement to members by a company chairman is an influential part of the annual report and is widely read by shareholders. In essence the statement offers an opportunity for a chairman to report in unquantified and unaudited terms on the performance of a company during the past financial period and on likely future developments. The chairman will usually take the opportunity to comment on directors and other employees, and on the efforts of the management team and the workforce. Quite often, the statement will be used to make political or social comments about government, taxation, accounting standards or whatever else exercises the chairman at the time of writing.

There is no format, other than the general one that the statement is usually addressed to the shareholders and is conventionally signed and dated by the chairman, and there are no standard or even recommended contents.

Chairmen's statements range in length from half a printed page to more than seven or eight pages. In the latter case, the contents will include a reasonably thorough description of each of the main areas of activity.

Although the chairman's statement is not audited as such, the auditors would be expected to review it to ensure that the information disclosed is neither misleading nor incompatible with the financial statements. However, whether audited or not, there is little doubt that the users of annual reports find the chairman's statement to be of real value in assessing a company and its prospects. Lee and Tweedie (1981) found that professional institutional investment specialists considered the chairman's statement to be an important part of the annual report. The most important were the profit and loss account and the balance sheet, and the chairman's statement was next. It is salutary to add here that the auditors' report was considered the least important part of the annual report. Of the 214 readers of annual reports surveyed by Lee and Tweedie, all except one read the chairman's statement briefly or thoroughly; of those readers, the great majority did not read the auditors' report at all.

This relatively wide readership of the chairman's statement led the Committee on the Financial Aspects of Corporate Governance ('Cadbury Report' 1992) to note (p. 34) that 'it is therefore of special importance that it [the chairman's statement] should provide a balanced and readable summary of the company's performance and prospects and that it should represent the collective view of the board'.

The Cadbury Report also noted that the chairman should be able to stand back from the day-to-day running of the company to ensure that the board is in full control of the company's affairs and alert to its obligations to shareholders. There is no doubt that, divorced from the strict requirement of the law and the regulatory bodies, the tone and approach of a chairman's statement are valuable indicators of a company's 'state of mind' and as such the statement is clearly helpful to readers.

The role of the chairman of a company was, in the past, often combined with the role of chief executive. However, a chief executive is someone who is actively involved in the implementation of board decisions and the day-to-day management of a company, which is in direct contrast with the role of a chairman who is meant to be able to stand back from all of this. The Cadbury Report therefore recommended in its code of best practice that the roles of chairman and chief executive should be split with 'a clearly accepted division of responsibilities at the head of a company, which will ensure a balance of power and authority, such that no one individual has unfettered powers of decision'. Although this was not a requirement, most major companies have separated the roles of chairman and chief executive and it is usual for each to provide a statement or review.

BOC follows this practice and includes in its 1997 report and accounts both a statement by the chairman (Mr David John) and a review by the chief executive (Mr Danny Rosenkranz). Neither of these are reproduced in full in Appendix A and so it might be useful to consider extracts from these here.

The chairman's statement begins by commenting on how a good performance has been masked by the rise and continuing strength of the pound sterling. The chairman also draws attention to the ongoing review by the board of the Group's businesses and strategies which was due to be completed by March 1998. Corporate Governance is also addressed and the chairman welcomes the work that has been done on this and confirms that the principal requirements of the existing codes and guidelines are complied with. The recent listing on the New York Stock Exchange is also noted and it is pointed out that rather than the full 108 page version of the annual report and accounts, shareholders can elect to be sent an abbreviated annual review of only 40 pages. Less than 5 per cent of shareholders had asked for the full version to be sent to them.

The chief executive's review

The chief executive's review provides a summary of the financial performance for the year and, like the chairman's statement, draws attention to the impact of the strength of the pound sterling on sales and profit. The chief executive also comments on BOC's previously announced plans to sell the group's health care business Ohmeda. At the beginning of his review the chief executive draws attention to four areas that are commanding significant management attention. These are: growing sales; continuous improvement; ethics; and enablers. The review elaborates on these and explains that 'ethics' covers such areas as impact on the environment and communities in which the group operates, how suppliers are treated and the health and safety of employees and that 'enablers' are the factors that enable the group to achieve growing sales, continuous improvement and ethical standards. These are stated to be the employees and particularly the managers of BOC and the chief executive confirms the high priorities attached to developing the skills and experience of managers and also to information management.

Perhaps one of the most important features of either the chairman's statement or the chief executive's review is the opportunity they provide to give some indication of the prospects of a company. Most users of financial statements will be particularly interested in the future and yet it is very rare for formal quantified forecasts of the future performance and financial position of a company to be provided. Thus any qualitative pointer to future performance that might be provided by the chairman or chief executive is often the closest approximation that there is to a forecast and as such it will be considered carefully by users.

The chief executive of BOC provides the following example of an assessment of future performance.

> I believe our prospects continue to be good. All our businesses have opportunities for growth and further improvements in profitability. We continue to invest very heavily, particularly in our gases business. Capital expenditure in this business is running at about £700 million a year; but our cash flow, balance sheet and all the key financial ratios remain healthy and will enable us to fund future growth.

The chief executive concluded his review by thanking the group's managers and other employees for their commitment to the company and its goals, and for their efforts and achievements.

7 The directors' report and the operating and financial review

The basic purpose of the directors' report is to provide a narrative supplement to the financial information. The 1985 Act (as amended) requires certain information to be included in the directors' report. Additionally, the Listing Agreement of the Stock Exchange occasionally calls for wider disclosure than that required by statute or accounting standard, and more recently the Cadbury Report has recommended specific items that should be reported on by directors.

There are no formats specified, but the directors of a company are required to give details of, and information on, the company's activities, its directors, substantial holdings of its shares, its employees and its charitable and political donations in the year under review. The quantity of those details and information vary considerably from company to company. However, all companies are required to present a directors' report and the same broad pattern is followed by most.

Activities and trading results

The directors are required to give details of the principal activities of the company and its subsidiaries during the year, and of any significant changes in those activities. Definitions or examples of principal activities are available, and the following offers a useful guide.

Principal activities are usually taken to mean important categories of diversification, generally in terms of distinct classes of industrial or commercial activity – engineering, leisure, retailing, etc. Vertical classification is not required.

In terms of changes to the company's activities, it is generally suggested that a positive statement be made if there has been no change or that sufficient details be given of any major changes, such as withdrawal from an industrial sector or a significant class of business.

Where a company that is quoted on the Stock Exchange has published a forecast of its performance and subsequent trading results reveal a material difference from the forecast, then the report of the directors should provide an explanation for the difference.

The operating and financial review

Additionally, the directors are required to give a fair review of the development of the company and its business during the period, and the position of the company and its subsidiaries at the end of the period. They must give details of any important occurrences affecting the company during the year, and present an assessment of likely future developments.

Although the Companies Act gives no guidance as to what constitutes a fair review, the Cadbury Report's code of best practice notes that the report and accounts of a company should contain a coherent narrative, supported by the figures, of the company's performance and prospects. The Cadbury Report went on to recommend that the directors of a company should provide a forward looking operating and financial review (OFR) along the lines of the ASB's statement of best practice ('Operating and Financial Review') published in 1993. This statement, which is persuasive rather than mandatory, makes it clear that the OFR is intended as a report on the year under review, not a discussion of future performance. It should nevertheless draw out those aspects of the year under review that are relevant to an assessment of future prospects.

The operating review

The purpose of the operating review is to identify and explain the main factors that underlie the business and any past changes or expected future changes in these factors. It should include a discussion of:

- the significant features of the operating performance for the period including changes in market conditions, new products and services introduced, changes in market share, changes in turnover and margins, changes in exchange rates, and new and discontinued activities;
- the factors that might have a major effect on future results including dependence on major suppliers or customers, scarcity of raw materials, skills shortages, patents licences or franchises, product liability, health and safety, environmental protection costs, exchange rate fluctuations;
- the extent to which directors have sought to maintain and enhance future income by capital expenditure, marketing and advertising campaigns; pure and applied research, training programmes, maintenance programmes and new product development;
- the overall return to shareholders in terms of dividends and increases in shareholders' funds and the contributions of different business units;
- the dividend policy of the directors;
- any subjective judgements to which the financial statements are particularly sensitive.

The financial review

The purpose of the financial review is to explain the capital structure of a company, its treasury policy and its sources of liquidity, including the implications of the financing requirements arising from capital expenditure plans. It should include a discussion of:

- the capital structure of the company;
- the capital funding and treasury policies and objectives including the management of interest rate and exchange rate risks, and the maturity profile of borrowings;
- the reconciliation between the actual and standard tax charges;
- the cash from operations and other cash inflows and any special factors affecting these;
- liquidity at the end of the period;
- restrictions on the ability to transfer funds between different parts of the group;
- debt covenants and breaches of covenant;
- the ability to remain a going concern;
- the strength and resources of a company whose value is not fully reflected in the balance sheet.

Prior to the implementation of the Cadbury code of best practice, a discussion of many of the above items would have been contained in the directors' report. BOC do not, in fact, include in their annual report for 1997 a statement that bears the title 'Directors Report'. However, they do provide ten pages of performance review and a further five pages of finance and treasury review. In addition a separate page of information on research, development and information technology is provided. It is these pages that contain the discussion of many of the above items.

Directors

The Companies Acts and other regulatory pronouncements are quite clearly concerned with ensuring the disclosure of all significant information about the directors of a company and their relationship with it. The basic requirements are as follows:

- the names of all directors at any time during the period in question;
- the interest of directors in shares and debentures of the company and/or its subsidiaries at the beginning of the period and at the end.

Listed companies must distinguish between beneficial and non-beneficial holdings, and information about the interests of directors' close families is usually provided.

In certain circumstances, details must be given of a director's service contract with the company – usually when he or she is eligible for re-election. Full details of all transactions and arrangements with directors – particularly loans, quasi-loans and credit facilities – must be presented in the financial statements.

Directors' remuneration

It was pointed out in Chapter 2 that the Company Accounts (Disclosure of Directors' Emoluments) Regulations 1997 have brought about significant changes in the disclosure of directors emoluments and the requirements are summarized on page 45. For the most part these changes were based on the recommendations of the Study Group on Directors' Remuneration (the Greenbury Committee), which reported in July 1995. The report also recommended that the remuneration of executive directors should be determined by a remuneration committee made up of non-executive financial directors and that the remuneration committee should make an annual report to shareholders to be included in the annual report and accounts. The Stock Exchange requires all listed companies to comply with these recommendations. BOC includes in its annual report a three page report of the management resources committee. The main function of this committee is to set the company's overall policy on executive employment conditions and remuneration, and to decide the specific remuneration, benefits and terms of employment for each executive director, including the chairman, the chief executive and a number of other senior executives. BOC's report of the management resources committee is then followed by six pages of detailed information concerning the remuneration of directors, including their pension contributions, and also the directors' interests in the company's shares, share options and share incentive units.

Employees

In note 6 to the financial statements (see pages 225–9) BOC provides information about the number of employees in each line of business and geographical region and also information on the costs of employees, share options and incentives held by employees and employee retirement benefits. A further two pages of information is also provided by the directors covering such issues as the employment policy of BOC and the training and development and reward and recognition of employees. The directors also state that the group is committed to maintaining 'a workplace free from discrimination for reasons of race, creed, age, disability, culture, nationality, gender, sexual orientation or marital status'.

Donations

The directors are required to report political and charitable donations by the company or group of companies, where those donations exceed £200. In addition, where donations are for a political purpose, the name of the recipient and the individual amount paid must be disclosed. There are considerable areas of confusion about the proper definition of a 'political purpose', but in general terms such payments are readily identified and should be reported. Given the degree of interest in the political donations of British companies, many reports make a point of stating categorically that no payments are made or donations given for political purposes.

Auditing and taxation matters

The appointment of a company's auditor is a matter for the shareholders in general meeting, but it is customary for the directors' report to refer to the auditor's willingness to be reappointed or, if appropriate, to mention and explain any proposed change to current auditing arrangements. Although the 1985 Act (as amended) does not require the directors' report to be audited, there is a requirement for auditors to draw attention in their reports to any inconsistency they find between the directors' report and the company's financial statements.

Where a company is held to be subject to the close company taxation liability of any company, that fact should be included in the directors' report; listed companies must report whether or not they are subject to close company provisions.

Corporate governance

The influence of the Cadbury Report on corporate governance has been significant. The report defines corporate governance as the system by which companies are directed and controlled and points out that boards of directors are responsible for the governance of their companies. The report (p. 53) notes that:

> No system of corporate governance can be totally proof against fraud or incompetence. The test is how far such aberrations can be discouraged and how quickly they can be brought to light. The risks can be reduced by making the participants in the governance process as effectively accountable as possible. The key safeguards are properly constituted boards, separation of the functions of chairman and of chief executive, audit committees, vigilant shareholders and financial reporting and auditing systems which provide full and timely disclosure.

The report's code of best practice includes the need for statements explaining the directors' responsibilities for preparing the accounts and the reporting responsibilities of the auditors. The statement of directors' responsibilities should cover the following points:

- the legal requirement for directors to prepare financial statements for each financial year which give a true and fair view of the state of affairs of the company (or group) as at the end of the financial year and of the profit and loss for that period;
- the responsibility of the directors for maintaining adequate accounting records, for safeguarding the assets of the company (or group) and for preventing and detecting fraud and other irregularities;
- confirmation that suitable accounting policies, consistently applied and supported by reasonable and prudent judgements and estimates, have been used in the preparation of the financial statements;
- confirmation that applicable accounting standards have been followed, subject to any material departures disclosed and explained in the notes to the accounts. (This does not obviate the need for a formal statement in the notes to the accounts disclosing whether the accounts have been prepared in accordance with applicable accounting standards.)

The code of best practice also requires directors to report on the company's system of internal control and on whether they consider the company to be a going concern. Under Stock Exchange requirements, the annual report and accounts of a listed company must include a statement by the directors that the company is a going concern and this statement has to be reviewed by the auditors before publication. Also, the Stock Exchange require listed companies to state in their annual report and accounts whether or not they have complied with the Cadbury code of best practice.

BOC include a section in their annual report on Corporate Governance. This contains a statement on internal controls which explains the system of controls that the company has developed and concludes by stating that:

> The directors believe that the Group's system of internal financial control provides reasonable but not absolute assurance that assets are safeguarded, transactions are authorized and recorded properly and that material errors

and irregularities are either prevented or would be detected within a timely period. Having reviewed its effectiveness, the directors are not aware of any significant weakness or deficiency in the Group's system of internal financial control during the period covered by this report and accounts.

The finance and treasury review of BOC's annual report and accounts contains a statement which confirms that the directors are confident that the Group has adequate resources for the foreseeable future and continues to be a going concern.

8 The auditors' report

The audit of the accounts of a company by independent experts has, for many years, been a key feature of corporate accountability and it is a statutory requirement that auditors' reports must accompany the annual financial statements that are presented to the shareholders of all companies above a certain size. Until recently there was a requirement for every company registered in the UK, whatever its size, to have an annual audit, but this is no longer a requirement for companies with an annual turnover of less than £350,000 and a balance sheet total of less than £1.4 million.

An audit is defined by the Auditing Practices Board as 'an independent examination of, and expression of an opinion on, the financial statements of an enterprise'. The audit provides an objective verification to shareholders and other users that the financial statements have been prepared properly and in accordance with legislative and regulatory requirements, that they present the information truthfully and fairly and that they conform to best accounting practice in their treatment of various measurements and valuations.

The auditors' duty is to the shareholders of a company and although the extent to which this duty does or should extend to other users of financial statements has frequently been debated, the issue would seem to have been clearly resolved by the ruling in the 1990 'Caparo Case'. In this case (*Caparo Industries plc* v. *Dickman and Others* (1990) 1 All ER568) the House of Lords ruled that unless there are special features the auditors do not have a duty of care to prevent loss to anyone relying on their report except (a) the company and (b) the shareholders as a body. In other words no duty of care is owed to individual shareholders, to purchasers of shares, to lenders to the company or to those doing business with the company. Until this ruling it had been widely accepted that third parties could rely on the audit report to enhance the integrity of financial statements. Also it was felt that if auditors had this duty to a wide range of users then this provided a means of ensuring the effectiveness of the audit process because auditors would strive to avoid negligence claims against them by being diligent in their duties. The ruling did very little to enhance the role of the audit and many commentators felt that the benefits of having accounts audited would become very questionable. However, it was also clear that the full extent of the auditors' responsibilities needed to be clarified and the House of Lords felt that to hold auditors liable to anyone who might rely on the audit report would be far too onerous. The potential magnitude of the liability would be out of all proportion to the size of the audit fee. Also it is the duty of the directors to produce true and fair view accounts and so to make the auditors carry all of the liability would seem to be unfair. It should be noted though that the House of Lords ruling could be affected if any 'special features' are present. An example of a special feature might be where the auditors know or can reasonably foresee that third parties would rely on the audit report when making specific decisions. Under such circumstances the auditors' duty of care could well extend to the third parties involved.

The Cadbury Report accepted the Caparo ruling and stated that 'it is unable to see a practical and equitable way in which the House of Lords could have broadened the boundaries of the auditors' legal duty of care without giving rise to a liability that was indeterminate in scope, time and amount, nor does it consider that the decision should be altered by statutory intervention at the present time.'

The Auditing Practices Board

Until 1991, the contribution of the accountancy profession to the development of auditing guidelines and standards was provided through the Auditing Practices Committee. In 1991 the Consultative Committee of the six principal accounting bodies in the UK and Ireland (the CCAB) established the Auditing Practices Board (APB) to replace the Auditing Practices Committee. The membership of the APB includes representatives of the accountancy and auditing professions and also representatives of the Bank of England, the Stock Exchange, the Department of Trade and Industry, the National Audit Office, the Audit Commission and the Securities and Investment Board.

The objectives of the APB are contained in a May 1993 statement ('The scope and authority of APB pronouncements') and are as follows:

- to establish high standards of auditing;
- to meet the developing needs of users of financial information; and
- to ensure public confidence in the auditing process.

The APB intends to achieve these objectives by:

- taking an active role in the development of statutes, regulations and accounting standards which affect the audit profession;
- promoting ways of increasing the value of audits and of ensuring their cost effectiveness;
- consulting with the users of financial information to ensure that the APB provides an effective and timely response to their developing needs and to issues raised by them;
- advancing the wider public's understanding of the roles and responsibilities of auditors; and
- establishing and publishing statements of the principles and procedures with which auditors are required to comply in the conduct of audits and other explanatory material to assist in their interpretation and application.

The pronouncements of the APB take the form of statements of auditing standards (SASs), practice notes and bulletins.

SASs contain the basic principles and essential procedures with which auditors are expected to comply. SASs also include material which is not meant to be prescriptive, but to help in interpreting and applying auditing standards. The Companies Act 1989 requires auditors of companies to be registered with a recognized supervisory body. If auditors fail to comply with SASs they make themselves liable to action by their recognized supervisory body, which could include the withdrawal of eligibility to perform company audits. Before SASs are introduced the APB issues exposure drafts and may also issue other consultative documents in order to provide the opportunity for widespread consultation on proposed standards.

Practice notes are intended to assist auditors when applying standards which have been written in general terms to the requirements of specific circumstances and industries.

Bulletins are intended to provide auditors with timely guidance on new or emerging issues. They are persuasive rather than prescriptive but are indicative of good practice.

Usefulness of audit reports

The objectives of the APB as outlined above are an attempt to counter much of the criticism that has been directed at external auditing in recent years. To some extent this criticism has occurred because of the gap between the public's expectations of what the audit achieves or should achieve in terms of assurances about financial statements and what the audit actually does achieve. This has become known as the expectations gap. For example, it is not the responsibility of auditors to guarantee that the financial statements are correct or that the company will not fail or that there has been no fraud, and yet there is strong evidence to show that a significant proportion of the public believes that the purpose of the audit is to provide reassurances about these matters.

The financial statements of a complex organization can never be 'correct' in the sense that there is only one set of figures that is 'correct'. The judgements and valuations required to prepare the accounts of a company mean that a range of possible outcomes could be generally accepted as 'correct'. The directors of a company are therefore not required to prepare accounts that are 'correct', but accounts that give a true and fair view. The responsibility of the auditors is to give an opinion on whether the accounts give a true and fair view and have been prepared in accordance with the requirements of company law.

Similarly, it would be clearly impossible for the directors or auditors to guarantee that a company will not fail given the risks and uncertainties inherent in the business environment. However, perhaps auditors should be expected to form an opinion on the going concern assumptions on which the accounts are based.

Finally, if auditors were required to guarantee that material fraud had not occurred then the audit costs arising from the very detailed checking that would be required would probably be unacceptably high. Even if every transaction were checked the existence of collusion could still lead to a fraud going undetected and so the expectation that an audit guarantees the absence of fraud is generally felt to be unreasonable. However, it might be appropriate for auditors to contribute to fraud minimization by reporting on the adequacy of internal control systems.

The Cadbury Report considered the above causes of the expectations gap and made the following recommendations:

- the APB should be encouraged to expand the format and content of audit reports so that a description of the key features of the audit process is provided together with a clear statement of the auditors' responsibilities for reporting on the financial statements;
- the directors should state in the report and accounts that the business is a going concern, with supporting assumptions or qualifications as necessary, and the auditors should report on this statement;
- the directors should make a statement on the effectiveness of their system of internal control and the auditors should report on this statement.

Format and content of audit reports

The APB issued in May 1993 SAS 600 ('Auditors' reports on financial statements'), which had the purpose of establishing standards and providing guidance on the form and content of auditors' reports. The basic elements of the auditors' report are as follows:

- an identification of the report's addressee(s);
- an identification of the financial statements audited;
- separate sections dealing with:
  (i) respective responsibilities of directors and auditors,
  (ii) the basis of the auditors' opinion,
  (iii) the auditors' opinion on the financial statements;
- the signatures of the auditors;
- the date of the audit report.

In an attempt to overcome the expectations gap the audit report should include an explanation that the financial statements are the responsibility of the directors and a statement that the auditors' responsibility is to express an opinion on the financial statements.

Auditors' reports should contain a clear expression of opinion on the financial statements and should explain the basis of their opinion by including in their report:

- a statement of their compliance or otherwise with auditing standards;
- a statement that the audit process includes:
  (i) the examination, on a test basis, of evidence relating to the amounts and disclosures in the financial statements;
  (ii) the assessment of the significant estimates and judgements made by the reporting entity's directors;
  (iii) the consideration of whether the accounting policies are appropriate, consistently applied and adequately disclosed;
- a statement that they planned and performed the audit so as to obtain reasonable assurances that the financial statements are free from material mis-statement, whether caused by fraud or other irregularity or error, and that they have evaluated the overall presentation of the financial statements.

The report of the auditors to The BOC Group is contained in Appendix A (page 208) and it can be seen that this follows the above requirements. The BOC audit report is an example of an unqualified opinion that the financial statements give a true and fair view and have been properly prepared in accordance with the requirements of the Companies Act 1995.

However, there are occasions when the view given by the financial statements might be affected by an inherent uncertainty which, in the opinion of the auditors, is fundamental. In such cases the auditors should include an explanatory paragraph which draws attention to the fundamental uncertainty. Providing the fundamental uncertainty is adequately accounted for and disclosed in the financial statements then the auditors might still be capable of giving an unqualified opinion. However, if the disclosures about the fundamental uncertainty are inadequate then a *qualified* opinion will have to be given. There are various circumstances that might give rise to the need for a qualified opinion and various forms that qualified opinions can take. These are outlined below.

Qualified opinion – disagreement   This occurs when the auditors disagree with the treatment or disclosure of a matter in the financial statements. The audit report explains the area of disagreement and states that except for this the accounts give a true and fair view.

Qualified opinion – adverse opinion   This occurs where the effect of the disagreement is so material or pervasive that the auditors conclude that the financial statements are seriously misleading. In these circumstances they would state that the accounts do not give a true and fair view.

Qualified opinion – except for limitation of scope   Where the scope of the audit is limited by the inability to obtain sufficient evidence or explanations or because proper accounting records have not been kept and this prevents an unqualified opinion being given then the opinion should be qualified.

Disclaimer of opinion   Where the possible effect of a limitation of scope is so material or pervasive that the auditors have not been able to express an opinion as to whether or not the financial statements give a true and fair view then a disclaimer of opinion is required. If the effect of the limitation is not so material or pervasive as to require a disclaimer then an opinion that the financial statements give a true and fair view, except for the possible adjustments that might have been necessary had the limitation not existed, is appropriate.

Examples of the wording that could be used for the various forms of qualified and unqualified audit report are provided in SAS 600 ('Auditors' reports on financial statements'). This standard also gives an example of the qualified opinion that should be used when a primary statement required by financial reporting standards has not been included in the financial statements.

Going concern statement

Although company law requires the accounts of a company to be prepared on the assumption that the company is a going concern, there is no explicit need for directors to be satisfied that this is a reasonable assumption. However, as was noted in Chapter 7, the Cadbury Report recommended that the directors should satisfy themselves that the going concern basis is appropriate and report accordingly to shareholders. The report also went on to argue that the scope of the audit should be extended to test the going concern assumption and that auditors should give an opinion on the directors' going concern expectations. Guidance for auditors on this is contained in APB Bulletin 195/1 ('Disclosures relating to corporate governance'). The APB notes that although it would be possible for auditors to give an opinion on the directors' going concern report, it would not be practical to do so. This is because the extra work involved would outweigh any benefits to the users of financial statements. Auditors are therefore recommended to report only by exception on the directors' statement on going concern. If the auditors consider that the directors' statement on going concern is inconsistent with other information of which they have become aware then a qualification might be appropriate

Internal control

The internal control systems of an organization cover a range of rules and procedures which provide the necessary checks and balances to ensure the early detection of errors or frauds. Examples might include systems for the safeguarding of assets or for the proper authorization of expenditure or for ensuring that all income is received and accounted for. Any well run organization will have such procedures and through the use of internal auditing or other forms of internal monitoring will attempt to ensure that the rules and procedures for effective internal control are complied with. The Cadbury Report pointed out that it was convinced that effective systems of internal control are essential for the efficient management of a company and, as was pointed out in Chapter 7, recommended that directors should report on the effectiveness of their systems of internal control. The auditors were also expected to comment on the directors' report and the APB's guidance on this is contained in Bulletin 1995/1. The APB recommend that the audit report on corporate governance matters should state whether or not the directors' comments on internal financial control are consistent with information the auditors are aware of from their audit work on the financial statements and should include a statement that no assurance on the effectiveness of the systems of internal control is expressed.

Code of best practice

In addition to the above audit reporting requirements, the Cadbury Report, as has already been mentioned, produced a code of best practice and recommended that all listed companies reporting for year-ends after 30 June 1993 should state in their report and accounts whether they comply with this code.

It was also recommended that this statement of compliance should have been reviewed by the auditors before publication. The London Stock Exchange has adopted listing rules which confirm the need for a statement of compliance. However, the listing rules do not specify that auditors should report on their review of compliance but APB Bulletin 1995/1 strongly recommends that they should.

Reports on compliance with the Cadbury code of best practice, including the going concern position and internal controls are recommended to be included either as a separate report within the annual report or as an additional section in the auditors' report on the financial statements.

BOC provide a separate report immediately after the directors' statement on corporate governance. The report (see page 197) makes it clear that the auditors did not carry out additional work to satisfy themselves as to the ability of the company to continue as a going concern or on the effectiveness of internal financial control systems. The auditors, do, however, confirm that the directors' statements on internal financial control and going concern are not inconsistent with the information they are aware of from their audit of the financial statements.

Part Two

Interpretation and assessment

9 Financial statement analysis and comparison

Objectives

Having described and examined the principal components of published financial statements, it is now time to focus attention on the means by which those statements may be analysed to extract information that will be useful in making financial decisions or judgements about a company. The principal tools of financial statement analysis have been developed over a long period and consist, in general, of first identifying the important items of both financial and non-financial data and then relating these to one another and also to factors external to the company. This process is usually referred to as ratio analysis. The ratios calculated can then be used in conjunction with other information such as the annual review and performance report or external analyst's reports. On their own, ratios, like the figures in the published financial statements, do not necessarily provide answers, but rather suggest questions that require answering. Perhaps they have identified that significant changes have occurred, but identification of the cause is still required.

But first, just as in the preparation of the accounts, it is necessary to identify the purpose of the financial analysis. The structure and strategy of a review is described in some depth in Chapter 14. The selected purpose will influence the approach and the extent of the analysis. This will provide part of the basis of the selection of critical items in the profit and loss account, cash flow statement and balance sheet. Size of item will also be another factor since a 10 per cent change in £500 million is much larger and thus possibly more important than a 100 per cent change in £1 million.

In general, key items in the profit and loss account are sales, operating profit and net profit after tax. In the balance sheet total assets and capital employed are important, particularly as they represent, respectively, the total resources working to earn the profit and the total long-term funds invested in the company to earn the return. Having made a cursory assessment of the key variables the more rigorous assessment can be made by ratio analysis.

Ratio analysis

The decisions facing different users may be quite varied, e.g. lenders will be interested in credit-worthiness, employees in information for wage-bargaining purposes, shareholders in profits and dividend prospects and so on. Potential and existing shareholders are concerned about the profitability of the company, the return on the shares, the availability of cash to pay the dividends, to name but three items. Strategic information is just as important to shareholders as it is to the company's management who will select ratios that help them in their daily operations. But it is also worth remembering that management usually has access to more information concerning the company and its competitors than persons external to the company. Nevertheless, it is true to say that just about all users will be interested in evaluating the current performance and financial position of the company and in making predictions about its future. It is necessary, therefore, to consider the role that financial statement analysis has to play in this process.

The figures contained in the financial statements – turnover, profit, current assets, total assets etc. – are absolute amounts that may not by themselves be very meaningful indicators of good or bad performance, or of a satisfactory or unsatisfactory position. For example, the balance sheet of a company may reveal that the current assets figure is £150,000 and the current liabilities figure is £75,000. Individually these items may not tell us very much. However, if they are related to one another in the form of a ratio, i.e. £150,000 to £75,000, the resultant 2:1 (or simply 2) may indicate whether there is a sufficient cushion of short-term funds in the business. Similarly, it is possible to take two profit and loss account items, such as net pre-tax profit of £40,000 and sales of £800,000, and examine their relationships. Any informational value that these two items may have when considered in isolation will be greatly enhanced by calculating the profit to sales ratio of £40,000 to £800,000, or 0.05: 1. This ratio is usually expressed as a percentage, in this case 5 per cent, which indicates the net profit percentage being earned on each pound of sales value. Further ratios can be obtained by relating items from both the profit and loss account and the balance sheet. For example, the net profit figure used above was £40,000 and an examination of the balance sheet may reveal a figure of £400,000 for total assets employed. By themselves, these figures are difficult to interpret, but if they are related to each other in the form of a ratio, i.e. £40,000 to £400,000, a ratio of 0.1:1 or 10 per cent is obtained. This may indicate the adequacy of the profit figure when considered against the total value of the assets available for earning such a profit.

Reducing the large number of financial statement items to a relatively small number of key ratios in this way can help to begin to answer the following questions about the economic aspects of a company:

■ Is the profit that is being earned satisfactory?
■ Is the management of working capital (cash, debtors, stock, creditors) efficient or at least adequate?
■ Is the long-term capital structure suitable?
■ Is efficient use being made of assets and other resources?

To answer these sorts of questions does require comparison with acceptable benchmarks, some of which will be discussed shortly. It is also true that the ratios calculated following a standardized procedure may throw up further questions that require investigation, such as the following:

- Why have certain expenses grown as a proportion of sales?
- Why has the proportion of production carried in stock declined?
- Are the loans still well covered?
- Why has the profit growth target not been achieved?
- Why has the sales growth outstripped that of the competition?

Like all financial information, ratios can also be used as targets and projections, just as absolute targets of profit or sales are made. As we shall see, ratio analysis can be as simple or as sophisticated as the user wishes it to be.

One general approach is to break the analysis down into two series: one being the horizontal or line-by-line comparison of the accounts with those of the previous year. This is sometimes called common size analysis. The second series is called vertical analysis, where each item in the balance sheet or profit and loss account is expressed as a percentage of the total. Horizontal analysis provides, over a number of years, a trend of changes, growth or decline, in these elements of the accounts. We can get annual percentage growth rates in profits, sales, stock or any other item for this approach. The vertical analysis on the other hand will provide evidence of structural changes in the accounts: increased profitability through more efficient production would show up in the profit and loss account, while from the balance sheet could be discovered greater dependence on borrowing to finance new investment etc.

Another approach is to make use of what is in effect a pyramid structure of ratios to select the level of detailed analysis required. Thus, for example, if profitability is being considered, then the ratio at the apex of the pyramid would be return on capital employed. This can then be broken down into its constituent elements of return on sales and asset turnover, as explained in Chapter 10. Each of these ratios can then be broken down further into more detailed ratios such as cost of sales to sales, administration cost to sales and research and development to sales.

Comparison of financial ratios

The calculation of ratios is only the first step in financial statement analysis. Although ratios provide a useful means of relating individual items in the financial statements to other items, some standard is needed against which those ratios can be assessed. Unfortunately, there is no such thing as an 'ideal' or absolute standard measure for this purpose. For example, it is not possible to state categorically that the ratio of net pre-tax profit to total assets for all companies should be 10 per cent and therefore that anything less than 10 per cent is 'bad' and anything greater is 'good'.

The lack of absolute ratio criteria has been overcome in practice in a number of ways. The first – and the one most frequently adopted – is to calculate the average ratios for all the companies in a particular industrial or commercial sector. This gives an 'industry' standard against which the ratios of a particular company can be evaluated. The second method involves calculating the relevant ratios for the company under analysis for each of a number of preceding years and using these ratios as a basis for assessing those for the current period. Figures for immediately preceding years are available in the current year's financial statements. In addition, the more important items are shown in summarized form for at least the past five years by all listed public companies. Perhaps useful trends will emerge from this.

From a strategic view it is necessary to make comparisons with similar and competing companies. Thus it may be possible to take published information for such companies, compute their ratios and make comparisons. The use of ratio analysis is not restricted to publicly available information. The managers of companies and other organizations make widespread use of ratio analysis techniques for internal control and evaluation purposes, and in these circumstances will have budgeted figures and ratios to use as standards or targets.

However, these 'standards' do have certain limitations. There is still no clear guide as to the optimal size of a particular ratio. For example, assume that the industry average for the ratio of current assets to current liabilities is 1.5. If a particular company in that industry has a ratio of 0.5, it is well below the 'standard' and can perhaps be thought of as 'bad'. However, another company in the same industry with a ratio well in excess of the industry average, say 2.5, cannot categorically be thought of as 'good'. Such a high ratio might be the result of cash being allowed to lie idle or of stock levels being higher than necessary. Both of these practices could be instances of bad management of current assets. The answer, therefore, might seem to be to evaluate a company in terms of its deviation below or above the average for the industry. Unfortunately, it is not so simple. Even within the same industry, companies have to face different situations that may justify a substantial deviation from the industry average. Thus, if a particular ratio is out of line with the average for the industry, such a deviation merely indicates an area for further examination. Moreover, it could be argued that the industry average is not the most appropriate standard. After all, the average incorporates the ratios of the best and the worst companies in the industry. Perhaps it might be better to have industry standards based on the ratios of the most successful companies in the industry. This is a form of benchmarking, using the best as a comparator or target. If this is not possible, then the groups can be broken up into quartiles to help as a guide. It should also be borne in mind that where the ratios making up the statistics for a particular industry are drawn mainly from the larger public companies, then the resultant standard is of limited relevance for smaller companies. A similar problem is encountered if the 'standard' is based on the ratios of the company in earlier years. Conditions are unlikely to be stable over time and the ratios obtained in previous years may be wholly inappropriate to the current environment in which the company has to operate. Thus, a deviation from the previous years' ratios does not permit instant 'good' or 'bad' classifications but might, depending on the size of the deviation, suggest that further examination is necessary.

By themselves, ratios are of limited value. It seems clear that if absolute ratio criteria did exist then ratio analysis would be a mechanical procedure requiring very little expertise. It is because there are no absolute criteria and because of the imperfections in the surrogate 'standards' that a great deal of skill and judgement are required in the evaluation and interpretation of ratios.

Similarly, individual ratios taken in isolation can be misleading, they need to be combined in order to present a composite picture of a firm. In Chapters 14 and 15, the uses and limitations of both inter-firm and intra-firm ratio comparisons are considered further.

Ratio calculation

When calculating ratios, a logical connection between the items being related to each other is essential. For example, the ratio of net profit to total assets is economically meaningful and the resultant statistic can be used in the evaluation of those profits against the asset base available. A ratio relating the income tax charge in the profit and loss account to the total assets employed, on the other hand, is of doubtful significance. The implications of this for financial statement analysis are that a few key ratios are in reality all that is needed. Additional support for the view that only a limited number of ratios are required stems from the high degree of correlation among the various ratios. This is mainly because many ratios are made up of items that also appear in other ratios from the pyramiding effect, and so correlation might be expected.

A further requirement that is often proposed for ratio calculation is that the components of the ratios should be determined in a consistent manner. For example, a frequently calculated ratio is that of sales to debtors, i.e. the debtor turnover ratio. However, the debtors figure occurs as a result of credit sales, while the reported sales figure usually includes both credit sales and cash sales. So the same valuation basis is not being used. Such an inconsistency in the method of calculating the components of ratios does not necessarily invalidate it, but merely suggests care in its interpretation.

It is often argued that the components of the ratios should have relationships that vary with each other; in other words, the components should be functionally related. For example, when calculating the ratio of net profit to sales, the profit figure is arrived at by deducting from the sales figure all the manufacturing and operating expenses of the company. Some of those expenses will vary more or less directly with the level of sales, but others will be fixed, whatever the level of sales. Thus, the resultant profit figure is not linearly related to the sales figure.

Depending on the length and positioning of time periods used for the analysis, it is possible that short-run fluctuations are hidden. Similarly, there might be a situation where rapidly changing prices affect different items at different rates. In these cases caution is needed in the interpretation of the ratios, particularly when trying to assess trends.

Ratios, do not, of course, have to be restricted to financial items. In recent years, much more use has been made of non-financial data. Employee-related data are an obvious example of this, and ratios of sales per employee or profit per employee are now quite common. Other ratios of a similar nature will depend on the types of activity carried on by a company. For a road haulage company, for example, a useful ratio for comparative purposes might be profit per road mile travelled or per ton carried, for an airline, profit per passenger mile or costs per passenger mile might be useful statistics.

Internally, companies make much more use of non-financial ratios. For example, when measuring the level of quality; the percentage of output requiring reworking or the percentage of output scrapped might be useful; or for the marketing activity, ratios concerned with market share or market penetration could be calculated.

Problems in ratio analysis

Some of the problems surrounding ratio calculation and finding suitable bases for comparison have been mentioned earlier. In this section, attention is focused on some of the other frequently cited problems in ratio analysis.

Lack of uniformity in accounts preparation

It was shown in Part One that accountants preparing financial statements are free, within broad limits, to choose from a wide range of generally accepted accounting principles. Thus, two firms that are identical in every respect may show quite different figures for profit and balance sheet valuations, owing to the use of differing accounting policies. The efforts of the Accounting Standards Board and its predecessor body have done much to reduce the range of permitted accounting policies, but choices still exist for the valuation of stocks and work in progress, depreciation methods, deferred tax treatment of intangibles and goodwill, accounting for leases and many other areas. The consequences for ratio analysis are readily apparent. Comparisons are a very important feature of ratio analysis, yet without uniformity in the preparation of financial statements it is impossible to determine whether variations in ratios are due merely to accounting policy differences or to real economic differences.

Even if uniformity of accounting policies existed (e.g. a mandatory requirement for straight-line depreciation in all circumstances), differences in estimates of asset lives would still result in variations in depreciation charges. Thus, only total uniformity, with both depreciation method and asset lives being prescribed, would produce truly comparable bases for ratio preparation. Such requirements would, of course, be anathema to the British business community. Different companies do use identical assets in different ways and, therefore, in reality, there will be differences in asset lives. Accounting for economic reality, and not simply accounting in accordance with the rules, is a cornerstone of accounting philosophy in the UK.

Furthermore, because of the need for speedy reporting by companies, many of the figures incorporated in the published accounts are based on an element of estimation. Buildings being valued by different professional valuers can produce significantly different results. Although the company and the auditors may believe the valuation to be a true and fair view estimate, it does mean that the accuracy of the ratios cannot be guaranteed any more than that of the underlying data.

Finally it must be recognized that the use of historic cost accounting has also, during times of rapidly changing prices, had the effect of making ratio comparison an exercise of doubtful validity. Using, once again, the ratio of net profit to total assets as an example, it is evident that the denominator of the ratio (total assets) will be different for a firm with assets purchased more recently than it would be for a firm with equivalent assets purchased some time ago at lower prices.

Diversified companies and multinationals

The growth by acquisition and merger of companies still continues. The merger boom of the 1960s and early 1970s started a movement which has produced a large number of highly diversified companies. Because, by definition, diversified companies operate in different industries with different degrees of risk and different expected profitabilities, the calculation of ratios based on the aggregated figures is of limited use in financial statement analysis. The problems of aggregating the results of diversified companies have been recognized for a long time. The obvious solution is to report separately the results of the segments of a company that operates in different industries. That will facilitate comparisons by permitting the calculation of ratios not only for the diversified group as a whole but for each of the industrial sectors in which the company operates. Unfortunately, segment reporting is still high on the list of unresolved problem areas in financial reporting. One of the difficulties in terms of ratio analysis is the allocation to individual segments of costs that are common to the whole company. Head office administrative costs, interest charges on loans and so on, are examples of common costs that are incurred by the company and have to be allocated on an arbitrary basis to each segment. Such a requirement can significantly distort the results of a particular segment. Nevertheless, thanks to the passage of time, greater consistency has come about in the methods and bases used by companies for their segmental reporting, and this has helped.

The 1990s have also brought about changes in corporate strategies based upon the concept of refocusing companies to a limited range of products or services. This has led to the breakup of many of the conglomerates into a number of separate entities, e.g. Thorn EMI became Thorn and EMI. But even within these newly separated and refocused companies there are still individual segments so the accounting problems still exist even if the scale is not as great.

A further development has been the large increase in the numbers of multinational companies. These companies with subsidiary operating companies based in many foreign countries, buy and sell in currencies other than pounds sterling. The annual combining of the accounts of those companies based in different local currencies into one consolidated group set of accounts in one currency, sterling, is not without its difficulties, in particular when exchange rates with sterling have not been particularly stable during a year.

These problems and difficulties of using financial information for ratio analysis reinforce the need for the analyst to make full use of the details provided in the notes to the accounts and not just take the figures in the balance sheet and profit and loss account at face value.

Lack of conceptual foundation

It was claimed earlier that the purpose of financial statement analysis is to extract information useful for decision making purposes. It was also stated that ratio analysis is the principal tool of financial statement analysis. It might therefore be reasonable to assume that ratio analysis would figure largely in microeconomic theories about asset valuation and in theories about securities analysis. However, an examination of the literature in those areas reveals that this is not the case. This is because of the lack of any conceptual foundation surrounding ratio analysis and decision making. It has been assumed that ratios will be useful without ever establishing that usefulness. Moreover, the strong support for the efficiency of capital markets, which argues that share prices at any time always reflect fully all publicly available information, implies that securities analysis is of little use in assessing share prices.

That statement is too sweeping and thus somewhat misleading since it is only in the long term that the market reflects the information. Some of the information is that which is derived from ratio and other analysis. There are plenty of examples of how, in the short term, users of this type of information have made gains.

So ratio analysis is still used in practice. In spite of its apparent limitations, a great deal of time and effort is spent on calculating and comparing ratios. In fact, as will be described in Chapter 15, decision models consisting of a combination of ratios have proved very effective in making predictions about companies. However, before considering these it is necessary to examine in detail the mechanics of ratio analysis; this is done in the next four chapters, before combining this knowledge in a structured approach to ratio analysis in Chapter 14.

As previously, the financial information prepared and produced by The BOC Group plc is used as the basis and source for the ratios computed, explained and analysed in the next few chapters. Appendix A includes a complete copy of The BOC Group plc annual financial report which includes the group five year record, the finance and treasury review, the statements on corporate governance, the reports of the auditors and the management resources committee and the financial statements and accompanying notes. Appendix B is a copy of the print-out of the financial information on BOC Group plc found on the FAME (Financial Analysis Made Easy) database. This is prepared and sold commercially by Jordans Ltd.

In Appendix B, which is derived from the annual financial accounts and notes of BOC Group plc, can be found both basic financial information and sets of ratios based upon that information. Five years of information is provided and analysed. Note as you go through the next few chapters that you will find differences between the values computed for a few ratios and those explained here. This is due to alternative interpretations and methods being chosen and used in the two places. This is a good chance therefore to remind readers that if and when they use financial information prepared by others they comprehend the basis upon which it has been prepared. Reference will be made to pages in Appendices A and B for source material and/or comparisons as we go through the next few chapters.

10 Profitability and performance

In Chapter 2 it was shown how information concerning the profit of a company is presented in the annual financial report. Although such information is useful in establishing the absolute level of profit earned during a period, it fails to indicate the performance of a company because it does not take account of the resources available for the generation of the profit. A measure of profitability is therefore required that relates profit earned to other relevant factors. There are several widely used indicators of profitability; this chapter introduces some of the more important of these.

Return on capital employed

Return on capital employed, which is usually expressed as a percentage, is calculated as

$$\frac{\text{Profit}}{\text{Capital employed}} \times 100$$

This ratio concentrates on the efficiency with which capital employed has been utilized. Thus, if two companies are being compared and the reported profit of Company A is £10,000 and that of Company B is £15,000, then Company B has clearly earned the greater profit. However, if it is then observed that the capital employed of Company A was £50,000 and that of Company B was £150,000, the return on capital employed for each company is as follows:

$$\text{Company A} \quad \frac{10,000}{50,000} \times 100 = 20 \text{ per cent}$$

$$\text{Company B} \quad \frac{15,000}{150,000} \times 100 = 10 \text{ per cent}$$

It is now apparent that, when the profits earned by the two companies are related to their respective investment bases, Company A achieved the better return on capital employed and might therefore be regarded as the more successful. It is at this point, however, that the problem is first encountered of establishing precisely what is meant by the components of financial ratios, and also the methods by which these components may be calculated. Both 'capital employed' and 'profit' can quite sensibly have different meanings attached to them, and, before comparisons between the ratios of different companies can be made, it is obviously essential to ensure that like is being compared with like.

Capital employed is usually taken to be either the total assets of the company, i.e. fixed assets plus current assets, or the net total assets, i.e. fixed assets plus current assets minus current liabilities. If the amount of total assets is used, the resultant profitability measure is intended to focus attention on the efficiency with which all of the resources available to the managers of the company have been utilized. The argument for the use of net total assets is that the level of current assets is inextricably linked with the level of current liabilities and is very much dependent on the working capital policy of the company. In other words, only the net total assets can be thought of as a resource that is completely at the disposal of management. Any distortions caused by variations in working capital policy will be minimized by netting off current liabilities against current assets, so that a more comparable asset base is obtained. These are the assets financed by long-term funds such as the shareholders' capital and long-term loans.

In the examples that follow, ratios of return on capital employed have been calculated for The BOC Group plc, based on each of the alternative definitions discussed above. One point concerning capital employed relates to the date at which this should be calculated. Because the numerator of the ratio represents a flow of profit earned over the entire accounting period, the denominator ought to reflect the average amount of capital employed during the period. It is usually sufficient for this purpose to take an average of the amounts of capital employed at the beginning and end of the accounting period.

It is also evident that the basis on which the assets have been valued will have important implications for profitability analysis. At times of rising prices, the historical cost of the assets will usually be lower than their current values. This can make comparisons extremely difficult between firms with different asset age structures.

During the late 1970s and early 1980s, many companies included in their annual reports supplementary financial statements prepared according to the principles of current cost accounting. This enabled ratios based on current cost as well as historic cost to be prepared. Nowadays it is usual for the only amendment to the historic cost of assets to be through the frequent revaluation, where appropriate, of the fixed assets to reflect their current values. Note 7 to the accounts of The BOC Group plc (see Appendix A, pages 230–1) shows that there was no revaluation of tangible fixed assets in 1997, but assets with a net book value of £7.3 million for 1996 had been revalued.

The detailed financial review of The BOC Group plc for the year ended 30 September 1997 is reproduced in Appendix A (pages 188–242). As the profit and loss account (see page 209), balance sheet (see page 210) and cash flow statement (see page 211) are referred to extensively during this and succeeding chapters, they are reproduced in this section in Tables 10.1, 10.2 and 10.3 respectively.

Before calculating a company's ratios, it is useful to read through the statement on the accounting policies used by the company in its preparation of the figures. This is important to help maintain comparability between firms or time periods, since firms do change policies from time to time and also may have some variations from those of the

Table 10.1 The BOC Group plc – consolidated profit and loss account (year ended 30 September 1997)

	Notes	1997 (£ million)	1996 (£ million)	1995 (£ million)
Turnover				
Continuing operations		**3,929.9**	4,014.4	3,704.8
Acquisitions		**33.7**	5.1	47.1
Turnover, including share of associated undertakings	1(a)	**3,963.6**	4,019.5	3,751.9
Less associated undertakings' turnover		**285.9**	267.4	208.0
Turnover of subsidiary undertakings		**3,677.7**	3,752.1	3,543.9
Cost of sales	2(a)	**(2,105.5)**	(2,115.5)	(1,986.6)
Gross profit		**1,572.2**	1,636.6	1,557.3
Net operating expenses	2(a)	**(1,093.4)**	(1,154.7)	(1,106.3)
Operating profit				
Continuing operations		**478.5**	481.7	447.7
Acquisitions		**0.3**	0.2	3.3
Profit of subsidiary undertakings		**478.8**	481.9	451.0
Share of profit of associated undertakings		**61.6**	57.5	45.4
Operating profit	1(b)	**540.4**	539.4	496.4
Interest (net)	3(a)	**(95.2)**	(94.5)	(94.2)
Profit on ordinary activities before tax		**445.2**	444.9	402.2
Tax on profit on ordinary activities	4(a)	**(129.1)**	(137.9)	(128.6)
Profit on ordinary activities after tax		**316.1**	307.0	273.6
Minority interests		**(28.5)**	(28.7)	(24.6)
Profit for the financial year		**287.6**	278.3	249.0
Dividends including non-equity	12(a)	**(140.4)**	(130.1)	(118.8)
Surplus for the financial year		**147.2**	148.2	130.2
Earnings per 25p Ordinary share, net basis, undiluted	2(c)	**59.31p**	57.74p	51.97p

Table 10.2   The BOC Group plc – consolidated balance sheet (at 30 September 1997)

	Notes	1997 (£ million)	1996 (£ million)
Fixed assets			
Tangible assets	7	**2,953.7**	2,747.6
Intangible assets	8	**28.8**	33.4
Investment in own shares	9	**24.0**	22.6
Other investments	9	**295.5**	263.7
		3,302.0	3,067.3
Current assets			
Stocks	10(a)	**354.3**	403.4
Debtors due within one year	10(b)	**901.7**	906.1
Investments		**16.7**	7.7
Deposits and cash due within one year	10(c)	**222.2**	155.8
Assets due beyond one year	10(d)	**101.9**	95.7
Current assets		**1,596.8**	1,568.7
Current liabilities			
Creditors: amounts due within one year			
Borrowings and finance leases	10(e)	**(620.4)**	(623.1)
Other creditors	10(f)	**(886.2)**	(911.9)
Current liabilities		**(1,506.6)**	(1,535.0)
Net current assets		**90.2**	33.7
Total assets *less* current liabilities		**3,392.2**	3,101.0
Long-term liabilities			
Creditors: amounts due beyond one year			
Borrowings and finance leases	11(a)	**(1,001.2)**	(767.4)
Other creditors		**(23.5)**	(26.3)
Provisions for liabilities and charges	11(b)	**(229.7)**	(245.8)
		(1,254.4)	(1,039.5)
Total net assets		**2,137.8**	2,061.5
Capital and reserves			
Called up share capital			
equity capital	12(b)	**121.8**	120.8
non-equity capital	12(b)	**2.5**	2.5
Share premium account	12(c)	**272.4**	259.4
Revaluation reserves	12(c)	**63.8**	71.9
Profit and loss account	12(c)	**1,320.7**	1,252.5
Associated undertakings' reserves	12(c)	**111.6**	111.6
Shareholders' funds		**1,892.8**	1,818.7
Minority shareholders' interests		**245.0**	242.8
Total capital and reserves		**2,137.8**	2,061.5

Note:
The financial statements were approved by the board of directors on 28 November 1997 and are signed on its behalf by Danny Rosenkranz (Director) and J. Howard Macdonald (Director).

Table 10.3　The BOC Group plc – consolidated cash flow statement (year ended 30 September 1997)

	Notes	**1997** **(£ million)**	*1996* *(£ million)*	*1995* *(£ million)*
Net cash inflow from operating activities	14(a)	**733.8**	625.1	647.4
Returns on investments and servicing **of finance**				
Interest paid		**(113.3)**	(108.9)	(107.8)
Interest received		**15.9**	23.5	14.4
Dividends paid to minorities in subsidiaries		**(6.3)**	(5.9)	(9.3)
Interest element of finance lease rental payments		**(0.2)**	(0.4)	(0.7)
Preference dividends paid		**(0.1)**	(0.1)	(0.1)
Returns on investments and servicing **of finance**		**(104.0)**	(91.8)	(103.5)
Tax paid		**(109.5)**	(115.8)	(105.8)
Capital expenditure and financial investment				
Purchases of tangible fixed assets		**(650.8)**	(533.6)	(407.4)
Sales of tangible fixed assets		**34.5**	47.1	36.7
Purchases of current asset investments		**(9.0)**	(4.7)	—
Capital expenditure and financial investment		**(625.3)**	(491.2)	(370.7)
Acquisitions and disposals				
Acquisitions of businesses	15(a)	**(31.7)**	(25.8)	(49.9)
Net cash/(overdrafts) acquired with subsidiaries		**0.5**	0.2	(11.8)
Disposals of businesses	15(a)	**23.8**	13.8	28.7
Net overdrafts disposed of with subsidiaries		**—**	2.0	—
Investments in associated undertakings		**(26.3)**	(12.1)	(2.5)
Acquisitions of intangibles		**(1.2)**	(3.9)	—
Purchases of trade investments		**(13.4)**	(4.9)	(11.8)
Sales of other investments		**9.7**	17.0	9.9
Acquisitions and disposals		**(38.6)**	(13.7)	(37.4)
Equity dividends paid		**(121.5)**	(121.1)	(111.3)
Net cash outflow before use of liquid **resources and financing**		**(265.1)**	(208.5)	(81.3)
Management of liquid resources				
Net (purchase)/sale of short-term investments		**(62.3)**	(19.8)	0.2
Financing				
Issue of shares		**22.1**	20.7	7.6
Increase in debt	14(d)	**342.1**	182.2	103.3
Net cash inflow from financing		**364.2**	202.9	110.9
Increase/(decrease) in cash		**36.8**	(25.4)	29.8

Note:
A reconciliation of the increase/(decrease) in cash to the movement in net debt in the year is given in note 14(b).

firm to which they are being compared. For BOC the note on accounting policies is given on pages 214–15.

From this it can be seen that the accounts are based on the traditional historical cost accounting convention, but they include the revaluation of certain land and buildings. BOC plc revalues its land and buildings periodically, basing the revised value on the purchase cost in the open market for the type of property, which is then depreciated to reflect the age of the buildings.

As far as the profit component of the ratio is concerned, comparability will be improved by using a profit figure that reflects the sustainable ordinary trading activities and excludes the effects of any extraordinary and exceptional items that may have occurred. Analysts and financial reports call this the headline earnings. They argue that their approach, though at odds with that of the FRS, provides a more standardized approach to reported profit from trading. The approach is perceived to provide a sharper focus on the results from a company's ongoing trading activities.

By showing exceptional items separately it highlights to the reader the material costs or revenues from within the ordinary trading activities caused by some significant event(s). One such event might be a major strategic decision to downsize part of the operations. Further elaboration and description of these exceptional items ought to be found in the notes to the accounts and elsewhere in the Directors' Report. For BOC, the only exceptional items were in 1994 caused by restructuring the company and amounted to £85 million (see the five-year record in Appendix A, pages 188–9). The five-year record can give the reader an indication of the trend of the headline earnings and the regularity/or otherwise) of the incidence of these exceptional items. Clearly, the inclusion of the exceptional items can significantly affect the trend.

FRS 3 treats the profit on ordinary activities before interest, which are post exceptional items, as the company's profits from its year's commercial activities, but it is not the sustainable profit figure. The debate as to which profit figure, operating profit or profit on ordinary activities before interest, to use as the numerator, continues but analysts still tend to focus on the operating profit before exceptional items. Note how the BOC five-year trend in operating profit and earnings per share (EPS) is affected by the 1994 exceptional items.

Comparability is similarly improved by using a profit figure before deductions for interest and taxation. The amount of taxation paid by a company depends on a variety of circumstances, not all of which are under the control of the company. Distortions caused by differences in liabilities to taxation can therefore be avoided by concentration on the before-tax position. The rationale for excluding interest charges is that the resultant profit figure is then consistent with the calculation of capital employed. If capital employed is taken to represent the total assets of the company, then it is evident that these have been partially financed by the creditors; therefore the profit figure should be the amount before any interest payments to creditors have been deducted. If capital employed is taken to represent the net total assets, then strictly speaking it would be correct to exclude only the long-term interest payments. The interest paid on current liabilities, or received on current assets, should be included in the calculation of profit.

BOC, in note 3 to the financial statements, give some details concerning interest paid and received, but this does not include information on interest paid to short-term creditors on loan, etc., maturing within one year. Therefore any adjustment to the operating profit for short-term interest paid has to be ignored because it cannot be made through lack of information. With many companies the amounts involved in interest paid on short-term creditors is small and thus ignored.

Return on total assets

The formula for return on total assets is

$$\frac{\text{Trading profit before interest paid, taxation and exceptional items}}{\text{Average total assets for the period}} \times 100$$

The average total assets for the period can be determined from Table 10.2. The total assets figure at the end of the period (30 September 1997) is the sum of the fixed assets of £3,302.0 million and the current assets of £1,596.8 million, i.e., a total of £4,898.8 million. Similarly, the total assets figure at the beginning of the period (30 September 1996) is made up of fixed assets of £3,067.3 million and current assets of £1,568.7 million, i.e. a total of £4,636.0 million.

The trading profit before interest, taxation and exceptional items can be obtained by referring to Table 10.1; it consists of the amount shown as 'operating profit' of £540.4 million.

The return on total assets (ROTA) can now be calculated as

$$\text{ROTA} = \frac{540.4}{\frac{1}{2}(4,898.8 + 4,636.0)} \times 100 = 11.3 \text{ per cent}$$

Return on net total assets

The formula for the return on net total assets, which is also called the return on capital employed (ROCE), is

$$\frac{\text{Trading profit before interest, taxation and exceptional items}}{\text{Average net total assets for the period}} \times 100$$

The net total assets figure is the same as the capital employed figure; the latter being made up of the sum of the long-term liabilities and the capital and reserves, i.e. the long-term funding element of the total assets. In 1997 the capital employed for BOC from Table 10.2 is made up of the sum of the long-term liabilities of £1,254.4 million plus capital and reserves of £2,137.8 million, which is £3,292.2 million; the same as the total assets less current liabilities. Thus, the alternative but preferred name to return on net total assets is return on capital employed.

The net total assets are referred to in Table 10.2 as 'total assets less current liabilities'. At the end of the period these amounted to £3,392.2 million and at the beginning of the period to £3,101.0 million. The operating profit for the year was £540.4 million.

The return on net total assets is

$$\text{ROCE} = \frac{540.4}{\frac{1}{2}(3,392.2 + 3,101.0)} \times 100 = 8.3 \text{ per cent}$$

Where inter-firm comparisons are being made it is not possible to state categorically which of the alternatives of return on total assets or return on net total assets is the 'correct' one to use. It all depends on the particular aspects of the company on which the analyst wishes to concentrate, either long-term capital employed, or the complete economic unit. Provided that the components of the ratios are defined in the same way for the companies being compared, then the comparisons should be meaningful. It is also usual to compare the performance of a particular company over time, and ideally a sequence of the above ratios calculated for BOC for 1997 and earlier years would enable the establishment, or otherwise, of a trend in the return on capital employed (see Table 14.2).

However, BOC has its own method of calculating net total assets/capital employed and as the only information available for years prior to 1996 is that given in the five-year record on pages 188–9, it will be necessary to use the BOC definition for the purpose of time series comparisons. The BOC definition for capital employed differs from that in the balance sheet in Table 10.2 in so far as all short-term borrowings and finance leases are included, but are reduced by the deposits and cash. It is shown in BOC's five-year record (see page 189).

The calculation of the capital employed figure used by BOC for 1997 is as follows:

	£ million
Total assets less current liabilities	3,392.2
(i.e. net total assets)	
Add	
Borrowings and finance leases falling due within	
one year (see note 3)	620.4
	4,012.6
Less	
Deposits and cash (see note 3)	246.3
'BOC capital employed'	£3,766.3

The figure of 'capital employed' for 1997 and the corresponding figures for the four previous years are to be found in the five-year review on pages 188–9. Because of the adjustments to the net total assets figure by BOC indicated above, the operating profit figure given in the profit and loss account in the five-year review needs no further adjustment. Therefore, using the BOC review figures, for 1997 and 1996 the returns on average capital employed have been calculated as follows:

$$\text{ROCE 1997} = \frac{540.4}{\frac{1}{2}(3,766.3 + 3,564.2)} \times 100 = 14.7 \text{ per cent}$$

$$\text{ROCE 1996} = \frac{539.4}{\frac{1}{2}(3,564.2 + 3,241.5)} \times 100 = 15.9 \text{ per cent}$$

If the analysis is extended to years before 1996 the fluctuations in the return on capital employed since 1993 are evident, with an overall decline of approximately 1.0 per cent. But over the same five-year period, operating profit has shown an increasing trend in headline earnings from £420.8 million in 1993 to £540.4 million in 1997, an increase of 28.3 per cent. The use of trend (time series) analysis is discussed more fully in Chapter 15. (In 1997 BOC added a further degree of sophistication not available to the external reader by calculating the average capital employed on a monthly basis. This resulted in a lower average capital employed than the simple averaging of the opening and closing capital employed as used in the above calculation, and produced a return on average capital employed of 15.0 per cent).

Some analysts argue that a number of firms use bank overdrafts as a form of long-term borrowing, and that this is particularly true of small firms. In such cases it is suggested that the bank overdraft should be included as part of the capital employed, and any cash-in-hand balances should be netted off against the overdraft and 'short-term' borrowing, with no interest being deducted from the operating profit. This would also appear to be BOC's logic. BOC has included all interest bearing borrowings in its capital employed less any deposits and cash held.

Return on equity

The purpose of the return on equity ratio is to show the profitability of the company in terms of the capital provided by the owners of the company, i.e. the ordinary shareholders. Return on equity is usually calculated as follows:

$$\frac{\text{Profit after interest and preference dividends but before tax}}{\text{Average ordinary share capital, reserves and retained profit for the period}} \times 100$$

This ratio therefore focuses attention on the efficiency of the company in earning profits on behalf of its ordinary shareholders, by relating the profits to the total amount of shareholders' funds employed in the company. As with return on capital employed, it is usually more appropriate to take the figure of profit before tax, to avoid distortions caused by differences in the taxation liability of different companies.

In the following ratios, calculated for BOC for 1997, the numerator is the amount described in each of the consolidated profit and loss accounts as profit before tax minus the preference dividend of £0.1 million (see note 2 to the financial statements). The denominator is the average of the opening and closing amounts described in each of the consolidated balance sheets as shareholders's funds in the 'capital and reserves' section, minus the issued preference share capital of £2.5 million (see note 12 to the financial statements). As it is the intention to concentrate on the returns attributable to the shareholders in BOC, the minority shareholders' interests (i.e. the interest of outside shareholders in consolidated subsidiary companies) should not be included in the calculation. The minority interest of £28.5 million in the 1997 profits of BOC has therefore been deducted.

$$\text{Return on equity} = \frac{445.2 - 0.1 - 28.5}{\frac{1}{2}(1{,}892.8 - 2.5 + 1{,}818.7 - 2.5)} \times 100 = 22.5 \text{ per cent}$$

In Appendix B, page 247, the ratio Return on Shareholder Funds (Return on Sh. F) can be found. This is another name for return on equity. However the numbers above and on pages 245–8 differ because of small differences in defining the numerator and denominator. FAME have made no adjustments for the minority interest in profit and the dividends and capital of the preference shareholders.

This is a good example of two interpretations of the same ratio. We would argue ours is more conceptually sound, but more time consuming to compute.

Earnings per share

Earnings per share (EPS) is a much more widely used variation of the return on equity indicator of profitability. The numerator of this represents the total amount of earnings available to ordinary shareholders after all deductions have been made, i.e. the profit after exceptional and extraordinary items, interest, taxation, minority interests and preference dividends. The denominator represents either the number of ordinary shares issued by the company at the year-end or, if substantial changes have taken place during the year, the average number of shares outstanding during the year. It is now standard practice for EPS information to be given in the published accounts of a company (as required by FRS 3); it is therefore normally unnecessary for the analyst to have to calculate this ratio. However, it might be useful to consider briefly the steps that are involved in this calculation. In the group five-year record, as shown on pages 188–98, two different EPS figures are given.

The EPS figures in the accounts have been calculated on the 'net basis', i.e. after deduction of all elements making up the tax charge, which is in line with the accounting standard. When a company pays a dividend, it is at the same time required to pay to the Inland Revenue an amount of advanced corporation tax (ACT) equal to the tax credit on the net dividend paid out. When the corporation tax charge on the assessable profits of the company is eventually computed, then all that has to be paid on the normal corporation tax payment date is the difference between the total liability for corporation tax for the year and the ACT. There are additional complications for those companies with overseas income and taxes to pay, but we shall not concern ourselves with those here. It is, of course, possible for a company's ACT to exceed its liability to corporation tax, making some of the ACT irrecoverable and thus increasing the cost to the company of paying a dividend.

The undiluted EPS ratio for 1997 can be computed as follows:

	£ million
Earnings	287.6
Less preference dividend	0.1
	287.5

Average number of ordinary shares 484.8 million.

$$\text{EPS} = \frac{287.5}{484.8} = 59.31\text{p per share}$$

In the past, information has been provided in the BOC financial statements of the 'fully diluted' EPS. The calculations for these particular ratios are similar to that described above, except that the denominator now reflects the number of shares that would be in issue if all of the options to take up shares were to be exercised. For example, note 6 provides information on the ordinary share options outstanding under the various share-option schemes. If these options were exercised, then more ordinary shares would have to be issued and, as a result, the existing equity base would be diluted. The effect of these adjustments would be captured by the fully diluted EPS ratio.

Under FRS 3 the earnings to be incorporated into the EPS calculation are earnings after interest, tax and any preference dividends paid. With the changes in definition of exceptional items (see Chapter 2) and their incorporation above the line it is possible for the profit for the year to be materially influenced by the size of the exceptional item(s). This was the case for BOC in 1994. The charging of £85.0 million for restructuring costs and a further £16.6 million for losses on disposal of operations sold made a significant impact on the 1994 profits and EPS calculations. Note in the five-year record (see page 188) the EPS based as above, on published profit was 23.82p per share, but by excluding the two exceptional items it became 43.87p per share.

FRS 3 allows a company to compute an additional EPS based on the normal or maintainable profit. Generally this is known as the headline profit, the profit derived from the ongoing activities of the business prior to charging such exceptional or one-off expenses. The UK based Institute of Investment Management and Research (IIMR) has also made recommendations which seem to provide the basis for the method used by the market analysts. The recommendation is to allow the company to adjust the profit after tax by adding back only the cost of reorganization and restructuring. BOC in their computations followed the FRS 3 requirement and wrote-off all the exceptional items hence the 23.82p EPS, but by adding back the restructuring costs which, after tax, amounted to £95.53 million gave rise to the revised EPS of 43.87p. A review of the five years of the EPS for BOC highlights one of the limitations of the FRS 3 based EPS figure. Note the significant dip in EPS in 1994, the year of restructuring, and note the much smoother trend in the adjusted set of figures. The Accounting Standards Board would argue that when such a situation occurs the required method has served its purpose by highlighting to the market that the company has taken decisions which in the short term have cost a considerable amount, but which it hoped, will have long-term benefits.

So in spite of its widespread use, the EPS ratio does have several limitations. For example, if the ratio is used to compare the profitability of different companies, it may be misleading because it is based on the number of shares in issue. Two companies that are identical in every respect except for the nominal value of their ordinary shares will clearly have a different number of shares outstanding and will therefore have different EPS. If the profitability of the same company over time is being compared, the ratio will be affected by any bonus issues that have taken place. This has the effect of increasing the number of shares but does not provide any additional capital for the company. Also, because of the effect of retained earnings on the profit of a company, the EPS changes will be difficult to interpret correctly. For example, if a company has equity capital of £50,000 (in £1 ordinary shares) on which it currently earns an after-tax return of 20 per cent, then its earnings available to equity will amount to £10,000 and the EPS figure will be 20p per share. Of the earnings of £10,000, £2,000 might be distributed as dividends and the balance retained. The equity will now amount to £58,000 and, if the same return on equity is achieved in the next accounting period, then the earnings will be £11,600 and the earnings per share will increase to £11,600/50,000, i.e. 23.2p per share. Thus the EPS will have increased, although there has been no corresponding increase in the underlying performance of the company as measured by return on equity.

Price–earnings ratio (PER)

This ratio is calculated by dividing the market price of ordinary shares of a company by the EPS figure described above. The ratio is therefore made up of a component that reflects the expectations of the market concerning the future earnings of a company (i.e. the market price of the shares) and a component that reflects the earnings available for each ordinary share based on the results of the most recent past accounting period. For example, supposing the current market price of a BOC ordinary share is £8.67 and, using the EPS for the year ended 30 September 1997 of 59.31 pence, then the price–earnings ratio is

$$\frac{8.67}{0.5931} = 14.6 \text{ times}$$

What this means is that if £8.67 is paid for these shares, then 14.6 years of earnings of 59.31 pence per share are being bought. Because the current market value of a share reflects the expectations of investors concerning the future profits of a company, the ratio is effectively measuring the market's anticipation of future earnings. If the price–earnings ratios of different companies are compared, then, all other things being equal, the company with the higher ratio will be the one that is expected to have the better prospects. Price–earnings ratios differ from other measures of profitability so far discussed in that the latter are based on the actual reported profit and financial position for a past period. Those might therefore offer a better basis for inter-firm comparisons than the price–earnings ratio, which is very much dependent on the subjective opinion of investors concerning future profitability.

A quick indication of whether the company is highly or lowly rated is obtained by computing the Price–Earnings Ratio relative. (PER relative). This ratio is the result of comparing the PER of a company with the PER of the market, which is usually the FTSE All-share PER.

$$\text{PER relative} = \frac{\text{PER of BOC Group}}{\text{PER of market}}$$

For BOC, when its PER was 14.6, the FTSE All-share PER was 19.9, therefore

$$\text{PER relative} = \frac{14.6}{19.9} = 0.73$$

Similar relatives can be computed using a company's industry PER, which was 15.43 giving a PER relative with the industry of 0.95. This implies the market is seeing BOC as an average member of its industry grouping. A high PER relative would suggest either a market leader or an overvalued share; a low PER relative the opposite.

Return on sales and asset turnover

The profitability ratios that have been described so far relate profit earned to a specific investment base. An alternative way of examining the performance of a company is to make use of ratios that bring out the relationship between profit and sales, and the relationship between sales and capital employed. The first of these is the return on sales, or profit-margin, ratio and this is calculated as

$$\frac{\text{Profit}}{\text{Total sales}} \times 100$$

The purpose of this ratio is to indicate the performance of the company in achieving the maximum sales possible, while at the same time keeping costs to a minimum. The ratio can be thought of as expressing the profit in pence generated by each pound of sales; in general, the higher it is the better. However, such a ratio by itself may be misleading because it fails to take account of the assets or capital used to achieve the profit margin. In other words, a high return on sales may have been achieved, but only after making a considerable investment in resources, resulting in a low return on capital employed.

This problem can be overcome by introducing the asset-turnover ratio, which is calculated as

$$\frac{\text{Total sales}}{\text{Assets}}$$

This ratio is used to measure the performance of the company in generating sales from the assets at its disposal. It is described as the asset-turnover ratio because it is, in effect, expressing the number of times assets have been 'turned over' during a period to achieve the sales revenue. If one divided total sales by the capital employed the ratio could be called the capital-turnover ratio. The underlying principle is the same for both ratios.

The profit-margin ratio and asset-turnover ratio, if considered together, provide a useful means of breaking down the return on investment ratios described previously. The relationship between all three ratios can be seen to be

$$\frac{\text{Profit}}{\text{Total sales}} \times \frac{\text{Total sales}}{\text{Assets}} = \frac{\text{Profit}}{\text{Assets}}$$

Obviously, for such a relationship to hold, the numerator and denominator of each ratio need to be defined in a consistent manner. For example, if we refer to the return on capital employed ratios described earlier, several ways of defining both profit and capital employed were identified. The latter could be the total assets, the net total assets or, in the case of BOC, the net total assets after adjusting for short-term cash items. For the purpose of comparing the profit-margin and asset-turnover ratios of BOC in 1997 with the equivalent ratios for 1996, it will be convenient to use their own definition of capital employed.

From Table 10.1 it can be seen that the trading profit of £540.4 million in 1997 was earned from sales (turnover) of £3,963.6 million. Similarly, the 1996 trading profit of £539.4 million was earned from sales of £4,019.5 million. Both turnover and operating profit include the appropriate shares of the amounts made by the associated companies. Armed with this information, it is possible to calculate profit-margin ratios as follows:

$$\text{Return on sales (profit margin) 1997} = \frac{540.4}{3,963.6} \times 100 = 13.6 \text{ per cent}$$

$$\text{Return on sales (profit margin) 1997} = \frac{539.4}{4,019.5} \times 100 = 13.4 \text{ per cent}$$

There has been a marginal improvement between the two years in the profit margin which did not result in an increase in the ROCE, as shown on page 118. This would suggest that the use of the capital employed in generating sales has declined. For confirmation of this it is necessary to calculate the asset-turnover ratios for each year. For consistency we use the BOC calculated capital employed figures in the denominator, see page 118 for explanation and pages 188–9 of the BOC five-year record for figures. The ratios are as follows:

$$\text{Asset-turnover ratio } 1997 = \frac{3,963.6}{\frac{1}{2}(3,766.3 + 3,564.2)} = 1.08 \text{ times}$$

$$\text{Asset-turnover ratio } 1996 = \frac{4,019.5}{\frac{1}{2}(3,564.2 + 3,241.5)} = 1.18 \text{ times}$$

The relationship between profit margin, asset-turnover rate and return on capital employed can now be expressed as follows:

	Profit margin	*Asset turnover*		*ROCE*
1997	13.6	× 1.08	=	14.7 per cent
1996	13.4	× 1.18	=	15.9 per cent

It is evident that the slight increase in the profit margin has been partially offset by the decline in the asset turnover to give a fall in the return on capital employed. As the profit margin in 1997 has not increased much but the asset turnover has decreased proportionally more, the return on capital employed has declined significantly.

Analysing the profitability of the company in this way therefore provides a better explanation of the change in return on capital employed. Comparisons can now be made with similar companies in the same industry to determine whether the trends isolated for BOC are repeated elsewhere.

Profit-margin ratios and asset-turnover ratios can of course be related to other returns on investment ratios, such as return on equity or earnings per ordinary share. Provided that the numerator and denominator of the ratios are calculated consistently, the break-down of these measures of return can provide a useful analysis of profitability for inter-firm and time-series comparisons.

Segmental analysis

So far the analysis of the profitability of BOC has made use of the figures contained in the consolidated financial statements. The process of consolidation involves the aggregation of the results of many subsidiary companies with those of the parent company to produce one single figure for trading profit, for tangible fixed assets and so on. However, with a diversified company such as BOC, the various companies making up the group are involved in a variety of lines of business or operate in different parts of the world, and an analysis based simply on the aggregate position might fail to reflect the performance of the different industrial or geographical segments of the group. Differences in profitability and risk are likely to attach to different industries and to different geographical locations, and comparability, either with other companies or over time, will be improved by extending the analysis of profitability to the major segments of The BOC Group's activities.

Table 10.4 Return on capital employed

	1997	1996
Gases and related products	$\dfrac{415.6}{3,019.1} \times 100 = 13.8\%$	$\dfrac{408.3}{2,781.5} \times 100 = 14.7\%$
Health care	$\dfrac{44.5}{338.1} \times 100 = 13.2\%$	$\dfrac{53.1}{327.1} \times 100 = 16.2\%$

Segmental information concerning BOC is given in note 1 to its financial statements. The profit figure used is that described in Table 10.1 as 'operating profit'. The capital employed is the net total assets after adjusting for short-term cash items. Using this information, it is possible to isolate the profitability of each line of business or geographical location. For example, for two of the principal areas of business activity in terms of contribution to overall profit – gases and related products and health care – the position is shown in Table 10.4.

Financial information for each region and segment is provided for three years so we shall continue to use the average capital employed for each of the two years in the example.

Such an analysis is useful for highlighting the changes that have taken place in the profitability of each major segment, and it may help to create a better picture of the performance of the company in past periods and also of the prospects for the future profitability of the group as a whole. Moreover, comparisons can now be made with companies in the same industry, e.g. with other companies, or segments of other groups, operating in the industrial gases industry.

Segmental analyses need not, of course, be limited to return on capital employed; they could also concentrate on profit-margin and asset-turnover ratios as described previously. Once again using the information contained in note 1 to the BOC financial statements, the picture that emerges for the two business segments of gases and related products and health care is as shown in Table 10.5.

The decline in the return of capital employed on gases and related products can be seen to be due almost entirely to the decline in the asset turnover. For health care there was a general decline in both margins and asset turnover. Further reading of the chairman's statement, the review of operations and note 1 of the financial statements should provide some explanation for the changes highlighted by the ratios. The capital expenditure in the gases and related products segment has increased significantly over the past three years, as mentioned in the operating review. The company is attempting to sell off the health care division at the time of the annual report.

Obviously, where diversification does exist, the ability to be able to undertake this kind of detailed profitability analysis for the principal industrial and geographical segments should provide a useful supplement to the analysis of overall group profitability.

The segmental reports and their ratios help attest to the statements in the operating review of the annual report, helping to explain the much greater level of investment needed to support the gases and related products division. Likewise the same ratios when computed for the geographical regions can help explain those regional

Table 10.5 Profit-margin and asset-turnover ratios

	Profit margin (1)	Asset turnover (2)	ROCE (1) × (2)
Gases and related products			
1997	$\dfrac{415.6}{2,829.9} = 14.7\%$	$\dfrac{2,829.9}{3,019.1} = 0.94$ times	13.8%
1996	$\dfrac{408.3}{2,814.2} = 14.5\%$	$\dfrac{2,814.2}{2,781.5} = 1.01$ times	14.7%
Health care			
1997	$\dfrac{44.5}{477.4} = 9.3\%$	$\dfrac{477.4}{338.1} = 1.41$ times	13.2%
1996	$\dfrac{53.1}{505.9} = 10.5\%$	$\dfrac{505.9}{327.1} = 1.55$ times	16.2%

Table 10.6 The BOC Group – regional profitability

	Ratio	Europe	Africa	Americas	Asia/Pacific	Overall
1997	Profit margin (%)	18.7	18.6	7.00	14.1	13.6
	Asset turnover (×)	1.00	1.33	1.11	1.08	1.08
	ROCE (%)	18.7	24.6	7.70	15.3	14.7
1996	Profit margin (%)	16.4	18.6	9.3	13.0	13.4
	Asset turnover (x)	1.06	1.5	1.24	1.19	1.18
	ROCE (%)	17.4	27.9	11.5	15.5	15.9

differences. These are reproduced in Table 10.6 which serves to highlight the breadth of the dispersions of the regions' results from the overall range. The basic information was taken from note 1 to the financial statements (see pages 216–17). FAME, (see Appendix B, pages 245–7) provides general profitability ratios, but not the detailed segmental ratios. It has used the year end values for its capital and asset denominators and the net profit after interest but before tax for its numerators thus giving a different set of figures from those prepared here.

Cash flow returns

The publication of the consolidated cash flow statement (see Table 10.3 and Appendix A, page 211) is designed to aid users in making judgements on the amount, timing and degree of certainty of future cash flows. It has a further purpose, that of helping to indicate the relationship between profitability and cash generating ability, and thus the quality of the profit earned.

Quality of profit

The quality of profit earned ratio is expressed as a percentage and calculated as

$$\frac{\text{Net cash inflow from operations}}{\text{Operating profit}} \times 100$$

The ratio focuses attention on the company's ability to generate cash as opposed to profit and shows the proportion of profits actually earned as cash. This has obvious liquidity implications for interest, tax, dividend payments and future capital expenditure. These will be handled in Chapter 12. Given the relative size of the annual depreciation charge and various other non-cash expenses one would expect a company to have a quality of profit ratio in excess of 100 per cent. Note 14 to the financial statements of BOC provides the adjustments made to the operating profit to arrive at the figure for the net cash inflow from operations.

For the quality of profit ratios for BOC for 1997 the numerator is the amount of net cash inflow from operations, £733.8 million, which is taken from the consolidated cash flow statement. The denominator is the operating profit of £540.4 million in the profit and loss statement in Table 10.1.

$$\text{Quality of profit 1997} = \frac{733.8}{540.4} \times 100 = 135.8 \text{ per cent}$$

The ratio has improved considerably from the previous year, 1996, when it was 115.8 per cent. If turnover and profits start growing again, then as the ratio of annual depreciation charged to net profits declined, so too would the quality of profit ratio probably decline. If it ever came close to 100 per cent then analysts would start looking even harder at the company's liquidity ratios, though it is quite likely to occur in a business start-up situation.

Quality of sales

The quality of sales ratio is only possible if a company has chosen to use the direct method to report its net cash flow from operations, as this would include an amount for cash received from customers. The quality of sales ratio would be expressed as a percentage and calculated as

$$\frac{\text{Cash received from customers}}{\text{Sales}} \times 100$$

A ratio close to 100 per cent is desirable indicating that the company is keeping on top of the collection of cash from its debtors. Its value should be reviewed alongside any changes in the average collection period (see Chapter 11).

Cash return on capital employed

The cash return on capital employed is the cash equivalent measure of return on capital employed and is expressed as a percentage and calculated as

$$\frac{\text{Net cash inflow from operations}}{\text{Capital employed}} \times 100$$

To many users of financial statements it is the cash return on investment rather than the profit-based return on investment that is of greatest meaning and value. This is particularly so in the case of analysts using business valuation models and corporate projection models.

In the example here for The BOC Group the cash return on the average capital employed (calculated per BOC approach) will be shown. The BOC net cash inflow from operations is £733.8 million for 1997.

$$\text{Cash return on capital employed 1997} = \frac{733.8}{\frac{1}{2}\,(3{,}766.3 + 3{,}564.2)} \times 100 = 20.0 \text{ per cent}$$

Unlike the profit-based ROCE, the cash return on capital employed (Cash ROCE) increased from 1996 to 1997, from 18.4 per cent to 20.0 per cent. It is still early days to report whether or not the cash ROCE has replaced the profit ROCE in terms of practical importance, even though the conceptual case is a strong one.

11 Efficiency and effectiveness

The profitability ratios described in the previous chapter were concerned with the overall efficiency of a company in generating profits and cash from a given investment base. In addition it is often useful to calculate ratios that concentrate on the performance of the management of a company in terms of specific resources such as stock, debtors, employees etc. This chapter considers how such ratios might be calculated and interpreted for The BOC Group plc.

Debtor turnover and collection

It is established practice in British industry for sales to customers to be made on credit terms. In other words, the goods or services supplied are not paid for immediately, but after an agreed period of time. Such a policy requires part of the capital of a company to be used to finance these unpaid sales; the total amount outstanding at the end of the financial year is recorded as debtors in the balance sheet. The questions then arising are concerned first with whether the amount of resources tied up in debtors is reasonable, and second with whether the company has been efficient in converting debtors into cash. Because the level of debtors at the end of the year might be expected to vary with the level of sales during the year, these questions are usually examined by calculating the following ratios:

$$\text{Debtor turnover} = \frac{\text{Sales}}{\text{Debtors}}$$

$$\text{Average collection period (in days)} = \frac{\text{Debtors}}{\text{Sales}} \times 365$$

The sales figures used in these ratios should, of course, reflect only the credit sales of the period. Where there is a marked seasonal variation in sales, then it would be more accurate to relate the year-end debtors to the sales of the last few months of the year. However, information on the distinction between cash and credit sales, or on the timing of sales, is not usually given in published annual reports, and the following ratios for BOC have been calculated by using the total figure for sales (Table 10.1). This does not include turnover of associated companies. Similarly, the debtors figure should ideally be the amount outstanding in respect of credit sales, i.e. the 'trade debtors'. Note 10 to the BOC financial statements (see pages 233–4) gives a break-down of the total debtors figures included in the balance sheet. The trade debtors for 1997 and 1996 were £702.8 million and £703.3 million respectively. If the notes to a company's financial statements do not give a detailed break-down of debtors, then the total debtors can be taken as an approximation.

<table>
<tr><td colspan="2">*Debtor turnover*</td><td>*Average collection period*</td></tr>
<tr><td>1997</td><td>$\dfrac{3{,}677.7}{702.8} = 5.23$ times</td><td>$\dfrac{702.8}{3{,}677.7} \times 365 = 69.8$ days</td></tr>
<tr><td>1996</td><td>$\dfrac{3{,}752.1}{703.3} = 5.33$ times</td><td>$\dfrac{703.3}{3{,}752.1} \times 365 = 68.4$ days</td></tr>
</table>

There has been some decline in the debtor turnover and an increase in the average collection period between 1996 and 1997. It would be helpful to compute the average collection period for the earlier trading periods to see whether this is a one-off decline or a deteriorating trend. Comparisons with similar companies will give some indication of relative performance. The movement in the quality of sales ratios should be computed and compared to see if it confirms the increase in the average time taken to collect the debts. The trend series can be seen in Chapter 14 (page 163).

The average collection period can also be compared with the stated credit terms of BOC. For example, if the credit terms are 'thirty days', then this is usually taken to mean thirty days from the end of the month in which the invoice is issued. This would imply an average collection period of about forty-five days. Any variation between the stated and actual credit duration might be thought of as an indication of inefficiency in the collection of amounts due from debtors. However, as was pointed out in the previous chapter, the trading operations of BOC are undertaken in many different parts of the world and credit terms may differ from country to country, depending on local customs and practice. The product trading mix of BOC is also changing and not all its lines of business have the same credit terms. This too will influence the overall average collection period. A more meaningful analysis would therefore be to calculate the average collection period for different geographical locations and by product groups. Unfortunately, this is not possible because a suitable breakdown of debtors is not provided.

Creditor turnover and payment

The system of supplying goods and services on credit terms also affects the purchases of a company. Any purchases that have not been paid for by the end of the year are shown as creditors in the balance sheet. The above exercise for debtors can therefore be repeated for creditors to show the average time taken to pay for the goods and services purchased. Information on purchases is not usually provided directly, but an approximate amount can be obtained from the cash flow statement providing the company uses the direct method which gives details of the net payments to suppliers. Unfortunately BOC uses the indirect method which does not give sufficient detail. If the information is available then the creditors turnover and payment period will be calculated in a similar manner to the debtors ratios.

$$\text{Creditor-turnover ratio} = \frac{\text{Cash payments to suppliers during the period}}{\text{Trade creditors at the end of the period}}$$

$$\text{Creditor payment period} = \frac{365}{\text{Creditor-turnover ratio}}$$

The creditor-turnover ratio is measured in times, with the payment period in days. In theory the turnover ratio is purchases divided by creditors, but because total purchases for the period are usually not published many approximations or surrogates are used. These surrogate measures used have included amounts for cost of sales, or cost of sales adjusted for changes in stock values and or reduced by the depreciation expense.

The stock adjustment is to convert the expense into a purchase, whilst the depreciation adjustment is to remove some of the known non-purchase items from cost of sales. But whatever degree of improvization is undertaken in the ratio components, the implications of it must always be borne in mind when interpreting the results.

An approximate 'purchases' figure for BOC for 1997 can be obtained by adjusting the cost of sales figures in Table 10.1 as follows:

		£ million
Cost of sales		2,105.5
Less depreciation	276.5	
decrease in sales	29.0	305.5
Approximate purchases for 1997		2,411.0

The depreciation and increase in stock figures have been taken from note 14 (page 238) where it indicates the adjustments to the operating profit for non-cash items and working capital changes. Since this approximate purchases figure includes trade purchases, wages and services purchased the creditors figure used will consist of the sum of the trade and other creditors as shown in note 10. Presumably the latter figure includes the amount unpaid on services received such as rates, electricity and so on.

$$\text{Credit turnover ratio} = \frac{\text{Purchases}}{\text{Creditors}} = \frac{2,411.0}{(332.6 + 212.2)} = 4.43 \text{ times}$$

$$\text{Credit payment period} = \frac{\text{Creditors}}{\text{Purchasers}} \times 365 = \frac{544.8}{2,411.0} \times 365 = 82.5 \text{ days}$$

This is a marked reduction from 112 days for 1996. Because of the imprecision in the calculation of the components of this ratio, it can be used only as an approximate indication of the creditor payment policy of BOC. Generally speaking, the longer the credit period achieved the better, because the operations of the company are being financed interest-free by suppliers' funds. However, if too long a period is taken to pay creditors, the credit rating of the company may suffer, thereby making it more difficult to obtain supplies in the future. Given the length of the creditor payment period calculated, 82.5 days and general credit terms of 30 days, it would lead one to consider hard the use of this particular approximation in any meaningful analysis. Not surprisingly this ratio is computed less frequently than average collection period due to the lack of data available on the purchases of materials and services during the year.

The implications of the degree of improvization in the ratio components must always be borne in mind when interpreting the results.

Stock turnover

An important aspect of the management of a company concerns the levels of stocks that should be held. Very often a considerable amount of capital is tied up in the financing of raw materials, work in progress and finished goods. It is therefore important to ensure that the level of stocks is kept as low as possible. However, if the level falls too low there is the danger that customers' orders could not be fulfilled in time and sales may be lost to competitors. On the other hand it may be part of a company's marketing strategy that the level of stock required is sufficient to ensure that all customers are supplied within a stated time period. The shorter the time period the greater the stock to be carried. Similarly, the type of production system and type of product made have implications for the level of stocks held.

A sound system of stock management is therefore crucial. One way of assessing this is by calculating the stock-turnover ratio as follows:

$$\frac{\text{Cost of sales for the period}}{\text{Stock at the end of the period}}$$

If the closing stock figure is not typical of the amount of stock held during the period, an alternative way of arriving at the denominator of the ratio would be to use the average stock held. Because information is not given on the levels of stock held at different times of the year, a simple average of the opening and closing stock amount is often used. It is important to use the cost of sales rather than sales as the numerator of the ratio, because stock is generally valued at cost. The following stock-turnover ratios for BOC have been computed from Tables 10.1 and 10.2 using year end stock figures.

	Stock-turnover rate	*Stock-turnover period*
	$\dfrac{\text{Cost of sales}}{\text{Stock}}$	$\dfrac{\text{Stock}}{\text{Cost of sales}} \times 365$
1997	$\dfrac{2{,}105.5}{354.3} = 5.94$ times	$\dfrac{354.3}{2{,}105.5} \times 365 = 61.4$ days
1996	$\dfrac{2{,}115.5}{403.4} = 5.24$ times	$\dfrac{403.4}{2{,}115.5} \times 365 = 69.6$ days

The stock-turnover period ratios reveal that the average period for which stock was held before sale in 1996 was 69.6 days, and that this has fallen considerably to 61.4 days in 1997. Generally speaking the higher the stock-turnover ratio, or conversely the lower the stock-turnover period, the better, but whether these ratios should be classified as 'good' or 'bad' depends very much on the nature of the business. Manufacturing companies such as BOC might be expected to have longer stock-turnover periods than, say, a company primarily involved in food retailing. What is an optimal level depends on balancing such factors as the lead time for manufacturing processes, (e.g. zero for just-in-time – JIT) the need to hold reserve stock of raw materials to insure against uncertainties in supply, the length and types of the manufacturing process, the normal holding period of finished goods and the requirement to keep the amount of capital tied up in stock to a minimum. However, systematic changes over time, or deviations from the ratios of similar companies, might suggest that the stock position needs careful scrutiny, especially if it were a worsening situation. It would be useful to evaluate separately the levels of stocks held in raw materials, work in progress and finished goods, and thus highlight the area(s) causing the change in the overall picture. This point will be readdressed in Chapter 14 (see page 163) in more detail. At its simplest, purely from a cost of financing the stock, the lower the stock value, the lower the stock period.

In addition to the assessment of managerial performance in the use of resources and liabilities such as debtors, creditors and stock, these particular items also have important implications for the liquidity of the company and this will be considered in the following chapter. These resources can be combined into one ratio, the sales to working capital ratio, which is intended to indicate the adequacy of the total reservoir of liquid funds in supporting the level of sales.

Employee ratios

Note 6 to the BOC annual accounts (see pages 225–9) provides details about the human resources used in the group. It gives a break-down by business and region of the year-end number of employees and the average number employed during the year. It also indicates both present and future costs arising from these employees. The note reveals that the total employment costs of 1997 amounted to £909.2 million. The significance of this amount in terms of the overall operations of BOC can be appreciated by relating it to the sales figure of £3677.7 million. The wages to sales ratio is seen to be

$$\text{Wages to sales ratio} = \frac{909.2}{3,677.7} \times 100 = 24.7 \text{ per cent}$$

In other words, for every £1 of sales achieved, almost 25p is paid in employee costs. Its significance is even more striking if it is related to the amount of value added by the operations of BOC. (The value added is the wealth created by the activities of a company, the difference between total amount paid for bought in materials and services and the total amount earned when the products of a company are sold on to third parties. This value added is shared out amongst the employees by way of wages, etc., the government by way of taxes, the lenders by way of interest, the shareholders by way of dividends and the company by way of retentions.) The employee costs take up a large proportion of the value added, so employees are an important part of the inputs of a company. The efficiency with which this particular resource is utilized needs to be carefully assessed. The methods, approach and ratios described below could be just as usefully applied to other important resources of a company, e.g. area of floorspace in a retail company.

There are a variety of ratios that could be calculated to focus attention on the utilization of labour, such as sales per employee, profit per employee, value added per employee and so on. In Table 11.1, employee ratios analysed by line of business and geographic region have been determined for BOC for 1996 and 1997. Information on

Table 11.1 The BOC Group plc – employee ratios by line of business and by region

	Average number of employees		Sales		Sales per employee		Operating profit		Operating profit per employee		Capital employed		Capital employed per employee	
	1997	*1996*	*1997* (£ million)	*1996* (£ million)	*1997* (£ 000)	*1996* (£ 000)	*1997* (£ million)	*1996* (£ million)	*1997* (£ 000)	*1996* (£ 000)	*1997* (£ million)	*1996* (£ million)	*1997* (£ 000)	*1996* (£ 000)
Line of business														
Gases and related products	27,411	26,966	2,828.9	2,814.2	103.2	104.4	415.6	408.3	15.2	15.1	3,109.2	2,929.0	113.4	108.6
Health care	4,730	5,090	477.4	505.9	100.9	99.4	44.5	53.1	9.4	10.4	344.5	331.7	72.8	65.2
Vacuum technology	2,922	2,822	367.0	416.9	125.6	147.7	53.1	62.4	18.2	22.1	175.1	163.4	59.9	57.9
Distribution services	5,401	5,370	289.3	282.5	53.6	52.6	31.9	27.9	5.9	5.2	137.5	147.0	25.5	27.4
Corporate	269	247	–	–	–	–	(4.7)	(12.3)	–	–	–	(6.9)	–	–
Totals	40,733	40,495	3,963.6	4,019.5	97.3	99.3	540.4	539.4	13.3	13.3	3,766.3	3,564.2	92.5	88.0
Geographic region														
Europe	14,680	14,594	1,217.9	1,229.3	83.0	84.2	228.1	202.0	15.5	13.8	1,239.3	1,193.1	84.4	81.8
Africa	8,524	8,600	341.0	354.4	40.0	41.2	63.3	66.0	7.4	7.7	282.0	232.7	33.1	27.1
Americas	8,986	8,797	1,270.5	1,225.3	141.4	139.3	88.7	113.6	9.9	12.9	1,194.7	1,095.6	133.0	124.5
Asia/Pacific	8,543	8,504	1,134.2	1,210.5	132.8	142.3	160.3	157.8	18.8	18.6	1,050.3	1,042.8	122.9	122.6
Totals	40,733	40,495	3,963.6	4,019.5	97.3	99.3	540.3	539.4	13.3	13.3	3,766.3	3,564.2	92.5	88.0

average number of employees has been extracted from note 6 to the financial statements, and the sales, operating profit and capital-employed figures have been extracted from note 1. Note 6 also provides the year-end number of employees for both 1996 and 1997, which is also found in the five-year record from which the trend in employee numbers can be interpreted. There has been an overall increase in personnel involved in the continuing businesses of the group, both on the average and at the year-ends.

The segmental analysis in Table 11.1 does not reveal any significant positive trends, though it does help to highlight those lines of business that are most capital and person intensive, e.g., gases and related products, and the fact that in spite of increasing investment and manpower in health care and vacuum technology, sales and profits in absolute and relative terms took a considerable dive in those areas.

In the regional analysis the two regions with high per capita capital investment, the Americas and Asia/Pacific, did not necessarily come out better than the other regions in terms of sales and profit per capita. The big reduction in the American profits is not all due to the increase in the value of sterling against the dollar. They have been declining these past three years. The reasons for all these variations can be found in the company's operating review or in answers to questions put by interested shareholders at the company's AGM.

The advantages of segmental analyses of this nature are obvious. Analysts can compare the employee ratios with other directly comparable firms operating in each line of business. Assessments of future profitability of the whole group will be facilitated by a knowledge of the position in the principal segments and the variations in performance over time can be more meaningfully evaluated.

Other ratios

There are several other aspects of operational efficiency that could be highlighted by the use of ratios. These usually consist of attempts to break down, by using the pyramid concept, some primary measure of profitability (such as return on sales) into its component parts to try to pinpoint the reasons for differences in the profit margin from that of previous periods or from that of other companies. For example, in order for BOC to sustain total sales of £3,677.7 million in 1997, it was necessary to incur expenditure on administration, distribution, research and development and so on. Ratios that relate these expenditure items to sales could be calculated from the profit and loss account (Table 10.1) and the information in note 2 (see page 217). From these two sources it was possible to compare these expenditure items with the turnover that was created by their expenditure since BOC provides information on turnover and costs for the continuing and new business acquired during the year, or in the case of 1996 discontinued in the year.

The results from analysing the acquisitions and discontinued business cost ratios have to be treated with some care. It has been argued by some that if a new company is acquired early in the financial year its first year's profits could appear better than previously due to the benefit of the new management, but if the acquisition is late in the financial year the benefits will not be seen until the following year. It has been argued that new management can and sometimes has influenced pre- and post-acquisition profits by use of accounting provisions and accounting conventions in order to present gains from an acquisition in the best light. Whether post-acquisition profits

Table 11.2   Continued businesses and acquisitions cost ratios (proportion of sales)

	Continuing	Acquisitions	1997 total	1996 total
$\dfrac{\text{Cost of sales}}{\text{Sales}}$	$\dfrac{2{,}079.9}{3{,}644.7} \times 100 = 57.1\%$	$\dfrac{25.6}{33.7} \times 100 = 76.0\%$	$\dfrac{2{,}105.5}{3{,}677.7} \times 100 = 57.3\%$	56.4%
$\dfrac{\text{Distribution costs}}{\text{Sales}}$	$\dfrac{305.2}{3{,}644.7} \times 100 = 8.4\%$	—	$\dfrac{305.2}{3{,}677.7} \times 100 = 8.3\%$	8.3%
$\dfrac{\text{Administration costs}}{\text{Sales}}$	$\dfrac{705.6}{3{,}644.7} \times 100 = 19.4\%$	$\dfrac{7.8}{33.7} \times 100 = 23.1\%$	$\dfrac{713.4}{3{,}677.7} \times 100 = 19.4\%$	20.0%
$\dfrac{\text{Research and development costs}}{\text{Sales}}$	$\dfrac{80.6}{3{,}644.7} \times 100 = 2.2\%$	—	$\dfrac{80.6}{3{,}677.7} \times 100 = 2.2\%$	2.6%

are influenced by pre-acquisition provisions is a moot point but it should ensure that the investor treats with caution any attempts to isolate the pre- and post-implications on profits of an acquisition (see Smith 1996).

Taking each cost as a percentage of the appropriate amount of turnover provides the results given in Table 11.2.

As the results indicate, there have been small reductions in the proportion of administration and research and development costs which are almost equal to the increase in the ratio that relates the major cost component, cost of sales, to sales. This part of the analysis may be of more value when used internally by management on one company at a time and/or for those companies where a greater proportion of their costs are of a variable nature.

The asset-turnover ratio, as calculated in Chapter 10, could similarly be broken down to bring out the relationship between sales and specific categories of assets, such as plant and machinery, total fixed assets, total current assets and so on. Chapter 14 will include the values for these ratios in its structured review of The BOC Group plc's annual financial statements.

12 Liquidity and stability

An analysis of the profitability of a company may reveal a satisfactory position, and yet if there are insufficient funds available to pay bills as they fall due, the company will be unlikely to survive for very long. A problem that often faces highly profitable and fast-expanding companies is that of 'overtrading'. This situation arises when most of the profits are used to finance the additional fixed assets, stocks and debtors required to sustain the expanding level of business, producing a shortage of liquid resources for meeting short-term obligations. Therefore, it is important to assess not only the profitability of a company, but also its liquidity and stability. The principal methods adopted to focus attention on short-term liquidity are considered in this chapter.

Current ratio (working capital ratio)

The current ratio relates the current assets of a company to its current liabilities. Current assets consist of cash plus those items that can normally be expected to be converted into cash in the near future (i.e. debtors and stocks); together these are thought of as providing a reservoir of liquid resources for meeting the payments due to short-term creditors. The short-term creditors or current liabilities are defined as those requiring payment within twelve months of the balance sheet date. The working capital, or current, ratio is calculated as

$$\frac{\text{Current assets}}{\text{Current liabilities}}$$

From the balance sheet shown in Table 10.2 it is possible to calculate ratios for The BOC Group plc as follows:

$$\text{Current ratio 1997} = \frac{1{,}596.8}{1{,}506.6} = 1.06 \text{ times}$$

$$\text{Current ratio 1996} = \frac{1{,}568.7}{1{,}535.0} = 1.02 \text{ times}$$

Thus between 1996 and 1997 there has been a slight improvement of BOC's current ratio. As was pointed out in Chapter 9, it is not possible to state categorically what the ratio should be. Generally speaking, a ratio less than 1 might give cause for concern, because it would indicate that the liquid resources are insufficient to cover the short-term payments. Bearing in mind the time lag for converting debtors and stock into cash, it should perhaps be greater than 1. In the previous chapter it was shown that the average collection period for BOC's 1997 debtors was seventy days, and the average stock-turnover period was sixty-one days. This compares with the somewhat imprecisely calculated average payment period of trade and other creditors of eighty-three days. In addition, an examination of note 10 to the financial statements reveals that a substantial part of the total current liabilities of £1506.6 million is made up of items other than trade and other creditors.

The precise payment times for the loans and bank overdraft, taxes, dividends and so on may vary from almost immediately to several months in the future. Because of known and unknown variations in the time lags affecting the components of the working capital ratio, it might be considered safer for the ratio to be nearer to 2 than to 1. However, too high a ratio might be due to cash or stock levels being higher than is strictly necessary, and might therefore be indicative of the bad management of working capital requirements. Even a comparison with some 'standard' ratio for the industry might be misleading because of different circumstances facing individual companies.

Though the assets in the balance sheet are valued on a going concern basis, creditors are still interested in the value of the assets. They fear that if the company defaulted on its repayments of either capital or interest, the assets might not generate enough cash from an enforced sale to cover the amount outstanding. Hence, with a current ratio of 2:1 as a rule of thumb, the assets need only be realized for half their book value for the creditors still to recover their money. But since only debtors, stock and work in progress are likely to be sold off for less than book value, short-term creditors can still feel reasonably secure with a ratio between 2:1 and 1:1, but it does depend on the corporate circumstances.

Differences in accounting practices concerning the valuation of stocks and work in progress, and the susceptibility of the working capital ratio to 'window dressing', can cause problems with inter-firm comparisons. Window dressing involves manipulating the working capital position by accelerating or delaying transactions close to the accounting year-end. The following example shows how an inferior ratio could be improved by the use of window dressing, so that a healthier picture of the company's liquidity might be presented.

Supposing that, towards the end of the accounting period, a company forecast that if it follows its normal pattern of stock purchasing and creditor payment then the net current assets positions will be as follows:

Stock	£9,000
Debtors	5,000
Cash	6,000
	20,000
Less creditors	(15,000)
Net current assets	5,000

This will result in a current ratio of 20,000/15,000, i.e. 1.33.

This ratio could have been improved substantially by delaying stock purchases of, say, £4,000 until just after the end of the year. This would have reduced the stock figure to £5,000 and creditors to £11,000. The position could be further improved by using, say, £4,000 of the surplus cash to accelerate the payments to creditors, thereby reducing cash to £2,000 and creditors to £7,000. The net current assets would then appear as

Stocks	£5,000
Debtors	5,000
Cash	2,000
	12,000
Less creditors	(7,000)
Net current assets	5,000

Thus, although the net current assets position remains the same, the current ratio of 12,000/7,000, i.e. 1.71, would appear much healthier to external analysts.

Nevertheless, in spite of its imperfections, the working capital ratio is of use in providing an approximate indication of a company's liquidity, and is widely used as such.

Quick ratio (acid test ratio)

The working capital ratio is frequently criticized because the numerator includes items that are not very readily convertible into cash if the need arose to pay creditors at short notice. BOC is not untypical of manufacturing companies in having quite a lengthy stock-turnover period and therefore stock is generally thought of as lacking liquidity. The quick ratio overcomes this problem by excluding stock from the numerator. It is calculated as

$$\frac{\text{Current assets minus stocks}}{\text{Current liabilities}}$$

An examination of Table 10.2 reveals that the quick ratios for BOC are as follows:

$$\text{Quick ratio 1997} = \frac{1{,}596.8 - 354.3}{1{,}506.6} = 0.82 \text{ times}$$

$$\text{Quick ratio 1996} = \frac{1{,}568.7 - 403.4}{1{,}535.0} = 0.76 \text{ times}$$

This ratio, by concentrating on the more readily realizable of the current assets, is thought to provide a much stricter test of liquidity than does the working capital ratio.

The question of what is a 'good' or 'bad' ratio still depends on a variety of circumstances. In general, the quick ratio should not fall too far below 1 because this means that, if all of the creditors requested early repayment, there would be insufficient liquid, or nearly liquid, resources available to meet the request. In other words, the company will fail the 'acid test' of being able to pay the short-term obligations and would therefore be in danger of becoming insolvent. The ratio for BOC has improved between 1996 and 1997 but if the long-term trend is downwards the ratio of 0.82 might begin to give some cause for concern.

The quick ratio does provide a more useful indicator of potential liquidity problems and, because it avoids the distortions in stock valuation caused by different accounting practices, it gives a better basis than the current ratio for comparisons with other companies. However, the ratio can still be affected by 'window dressing' and it could be accused of oversimplifying the position. In reality the debtors of a company may not be very liquid. Certainly, the prepayments and accrued income may be difficult to convert quickly into cash and, at times of recession, the trade debtors may be seeking longer periods of credit because of their own liquidity problems. Attempts to press for earlier payment might force the debtors into bankruptcy. In fact, if recessionary conditions do exist, the raw materials component of the total balance sheet figure for stock may be more immediately realizable than the debtors. Even though the market for finished goods, and therefore work in progress, might be depressed, it should be relatively easy to sell raw materials, either back to suppliers or to other manufacturers.

One of the most important factors concerning liquidity appraisal is the extent to which loan and overdraft facilities are available. If a company has unused overdraft facilities that could be drawn on, then even in the extremely unlikely event of all of the creditors requiring immediate payment there would be a cushion to compensate for a low quick ratio. On the other hand, if overdraft facilities are currently being utilized up to the limit, a low quick ratio might be very serious. BOC indicate in note 3 to the financial statements (see pages 218–21) that they have unutilized contractually committed facilities available to the group of $420 million (£260.8 million at balance sheet date). This was available a year ago and is still untouched. Though only 17 per cent of the current liabilities it is a substantial backup for the company in an emergency.

Cash flow analysis

A disadvantage of both the current and the quick ratios is that they measure liquidity at a single point in time rather than over a period of time. The liquidity position of a company such as BOC will be constantly changing in response to the flow of cash into and out of the company, and therefore a ratio that merely reflects the liquidity at the balance sheet date fails to capture the extremely important relationship between cash inflows and outflows.

As we explained in Chapter 4, it is now standard accounting practice for a consolidated cash flow statement to be included in the annual financial statements of a company. This statement is extremely useful in providing the external analyst with an explanation for the changes in liquidity over the year.

An examination of the consolidated cash flow statement for BOC in Table 10.3 shows how in 1997 there was a considerable increase in cash inflow over that of 1996. The funds generated from operations was sufficient to cover all the outgoings such as servicing loan and equity finance and payment of taxes, leaving enough to cover approximately 60 per cent of the capital expenditure undertaken. This was also true in 1996. The balance of the funds needed to finance the capital expenditure, which has grown year-on-year for the past three years, has come predominantly from borrowing. This too has grown annually with £342 million being borrowed in 1997. This will impinge on the company's gearing levels which will be investigated in the following chapter. Note 3 on pages 218–21 indicates that the types of loan used were predominantly of medium- to long-term maturity. This is a good sign because companies that consistently fund long-term investment from short-term funds run the risk of damaging the liquidity and eventually the viability of the company. A major purpose of liquidity analysis is to try to assess the potential cash flow problems that a company may face in the near future.

A careful review of the information in note 3 will help here, as will the table provided in BOC's Finance and Treasury Review. This table shows how the total debt has increased from £1390.5 million in 1996 to the £1621.6 million in 1997 with its maturity lengthening. Note 3 also provides information on the type of borrowing undertaken, its type, source, currency and maturity. This can be evaluated if desired when assessing future liquidity requirements, or when reviewing the foreign currency hedging and matching arrangements the company has, given that it is an international business with trade and investments sourced in many currencies.

Cash interest cover

The cash interest cover ratio is the preferred complement for the traditional interest cover ratio which will be described in the next chapter. This ratio states the number of times the cash flow from operations covers the interest payments to lenders. This is of obvious importance to both lenders and shareholders since non-payment of interest, when due, can precipitate a company's liquidation. Using the information from the cash flow statement the ratio is calculated as

$$\frac{\text{Net cash inflow from operations and interest received}}{\text{Interest paid}}$$

In 1997 the net cash inflow from operations is £733.8 million and interest received is £15.9 million, shown in the consolidated cash flow statement (Table 10.3). From the same statement the 1997 interest paid is £113.3 million. The cash interest cover ratios are:

$$\text{Cash interest cover 1997} = \frac{733.8 + 15.9}{113.3} = 6.62 \text{ times}$$

$$\text{Cash interest cover 1996} = \frac{625.1 + 23.5}{108.9} = 5.96 \text{ times}$$

The cushion on the interest payment has increased in 1997, and there is a long way to go before the company risks default on its interest payments. BOC has included in its interest payments both interest capitalized and interest charged to the profit and loss account. This is the correct way to test coverage. The true figure for interest must include all interest paid regardless of whether or not it is capitalized since the default risk is no different for either category of interest.

Cash dividend cover

The cash dividend cover ratio has a similar purpose to the cash interest cover in that it signals the ability, or lack of it, of the company to cover the cash dividend payout. In general, companies do not want to be paying dividends out of funds generated other than by earned profits. That would be a case of robbing Peter to pay Paul, i.e. of paying dividends out of capital flows.

The cash dividend cover is a multiple and is calculated as

$$\frac{\text{Net cash inflow after tax from operations} - \text{Interest paid}}{\text{Dividends paid}}$$
$$+ \text{ Interest received} + \text{Dividends received from related companies}$$

A multiple in excess of 1 indicates sufficient cash earned from operations and investment and after paying off the financing charges to provide for a dividend and for the reinvestment of cash to help maintain the physical and monetary capital of the company.

Taking the information from the cash flow statement for BOC (see page 115), the net cash inflow from operating activities for 1997 is £733.8 million, the net outflow for returns on investment and servicing of finance is £104.0 million and this covers all the other items listed in the numerator. The tax paid is £109.5 million. The dividends paid in 1997 were £121.5 million.

$$\text{Cash dividend cover 1997} = \frac{733.8 - 109.5 - 104.0}{121.5} = 4.28 \text{ times}$$

$$\text{Cash dividend cover 1996} = \frac{625.1 - 115.8 - 91.8}{121.1} = 3.45 \text{ times}$$

The cash dividends paid in both 1996 and 1997 were well covered by the cash inflow from operations, leaving plenty of cash to be reinvested in the group for the maintenance of its capital.

Cash debt coverage

A company's ability to continue as a going concern is dependent not only on meeting its current interest payments but also on repayment of its loan capital. The cash debt coverage ratio can indicate how much of the maturing debt capital can be repaid out of the retained cash flow from operations. If the multiple exceeds unity the company will not need to reduce its asset base or raise additional external funds to repay the maturing loans.

The numerator is the net cash retained from operations after paying interest, tax and dividends. The denominator is the debt maturing in the next twelve months.

The cash debt coverage ratio is a multiple and is calculated as

$$\frac{\text{Net cash inflow from operations after interest, tax and dividends}}{\text{Debt maturing within the next twelve months}}$$

For the BOC group the numerator for 1997 is the net cash retained from that year's operations. This is made up of the £733.8 million net cash inflow from operations less the tax paid of £109.5 million and the net cash outflow from paying interest and dividends of £104.0 million and £121.5 million. These amounts are found in the cash flow statement (see page 115). The denominator is the figure for loans maturing within the next 12 months which are given in note 3 (see pages 218–21). For the BOC group in 1997 these maturing loans within a year total £620.4 million.

$$\text{Cash debt coverage 1997} = \frac{733.8 - 104.0 - 109.5 - 121.5}{620.4} = 0.64 \text{ times}$$

$$\text{Cash debt coverage } 1996 = \frac{625.1 - 91.8 - 115.8 - 121.1}{623.1} = 0.48 \text{ times}$$

In neither 1996 nor 1997 is the retained cash flow, earned through operations, sufficient to pay off the loans to be retired during the next 12 months. Link that fact with the fact that there is an increasing amount of cash reserved for capital expenditure highlighted in the cash flow statement and it will ensure analysts look carefully at the methods used by BOC to fund its cash flow needs. From note 3 we also learn that BOC has £222.2 million in cash and deposits of less than a year's maturity plus the previously mentioned $420 million (£260.8 million) unused credit facility. Before reaching for the panic button an historical review will indicate that the company has satisfactorily met its debt repayment requirements over the years in year-end situations not too dissimilar from the present.

As yet the definition of this ratio has not received widespread affirmation through usage and publication, unlike most others in this text. This is because it is only very recently that data to compute the ratio has become available. Some writers have argued that all debt should be incorporated into the denominator, others would include creditors too while others would net off the cash and deposits held by the company. Each possible alternative has a logical rationale to support it. The logic supporting the ratio defined above is that the ratio matches the long-term source of cash that is derived from operations, with the requirement to repay the maturing element of long-term finances. Any loans maturing beyond twelve months will be repaid out of profits earned in the future, while cash presently held is in general needed for the day-to-day trading operations, though it has to be conceded that the cash may have been built up by the company for the purpose of the loan repayment.

13 Capital structure and financial risk

In addition to an assessment of the short-term liquidity position of a company, it is also important to examine the overall means by which a company finances its operations. It is usual for a company to be financed partly by loans from banks and other lenders and partly by the funds of its ordinary shareholders. These two sources of finance are normally referred to respectively as debt and equity, and the relationship between the two gives a measure of the gearing of the company. Gearing has important implications for the long-term stability of a company because of its effect on financial risk. This is because debt and equity have quite different characteristics. The providers of loan capital require a fixed amount of interest to be paid to them each year, irrespective of the level of profits earned. The providers of equity capital do not enjoy a fixed reward each year, but are entitled to the residual profits after all other payments including interest charges have been met. This residual amount will vary depending on the fortunes of the company. Because the existence of loan capital imposes a fixed commitment in the form of interest charges, the higher the proportion of debt to equity in the capital structure of a company the more volatile the residual rewards available to equity will become and the greater will be the financial risk perceived by ordinary shareholders. For example, if an all-equity firm earns operating profits after tax of £200,000, then the amount accruing to ordinary shareholders, either as dividends or retained profits, will be £200,000. If in the next year the profits fall by 25 per cent to £150,000, then the amount accruing to ordinary shareholders will also fall by 25 per cent. However, if the company were geared, i.e. if it were financed partly by loans requiring an after-tax fixed-interest payment of, say, £75,000 per year, then the profits available to ordinary shareholders in the first year would be £125,000 (£200,000 minus interest of £75,000), but in the second year these would fall to £75,000 (£150,000 minus interest of £75,000), a decline of 40 per cent. Conversely, if profits had risen by 25 per cent to £250,000, the earning available to the ordinary shareholders in the geared company would have increased to £175,000 (£250,000 minus £75,000), an increase of 40 per cent.

A similar argument applies to the riskiness attached to capital repayments. In the event of the liquidation of a company, the providers of loan capital have priority over the ordinary shareholders as to capital repayment. Therefore, the higher the level of gearing, the greater is the chance of ordinary shareholders not being repaid in full.

It is not only the shareholders who are affected by gearing. Looked at from the point of view of creditors, it is clear that a high proportion of debt to equity will increase the risk of interest payments not being met, or the loan repayments and amount owing to suppliers not being made in full. Even though lenders have the benefit of priority over shareholders for annual interest payments and on liquidation, the value of this benefit steadily declines as more and more of the operations of the company are financed by the lenders and the 'cushion' that the equity-financed part provides becomes less and less.

Nevertheless, gearing does have its advantages. It might be reasonable to expect that the benefits of a fixed amount of interest every year and priority over shareholders on liquidation should make the cost of debt capital cheaper than that of equity. In other words, the average return expected by lenders should be lower than the average return expected by shareholders. Furthermore, the interest payable on loan capital is an allowable expense when determining taxable profit, whereas dividends are a distribution out of the after-tax profits. Thus, for a company that pays corporation tax at the rate of, say, 35 per cent on its taxable profits, the after-tax cost of interest payments will be reduced in the same proportion, because every £100 paid in interest will reduce taxable profit by £100 and therefore tax payable by £35. To the extent that debt is a less expensive source of finance than equity, then initially the use of gearing might be beneficial, providing that the advantages of lower-cost debt more than compensate for the disadvantages caused by increased financial risk. However, as gearing increases, the financial-risk effect will begin to outweigh the benefits of low-cost debt. This implies the existence of some optimal level of gearing that a company should try to achieve. Empirical evidence would suggest that companies no longer assume that one specific level of gearing is appropriate all the time and in all the circumstances. For example, during the downturn of an economic cycle companies will attempt to reduce their gearing and then reverse it on the upturn. This will minimize the risks concerning non-payment of interest in poor trading conditions on the one hand, and on the other hand enable the company to gain the benefits of the gearing on the upturn in profits.

The ever widening portfolio of types of long- and short-term capital available to a company may make life more complex for financial managers, but at the same time it will hopefully reduce the financial risks by the better matching of fund type with corporate need. This financial engineering brings with it further problems for the analyst since a careful examination of gearing is obviously of crucial importance in an evaluation of the capital structure of a company. In the following sections of this chapter, the gearing position of The BOC Group plc is analysed.

Capital structure ratios

There are several ways of examining the gearing position of a company, depending on whether it is the long-term capital structure or the overall financial structure that is being analysed.

Long-term debt to equity ratio

From the point of view of long-term capital structure, the most widely used ratio is that of debt to equity. This is calculated as

$$\frac{\text{Long-term loans} + \text{Preference shares}}{\text{Ordinary shareholders' funds}} \times 100$$

Preference shares are usually included in the numerator because preference shareholders are entitled to a fixed rate of dividend. (It should be noted, however, that preference dividends are payable only if sufficient profits have been earned, therefore if a dividend has not been declared it might be more appropriate to exclude preference capital from the ratio.) FRS 4 ('Capital instruments') has stated that preference capital is non-equity capital and should be treated as a liability in this context. FRS 4 in dealing with accounting for capital instruments has as liabilities all capital instruments that contain an obligation to 'transfer economic benefits' (including contingent obligations). So convertible debt is treated the same as ordinary debt until it is converted. Ordinary shareholders' funds are usually taken to mean the ordinary share capital plus retained profits and reserves. The treatment of provisions can be somewhat problematical: depending on their nature, they might be thought of as part of ordinary shareholders' funds or as liabilities that should be included with long-term loans. In the ratios calculated for BOC, provisions have been excluded because they are non-interest bearing and have no gearing implications for the profits available to shareholders. Later in the chapter, when assessing the amount of asset coverage for the company's liabilities, provisions will be included, because, as defined earlier, they are a liability. The components of each ratio are made up as follows:

Long-term loans plus preference shares (see notes 11 and 12 to the financial statements).

	1997 £ million	1996 £ million
Loans from other than banks	863.7	622.2
Bank loans	133.4	140.0
Financial leases	4.1	5.2
Preference share capital	2.5	2.5
	1,003.7	769.9

Obligations under finance leases represent the present value of the future rental payments for assets financed under leasing agreements. Because this method of financing asset acquisitions gives rise to an interest payment that is included in the rental amount, the capital element has been included with long-term loans in accord with financial reporting practice.

Ordinary shareholders' funds (the figures shown in the balance sheet in Table 10.2 have been used)

	1997 £ million	1996 £ million
Called-up ordinary share capital	121.8	120.8
Share premium account	272.4	259.4
Revaluation reserve	63.8	71.9
Profit and loss account	1,320.7	1,252.5
Associated undertakings' reserves	111.6	111.6
	1,890.3	1,816.2

The preference share capital of £2.5 million has been deducted from the called-up share capital amounts shown in the consolidated balance sheet.

The debt to equity ratios for BOC can now be calculated as

$$\text{Debt to equity ratio 1997} = \frac{1,003.7}{1,890.3} \times 100 = 53.1 \text{ per cent}$$

$$\text{Debt to equity ratio 1996} = \frac{769.9}{1,816.2} \times 100 = 42.4 \text{ per cent}$$

In the case of those companies, particularly small ones, that treat bank overdrafts as a form of long-term loan, then the value of a bank overdraft should be included as a long-term loan in the ratio calculations.

Long-term debt to total long-term finance ratio

An alternative way of considering the debt to equity relationship is to calculate the ratio in such a way that it expresses the amount of debt finance as a proportion of total long-term finance, i.e. by calculating

$$\frac{\text{Long-term loans} + \text{Preference shares}}{\text{Long-term loans} + \text{Preference shares} + \text{Ordinary shareholders' funds}} \times 100$$

Using this approach, the ratios for BOC are as follows:

$$\begin{array}{l} \text{Long-term debt to total} \\ \text{long-term finance ratio 1997} \end{array} = \frac{1,003.7}{1,003.7 + 1,890.3} \times 100 = 34.7 \text{ per cent}$$

$$\begin{array}{l} \text{Long-term debt to total} \\ \text{long-term finance ratio 1996} \end{array} = \frac{769.9}{769.9 + 1,816.2} \times 100 = 29.8 \text{ per cent}$$

Whichever method of comparing debt to equity is used, the resultant ratio is meant to clarify the relationship between funds requiring a fixed amount of interest and dividend to be paid each year and funds provided by ordinary shareholders. The higher the ratio, the higher the proportion of debt in the capital structure of a company, and therefore the higher the amount of interest charges that might be expected and the higher the level of financial risk.

In order to decide whether the level of gearing in 1997 and 1996 is appropriate or not, a knowledge of the optimal capital structure of the company is required. Although it is not possible to state precisely what this should be, a comparison with some industry 'standard' might give an indication of the appropriateness of the ratio. However, much depends on the individual circumstances facing each company. A company that experiences a low level of business risk, with operating profits tending to be stable from period to period, can withstand a higher level of financial risk, and therefore a higher level of gearing, than a company whose operating profits fluctuate widely. Companies that are well diversified might be expected to have relatively stable profits, because of the wide spread of activities, and so could operate at higher levels of gearing than non-diversified companies.

Total debt to total assets ratio

The gearing ratios that have been considered so far have concentrated on the long-term financial structure of BOC. An alternative way of examining gearing is to bring short-term debt into the picture to show the proportion of the total assets financed by borrowed funds, both short term and long term. This is the total debt to total assets ratio and is calculated as

$$\frac{\text{Long-term loans} + \text{Short-term loans}}{\text{Total assets}} \times 100$$

One advantage of including short-term loans is that this acknowledges that short-term bank loans and overdrafts are often almost automatically renewable, therefore being effectively a source of long-term finance.

To calculate the total debt to total assets ratio for BOC, the components of the ratio must be determined as follows:

	£ million 1997	£ million 1996
Total debt		
Long-term loans and obligations under financial leases (see note 11 to the financial statements)	1,001.2	767.4
Preference share capital	2.5	2.5
Short-term loans and obligations under financial leases (see note 10 to the financial statements)	620.4	623.1
	1,624.1	1,393.0
Total assets (obtained from the balance sheet (Table 10.2))		
Fixed assets	3,302.0	3,067.3
Current assets	1,596.8	1,568.7
	4,898.8	4,636.0

The following ratios can now be calculated:

$$\text{Total debt to total asset ratio 1997} = \frac{1,624.1}{4,898.8} \times 100 = 33.2 \text{ per cent}$$

$$\text{Total debt to total asset ratio 1996} = \frac{1,393.0}{4,636.0} \times 100 = 30.0 \text{ per cent}$$

This ratio shows that, of the total value of the assets of BOC at 30 September 1997, 33.2 per cent were financed by interest-bearing borrowed funds. This gives some indication of the extent to which interest payments will have to be made. Once again, it is not possible to state categorically whether this is 'good' or 'bad'. Another way of viewing the ratio is from the perspective of a possible liquidation. Were the total assets to be realized for less than 33p in the £1 then the lenders would not get all their money back. This is a little simplistic since there is a preferential payment ordering for creditor types in a liquidation or receivership and the interest-bearing loans would not necessarily be first in the queue. But at that level of 33.2 per cent the lenders ought to feel comfortably secure. However, BOC's financial review (see page 190) quotes borrowing as having grown from 34.5 per cent to 36.5 per cent in terms of capital employed.

Notice that the BOC gearing ratios do not agree with any of the ones computed above. Its ratios are based upon information in note 3 to the financial statement (see pages 218–21) and the five-year record (see pages 188–9). The derivation of the net borrowings and capital employed was discussed earlier on page 118 and the ratio is calculated as follows:

$$\frac{\text{Net borrowings and financial leases}}{\text{'BOC capital employed'}} \times 100$$

BOC net borrowings to capital employed ratio 1997

$$= \frac{1,375.3}{3,766.3} \times 100 = 36.5 \text{ per cent}$$

According to the information in note 3 of the financial statements only £115.7 million of the £1,621.6 million borrowed is secured, i.e. tied to some identified asset. In the event of a receivership or liquidation, the proceeds from the sale of these specific assets would have to be used first to repay the £115.7 million, and only the surplus over and above this amount could be used for the benefit of other unsecured creditors. This is a low proportion of secured debt, approximately 7 per cent, and the unsecured lenders ought to feel reasonably safe, in that the book value of the total assets is approximately three times the total borrowings. However, these lenders should note that there are other creditors too, and that many analysts combine all forms of liabilities to third parties and calculate the ratio of total owing to total assets.

Total owing to total assets

This ratio is a better indicator for unsecured lenders, including trade creditors, that the book value of the assets gives a comfortable surplus over the amount owing. To differentiate it from previous ratios, all amounts included in the short- and long-term liabilities are combined to form the total amount owing. Preference-share capital is not included in this because it ranks after debt in a liquidation. The ratio is calculated as

$$\frac{\text{All creditors (less than one year) + Long-term liabilities}}{\text{Total assets}} \times 100$$

Provisions for liabilities have been included, because they represent liabilities which, although of uncertain amount, are reasonably likely to occur. The figures have been taken from the balance sheet in Table 10.2.

	1997 *£ million*
Creditors: amounts falling due within one year	
Borrowings and finance leases	620.4
Other creditors	886.2
Creditors: amounts falling due after more than one year	
Borrowings and finance leases	1,001.2
Other creditors	23.5
Provision for liability and charges	229.7
Total owing	2,761.0

The ratio for BOC can be calculated as follows:

Total owing to total assets ratio 1997 =

$$\frac{2,761.0}{3,302.0 + 1,596.8} \times 100 = 56.4 \text{ per cent}$$

Total owing to total assets ratio 1996 =

$$\frac{2,574.5}{3,067.3 + 1,568.7} \times 100 = 55.5 \text{ per cent}$$

The total owing to total assets ratio indicates that 56.4 per cent of the business has been financed by third parties, some of whom require interest payments on their loans. However, there is still a very reasonable surplus of book value of assets over the total amount owing to third parties.

Capital gearing

An alternative way of analysing gearing is to concentrate on the income position rather than on the capital structure. Under this approach, capital gearing, as it is sometimes called, is a multiplier or factor which, when applied to fluctuations in operating profit, shows the greater changes that would occur in profits available for the shareholders, thus highlighting the results of financial gearing. The concept of this capital gearing factor is similar to the gear-ratio principle of a car's gearbox. The ratio is calculated as follows:

$$\frac{\text{Profit on ordinary activities before interest + Interest received}}{\text{Profit on ordinary activities before taxation}}$$

Taking the figures in the profit and loss account in Table 10.1 and note 3(a) (page 218), the capital-gearing ratio for 1997 is calculated as follows:

$$\text{Capital gearing 1997} = \frac{540.4 + 13.7}{445.2} = 1.24 \text{ times}$$

This means the proportionate change in profit before tax is 1.24 times that of a change in profit before interest paid. Thus if profit before interest paid rises by 20 per cent in 1998, i.e. £110.8 million, and if the amount of interest paid remains constant, the profit before tax will rise by the same £110.8 million, an increase of 24.9 per cent. This 24.9 per cent is 1.24 times the proportionate increase of 20 per cent in profit before interest paid. This relationship is only approximate because the level of gearing and interest paid on borrowing usually does not remain constant over the years. It holds for falls in profit before interest paid in exactly the same way. A similar ratio using profit after tax instead of profit before tax could be used, but its consistency could not be maintained because a company's effective tax rate changes from year to year. This change in the effective rate arises from tax allowances on changes in capital expenditure patterns, tax rate changes etc. Nevertheless, the capital gearing ratio does provide a rough guide to the extra change in profits attributable to the shareholders due to the level of gearing.

Interest cover

Before the cash flow statement was available this was the ratio calculated to focus attention on the relationship between interest payments and the profits available for meeting those payments. It showed the number of times interest is 'covered' by profits and therefore indicated the risk of non-payment of interest. The ratio, interest cover, is calculated as a multiple, as follows:

$$\frac{\text{Profit before interest and tax}}{\text{Gross interest payable}} =$$

$$\frac{\text{Profit on ordinary activities before interest + Interest received}}{\text{Gross interest payable}}$$

The numerator is the profit available to pay the interest, and so includes both profit from operations and interest received. Note 3(a) to the financial statements reveals that the gross interest payable by BOC amounted to £112.9 million in 1997 and £113.9 million in 1996. The amount of profit before interest and tax that was available for meeting these interest payments is the profit on ordinary activities before interest for each year, as shown in Table 10.1. Interest receivable of £13.7 million in 1997 and £17.8 million in 1996 (see note 3(a) to the financial statements) would also be available to meet interest payments and should therefore be included in the numerator.

As profits from associated companies are combined in the total operating profits, so too should their interest proportion be included in interest payable. Any interest capitalized should be excluded. Thus, the gross interest payable in note 3(a) is increased by the associated company interest payable and reduced by the interest capitalized, leaving interest payable through the profit and loss account for 1997 at £108.9 million and for 1996 at £112.3 million.

$$\text{Interest cover ratio 1997} \ = \frac{540.4 + 13.7}{108.9} = 5.09 \text{ times}$$

$$\text{Interest cover ratio 1996} \ = \frac{539.4 + 17.8}{112.3} = 4.96 \text{ times}$$

An alternative way of looking at this is to say that as the profits available for paying interest in 1997 are 5.09 times the interest payable in that year, then the profits could fall by a factor of 4.09 times the interest payable and there would still be a sufficient amount of profit to cover the interest payable. The inference is that the smaller the multiple the smaller the amount of profit earned and therefore available for the equity owners of the company. The company's prime purpose is to generate profits for the ordinary shareholders. The ratio is giving an indication of the gearing relationship between profit and interest and how much of the profits are going in interest payment to service the requirements of the third parties who lent money to the company.

Prior to the publication of the cash flow statement this ratio was used as a surrogate for the cash interest cover described on page 143. From the point of view of providers of loan capital, the ratio indicates the protection they have if profits fall; therefore, the higher the ratio the better. Ordinary shareholders would also like to see a high interest cover ratio because this will indicate that the risk of non-payment of dividends is reduced. As with capital structure ratios, the adequacy of the interest cover is very much dependent on the business risk facing the company. For a company with high business risk whose profits fluctuate a great deal from period to period, a cover of 5.09 times might seem satisfactory. For a company that achieves stable profits over time, the cover might be very secure.

Dividend cover

Dividend cover is a ratio similar to the interest cover ratio. It involves examining the amount by which profits could fall before leading to a reduction in the current level of dividends. The dividend cover ratio is calculated as

$$\frac{\text{Profits available for paying ordinary dividends}}{\text{Ordinary dividends}} =$$

$$\frac{\text{Profit for the financial year} - \text{Preference dividends}}{\text{Ordinary dividends}}$$

The ratio is the reciprocal of the dividend payout ratio, the proportion of profits available to the equity owner paid out in dividends. Neither measures the company's actual ability to pay out the dividend in cash. This has already been calculated in the previous chapter as cash dividend cover.

The numerator of the dividend cover ratio should be the final amount of profit left after all other deductions have been made. The profits available to the ordinary shareholders of BOC in 1997 are therefore taken as profit for the financial year of £287.6 million less the preference dividend of £0.1 million. Details of the dividends paid and proposed are given in note 12 and indicate the ordinary dividends paid and proposed amount to £140.3 million for 1997 and £0.1 million for the preference dividends. Even though some of the dividends were paid in scrip rather than cash it is the total dividend appropriated that is used to indicate the extent that profits have been used to reward the shareholder.

The dividend cover ratios are calculated as:

$$\text{Dividend cover ratio 1997} = \frac{287.5}{140.3} = 2.05 \text{ times}$$

$$\text{Dividend cover ratio 1996} = \frac{278.2}{130.0} = 2.14 \text{ times}$$

At face value, these ratios show that ordinary dividends were covered 2.14 times in 1996 and that this declined marginally in 1997 to 2.05 times. The cash dividend cover calculated in the previous chapter as 4.28 times for each year indicated the considerable degree of safety in paying the dividend at that level in each of the two years.

Some users of accounts prefer instead to use the payout ratio, defined as follows:

$$\frac{1}{\text{Dividend cover}} \times 100$$

For BOC the payout ratios of 1997 and 1996 are the reciprocals of the dividend cover ratios just calculated.

$$\text{Payout ratio 1997} = \frac{1}{2.05} \times 100 = 48.8 \text{ per cent}$$

$$\text{Payout ratio 1996} = \frac{1}{2.14} \times 100 = 46.7 \text{ per cent}$$

In 1997 BOC paid out 48.8 per cent of its available earned profits in ordinary dividends. It can also be said that BOC retained 51.2 per cent of its profits for reinvestment in the business for 1997.

14 A structured approach to reviewing financial statements

The preceding four chapters have shown how financial ratios for The BOC Group plc could be derived from the published annual report to focus attention on different economic aspects of the group's activities. The purpose of ratio analysis is to provide a profile of the past performance and the present financial strength of a company that might be useful for decision making. The use that is made of ratios will vary, therefore, depending on the decisions faced by users and on the amount of detailed information available. Managers, for example, will be interested in comparing their actual performance with some predetermined budget performance, and also with the performance in previous years, or with that of other competing companies. Because managers have access to a great deal of detailed information about the company, the ratios they can calculate will range from those that reveal overall performance down to those that concentrate on specific manufacturing or internal processes. The information available to external users, on the other hand, is usually restricted to what is provided in the annual financial report, supplemented by other published data such as industrial or economic statistics.

This chapter, like the preceding five, is primarily concerned with the use of ratios by external users, although the ideas, concepts, approach and techniques could well be of use to management in their daily tasks. Whether the external reviewer is an existing or potential shareholder, an existing or potential creditor or lender, or even a major predator, they will still find it necessary to conduct some ratio analysis of the financial performance and position of the company. The emphasis of their goals will differ, some reviewers being more interested in explanations of profitability, or the lack of it, others being more interested in past or potential cash flows and yet others being interested in asset backing and loan security. All, though, will be helped by having a structure to their review indicating the various links between the different ratios.

The extent to which an examination of past data, through ratio analysis, can be incorporated into models for predictive purposes will be discussed at greater length in Chapter 15. Many financial reviewers use a more subjective approach and basis to their predictions but, nevertheless, are guided significantly by what they discover from their structured financial analysis.

It seems reasonable to suggest that a starting point in the predictive process would involve an assessment of the current performance of a company by the use of ratio analysis, together with an analysis of the position in previous years and a comparison with other companies.

The aim of this chapter is to put together those ratios, the underlying concepts and a series of key questions that ought to be asked, thus enabling the reviewer to obtain an overall view of the current corporate performance. Though there are ten stages to the review described here, the individual stages can be read and acted upon separately, should the reviewer only need to look at one aspect of a company's performance. However, the reviewer should be reminded that in many instances the corporate performance in one area will almost certainly have repercussions in another, e.g. increasing sales and profitability will bring with it funding decisions with implications for sources of finance and liquidity.

Main stages of review

It is suggested that the review should consist of a number of stages, the sequence of which does not necessarily have to follow that listed here, though it would be worthwhile to review the company in general in stages 1 and 2 before selecting the specific area of investigation. The ten stages are as follows:

1 SWOT analysis;
2 strategic and major features review;
3 profitability;
4 operating efficiency;
5 growth;
6 liquidity;
7 finance;
8 investment;
9 management of financial risk;
10 conclusions.

Each stage will be introduced in a separate section using ratios already computed, and where appropriate introducing new ones. These ratios will be used to provide answers to key questions posed during each stage. In the final section some general conclusions on the overall picture presented by The BOC Group plc annual report will be made. But we repeat here that the accounts are being used to help make a number of learning points, and that this chapter is not designed to provide a very critical analysis of The BOC Group, such as can be found in the financial pages of the press or in analysts' reports.

SWOT analysis

SWOT analysis is an acronym taken from the four segments shown in Table 14.1. The analyst should attempt to identify characteristics of the company under each heading. Of course it is quite possible that an external reviewer may not have access to information that provides much depth for this analysis, though recourse to an analyst's report along with the chairman's report and items gleaned from the financial press during the year could be of great assistance.

This approach to analysis is just one of the number that strategic analysts offer as tools of analysis. One of its strengths is that it can be used as a basis for review in each of the narrower areas under review, e.g. under liquidity the reviewer can look at the

Table 14.1   SWOT

Strengths	Weaknesses (internal factors)
Opportunities	Threats (external factors)

system for generating, monitoring and controlling cash flows and thus identify operating as well as strategic attributes.

For BOC, under 'strengths' should be listed those areas of the firm's business where it is market leader, brand leader, etc. For example, it believes it is a world leader in its health care and vacuum technology divisions, particularly in vacuum systems, equipment and components. Information such as this can be gleaned from a company's review of operations and from trade associations, though it does depend on the extent of detail required by the analyst as to how far afield an investigator has to go to complete this part of the analysis. The corporate long-range plan could well be a very rich source for the information sought.

The corporate strengths are not solely in the product or operations area, since a review of the directors' report indicates that a significant proportion of the group's employees have some equity interest in the group's business thanks to the various employee share schemes. Thus it could be argued that the motivation and efforts of the workforce are the greater because of this.

Identifying the weaknesses, opportunities and threats is less easy, but still necessary. For example, BOC has itself identified various parts of its business that no longer fit into its corporate strategy or are not profitable enough, because these have been included in the discontinued business section of the analysis. An example of this was the sale in 1992 of the Glasrock operations. A weakness in the vacuum technology segment could be the heavy dependence (50 per cent) on one industry, the semiconductor industry.

There will be the usual cost–benefit analysis of the information gathering, the direction of which will be influenced by the major area of interest of the investigator, e.g. a bank's loan officer considering a multi-million pound loan will need to spend more time than an employee considering the sale of two hundred shares gained through the employee profit-share scheme.

Strategic and major features review

In each of the next stages, a leading question will be put with a series of follow-up questions to provide the reader with a framework from which to work. Here the leading question ties in with the SWOT analysis, and asks what the major features of the business are and how the business has performed in the period just ended.

The follow-up questions may at times be more appropriate to a single-country, single-market company, but can easily be amended for use with a multinational enterprise such as The BOC Group plc.

Before the detailed analysis of the financial statements, a general review of the chairman's statement, the directors' report and any survey of operations should be read for answers and clues for further questions and analysis. The results of the SWOT analysis will be used in a strategy review of the company, its past and its future, and because the direction of the analysis is one of a financial nature the emphasis of the review questions, analysis and conclusions will be oriented in that direction. Some of the stock questions to be addressed are: Is the company in a vigorous and growing sector of the economy? What are the perceived trends in profitability, operating efficiency, liquidity, finance and investment? What significant events, occurrences or transactions, if any, have there been during the past year? What is the mood of the board and chairman concerning the past performance and the future forecast? Is the stated support of the company for the standards of corporate governance recommended in the Cadbury Report reflected in compliance with the report's practice in both substance and form?

Turning specifically, now, to the financial statements, there are some general questions here worth mentioning. Is the audit report clean or have the auditors qualified it? All qualifications should put reviewers on their guard and cause them to make substantial further enquiries into the area or item mentioned in the qualification. From a review of the company's accounting policies, have there been any changes during the year, and if so with what implications? Do the accounting policies have a critical bearing on profits, or any of the other reported items? Do the accounting policies bear the hallmark of a management trying to present an optimistic or pessimistic picture, or are they just the typical set of policies one would expect to find? See Smith (1996) for examples as well as discussion of the effects and implications of the use of various accounting policies.

Not surprisingly, for The BOC Group plc the auditors gave a clean report. In the section on accounting policies, most of those reported would be considered typical of a company such as BOC.

The Annual Report of 1997 signalled to the world that the BOC Group was going to dispose of the Ohmeda health care business. This will leave the Group with a focused portfolio of three businesses that management believe can underpin the financial stability and performance in the future. Naturally an analyst would then attempt to identify the contribution that health care has given in the past and more importantly what may be lost to the Group in the future by the disposal.

Profitability

In Chapter 10 profitability was dealt with at considerable length, showing how various profitability ratios could be computed and interpreted. This section will use some of those ratios in an integrated manner, but first the leading question: is the reported profit real, adequate and maintainable? The first part of the question can be tackled by investigating the list of accounting policies to see if there have been any changes there and, if so, the implications these have for the profit figure. In the case of BOC there has been no change in 1997, but examples for other companies might include a change in the calculation of depreciation from reducing balance to straight line, or the revaluation of various assets with depreciation based on the revised figures.

However, in earlier years, starting with 1990, there have been changes in each year. In the first year change was due to a change in translating foreign currencies, in 1991 profits and losses on disposals and closures of businesses were included as part of operating profit, while in 1992, to comply with the then new UTIF pronouncement 3 ('Treatment of goodwill on disposal of a business'), a charge against the profit was made to reflect the goodwill on acquisitions which had previously been written-off against reserves. This charge against profit had to be made because the undertaking for which the goodwill had been paid in the past was disposed of in 1992.

Annually, the Finance and Treasury review of BOC (see pages 190–4) highlights the new accounting standards that the company has followed in the preparation of its accounts. For example in the 1997 accounts, for the first time, the US reporting requirements have been incorporated due to the Group's listing in September 1996, on the New York Stock Exchange. We are also informed that the Group cash flow statement for 1997 was prepared in accordance with the revised FRS 1 and the comparative figures restated accordingly. For 1997 the effects of accounting changes were presentational rather than quantitative. The five-year summary will also be amended for the comparatives when appropriate.

This five-year summary helps in a review of past trends and, with the future forecasts in the chairman's report, should help indicate whether the profit levels are maintainable and adequate, though confirmation of the latter ought to come from a comparison with profitability ratios of companies in the same industry.

Questions that also should be posed in this section include the following:

What is the company's return on capital?
What is the company' s return on sales and its capital turnover?
What are the returns on capital and sales for the different product groups of the
    company?
What is the operating profit per employee?
How do the results compare with those of competing companies or with averages for
    the industry and with a trend over time?
What is the forecast for next year's profit and turnover?

The method of computation of these ratios was explained in Chapter 10 with the values for The BOC Group for 1997 and 1996 computed. Some comments were made on any perceived changes between each year's figures. An extended trend analysis of growth is provided later in this chapter. At this stage, however, it is useful to consider the level and trend of profitability and the relationship with each of the major inputs that helped to earn it.

A brief summary of the main profitability ratios for The BOC Group plc for the five years 1993–7 is given in Table 14.2.

Table 14.2   The BOC Group plc – summarized profitability ratios

	1993	1994	1995	1996	1997
Return on sales (%)	13.7	10.0	13.2	13.4	13.6
Asset turnover (times)	1.14	1.47	1.21	1.18	1.08
Return on average capital					
employed (%)	15.7	14.8	16.0	15.9	14.7
Return on average equity (%)	14.2	15.7	23.9	24.0	22.5
Earnings per share (net)					
before exceptional items (p)	42.97	43.87	51.97	57.74	59.31
on published profit (p)	42.97	23.82	51.97	57.74	59.31
Dividends per share (p)	23.2	23.2	24.8	27.0	29.0
Operating profit per employee (£)	10,949	8,896	12,510	13,320	13,267

No obvious trends in profitability can be highlighted, though the asset turnover does appear to be downwards. In terms of returns to shareholders, though, both the return on average equity and earnings per share have grown markedly, as have the dividends per share. Efficiency in terms of utilization of employees, as measured by operating profit per employee, has improved by over 20 per cent in the five years. Further analysis is provided in the next section in an attempt to explain the profitability performance. The segmental and regional analysis, particularly if traced back five years would be of help here.

Operating efficiency

This stage is dedicated to inquiring more deeply into the efficiency of the operations that gave rise to the overall profit picture of the previous stage. The leading question for this stage is concerned with the identification of all improvements in operating efficiency in all areas of the company's operations.

The sort of follow-up questions that should be included are: What is the cost structure of the business? Are costs mainly fixed or variable, or of what mixture? What is the gross profit ratio? Have there been any changes in the corporate strategy which have affected the operating policy and efficiency, e.g. in the area of marketing through pricing changes? Not available from the financial accounts, but nevertheless important, are ratios of strategic areas of management, concerning level of market penetration by product and by market, competitor performance, competitors' costs, effects of advertising policies, plus many other ratios. These latter examples simply serve to reinforce the point that ratio analysis is not limited to publicly available information but is also a valuable technique for use by internal management.

A useful tool for this section is the vertical analysis of the profit and loss account converted to a common size. This expresses the annual turnover as a basis of 100 and converts all other costs and revenues to percentages of turnover. Table 14.3 gives a five-year time series of the common-size profit and loss account for The BOC Group plc.

Table 14.3 The BOC Group plc – consolidated profit and loss account common size vertical analysis, five years

	1993	1994	1995	1996	1997
Turnover*	100	100	100	100	100
Cost of sales	(55.1)	(57.2)	(56.1)	(56.4)	(57.3)
Distribution costs	(9.6)	(9.1)	(8.9)	(8.3)	(8.3)
Administration expenses	(19.9)	(21.5)	(20.0)	(20.0)	(19.4)
Research and development	(2.8)	(2.7)	(2.6)	(2.6)	(2.2)
Associated company profits	(1.1)	(1.2)	(1.3)	(1.5)	(1.7)
Operating profits	(13.7)	(10.6)	(14.0)	(14.4)	(14.7)
Exceptional items	—	(0.5)	—	—	—
Interest	(2.7)	(2.5)	(2.7)	(2.5)	(2.6)
Tax	(3.8)	(3.7)	(3.6)	(3.7)	(3.5)
Dividend	(3.6)	(3.4)	(3.4)	(3.5)	(3.8)
Profit retained	(3.1)	0	(3.7)	(3.9)	(4.0)

Note:
* Excluding associated companies' turnover

There are a number of discernible trends in Table 14.3, the first being the small increase in cost of sales, operating profits and dividends. The declining trend in distribution costs and administration are desirable and counter the cost of sales increase, but strategically the declining research and development would be seen by some as a retrograde move. The growing contribution from associated companies will be seen as welcome, especially when seen in light of the trend in Table 14.4.

	1993	*1994*	*1995*	*1996*	*1997*
Average collection period (days)	69.8	68.4	74.4	68.4	69.8
Stock-turnover period (days)	68.7	63.6	71.6	69.6	61.4

This series puts into better perspective the efforts at efficiency by management, particularly in reducing the amount of sales kept in stock, while noting that debtors still take, on average, a little more than two months to pay. Some companies provide a break-down of the stock and work-in-progress figure into the various elements of raw materials, work in progress and finished goods. Stock-turnover periods can be computed for each of these elements if thought useful.

Growth

The major issue at this stage is whether the business has achieved the desired and feasible growth rate. Of course, the two may be mutually exclusive if the desired rate is set too high. It is also probable that an external reviewer may be unable to answer that question because of lack of knowledge concerning the original growth targets.

Generally the two main targets are turnover and profit growth, and these can be computed as follows:

$$\frac{\text{This year's figures} - \text{Last year's figures}}{\text{Last year's figures}} \times 100$$

For example, the decline in turnover of BOC for 1997 on 1996 is

$$\frac{\text{Turnover (1997)} - \text{Turnover (1996)}}{\text{Turnover (1996)}} \times 100 = \frac{3,677.7 - 3,752.1}{3,752.1} \times 100$$
$$= -2.0 \text{ per cent}$$

The growth rate of operating profit in 1997 is computed using the same method and is just positive, thus indicating that profits have grown marginally faster than turnover, something that a simple visual comparison would confirm.

The follow-up questions will then be aimed at determining whether the decline was due to price changes; whether the annual change was a one-off or part of a trend; whether the decline in turnover and/or profits has been affected by internal growth or by external acquisition; and whether there are segmental differences (see pages 124–6). These indicate health care's difficult year.

Table 14.4 provides a horizontal analysis in common size for items in the profit and loss account for the five years 1993–7. This gives an insight into the separate annual

Table 14.4 The BOC Group plc – consolidated profit and loss account items common size horizontal analysis, five years

	1993	1994	1995	1996	1997
Turnover*	100	107.3	115.5	122.3	119.9
Cost of sales	100	111.5	117.7	125.3	124.8
Distribution costs	100	102.0	106.7	105.4	103.5
Administration expenses	100	116.0	116.0	122.6	116.6
Research and development	100	108.4	112.7	121.3	99.3
Associated company profits	100	118.0	140.6	178.0	190.7
Operating profits	100	83.3	118.0	128.2	128.4
Interest	100	113.2	113.2	113.6	114.4
Tax	100	111.4	111.4	119.5	111.9
Dividend	100	100.5	108.0	118.2	127.5
Profit retained	100	3.2	138.8	158.0	156.9

Note:
* Excluding associated companies' turnover

changes in the elements in the profit and loss account as well as the underlying trend in growth over the period.

The base year is 1993 and all other years' figures are related to this year and computed as in the following example:

$$\frac{\text{Turnover (1997)}}{\text{Turnover (1993)}} \times 100 = \frac{3,677.7}{3,067.5} \times 100 = 119.9$$

Table 14.4 presents a picture of gradual growth in both sales and costs over the five years, with the two not always in tandem, a point also identified in the earlier vertical analysis. It also reinforces the view that the company has made a conscious effort to increase its proportional expenditure on dividends as part of its strategy for gains for shareholders. This reflects stock market pressures on the company. The opposing trends in research and development and associated company profits have already been mentioned.

A review of the effects of price changes on growth is a useful tool but is not so straightforward for a multinational. This is because the sales and costs will be made up of many different currencies, each from a country with its own inflation rate. The approach adopted here has been to assume that the foreign exchange market is operating effectively and that all relative differences between the UK's rate of inflation and that of the foreign country are washed out by the change over the year in the foreign exchange rate, with the revised exchange rate being used as the basis for converting foreign transactions into sterling for consolidation purposes. Provided that assumption is a reasonably close approximation to the underlying reality, then the impact of price changes can be examined by using the annual average UK retail price index for all items for each year. Starting again with 1993, as 100, BOC's inflation-adjusted turnover and operating profit values are as follows:

	1993	1994	1995	1996	1997
Turnover	100	105.2	109.9	113.0	107.7
Operating profit	100	81.7	112.3	118.5	115.4

In real terms, turnover showed a distinct increase over the first four years, only to decline in 1997, and this recovery did flow through to the operating profits which for the past four years have been making up for the hiccup in 1994 and are now in real terms 15 per cent better than those of 1993. It has to be acknowledged that these adjusted figures for turnover and profits are only approximations, and care must therefore be taken in their interpretation.

Liquidity

The major question to be examined in terms of liquidity is whether the company is generating sufficient cash. In addition there are subsidiary questions concerned with the values of the current and quick ratios and the impact of changing working capital levels. Examples of the questions that might be asked are: Are there any trends or signals towards insolvency or poor asset management? Have there been any signs of attempted window dressing? Is there any information available suggesting possible changes in the liquid funds for the next year? For example, has the chairman announced a rights issue or new loan issue? Using data from BOC's financial statements for the years 1993–7, a five-year analysis of the main liquidity ratios discussed in Chapter 12 can be constructed. This is shown in Table 14.5.

A look at the longer-term trend of five rather than two years can put into starker relief any recent changes in ratios. In the case of the current and quick ratios the company seems to be able to maintain a relatively low pair of ratios with a current ratio hovering around 1.0 times and a quick ratio close to 0.80 times. The exception to that was 1994 when the current liabilities were much lower than average when a disproportionately large amount of commercial paper was repaid, thus enhancing the current and quick ratios. 1994 was also an exceptional year for the quality of the operating profit, due not to a big influx of cash but rather to a considerable reduction in profit. At the time analysts will have investigated in detail the causes for the fall in profit that year and these will have been explained in the financial review of that period. The cash interest cover and quality of operating profit are consistently at levels that engender confidence in the company, i.e. given the fact that over the year the company is receiving approximately 135 per cent of its profits in cash and that, in terms of cash, interest payable is covered well in excess of five times. Similarly dividends are well covered too.

Table 14.5 Five-year trend analysis of the main liquidity ratios

	1993	1994	1995	1996	1997
Current ratio (times)	1.06	1.24	0.99	1.06	1.06
Quick ratio (times)	0.79	0.93	0.76	0.76	0.82
Quality of operating profit (%)	138.8	177.1	133.1	115.8	135.8
Cash interest cover (times)	55.6	5.81	5.96	5.96	6.62
Cash dividend cover (times)	4.00	3.68	3.94	3.45	4.28

Finance

The finance stage follows on appropriately after the review of liquidity and prior to the consideration of investment. The major task of the analyst is to assess whether the financial structure of the company is both appropriate and adequate. Is the funding policy of the company broadly such that long-term commitments are financed by long-term finance? Do the ratios for the company's level of gearing, interest and dividend cover seem reasonable? Have there been any significant changes in the funding highlighted by the ratios and, if so, what do they indicate? Does the company appear to have plans to cope with the structural needs highlighted by the ratio changes? If so, what are the plans and are they appropriate? Finally, a question of increasing importance is whether there are signs of an expansion in the use of off-balance sheet finance, e.g. through increased numbers of operating leases of assets.

The mix of fixed and current assets will provide a starting point for the review of a company's financing needs. To calculate the ratio of fixed assets to total assets for BOC for 1997, the figures are obtained from the balance sheet in Table 10.2, giving fixed assets as £3,302.0 million and current assets as £1,596.8 million, which combine to give total assets of £4,898.8 million. The ratio is computed as follows:

$$\frac{\text{Fixed assets}}{\text{Total assets}} \times 100 = \frac{3,302.0}{4,898.8} \times 100 = 67.4 \text{ per cent}$$

The trend for this ratio is given in Table 14.6. The long-term funds invested in the company consist of the capital and reserves and the long-term liabilities. As can be seen from Table 10.2, these amount to £2,137.8 million and £1,254.4 million respectively, i.e. a total of £3,392.2 million. The ratio of long-term funds to total assets indicates how much of the total assets have been funded by long-term sources. Since there is also a long-term element in the need to carry stocks and debtors, many firms find it prudent to finance part of their current assets with long-term funds. The more conservative the funding policy, the higher the long-term funds to total assets ratio.

The ratio of long-term funds to total assets for 1997 is computed as follows:

$$\frac{\text{Long-term funds}}{\text{Total assets}} \times 100 = \frac{3,392.2}{4,898.8} \times 100 = 69.2 \text{ per cent}$$

This result of 69.2 per cent reinforces the point made earlier in the section on liquidity that the company depends heavily on short-term funds.

The five-year trend is given in Table 14.6. A more detailed break-down of the assets and fund structure can be found in Table 14.7, which uses the common-size approach in a vertical analysis of The BOC Group's balance sheets for 1997 and 1996. All items listed in the balance sheets in Table 10.2 have been converted to percentages of the *total* assets of that year.

Just as with the common-size profit and loss account in Table 14.4, the balance sheets for the past five years could be drafted to indicate the trends in the levels of different assets and liabilities over the period. This could be done by setting the 1993 figures equal to a base of 100 and computing the amount for the succeeding years in relation to 1993.

Though Table 14.7 only covers two years, 1996 and 1997, it clearly demonstrates the proportionate use of long- and short-term creditors, capital and reserves, as well as

Table 14.6 Trend of finance ratios

	1993	1994	1995	1996	1997
Fixed assets to total assets (%)	66.9	66.6	65.4	66.2	67.4
Long-term funds to total assets (%)	68.7	73.1	65.2	66.9	69.2
Total owing to total assets (%)	55.2	55.7	56.5	55.5	56.4
Total debt to total assets (%)	30.0	28.3	28.8	30.0	33.2
Long-term debt to equity (%)	44.5	56.9	40.5	42.4	53.1
Capital gearing (times)	1.25	1.38	1.30	1.25	1.24
Interest cover (times)	4.37	3.63	4.37	4.96	5.09
Dividend cover (times)	1.85	1.03	2.1	2.14	2.05

Table 14.7 The BOC Group plc – consolidated balance sheets common size vertical analysis

	1996	1997
Fixed assets		
tangible assets	59.3	60.3
intangible assets	0.7	0.6
investment in own shares	0.5	0.5
other investments	5.7	6.0
	66.2	67.4
Current assets		
stocks	8.7	7.2
debtors due within one year	19.5	18.4
investments	0.2	0.4
deposits and cash due within one year	3.4	4.5
assets due beyond one year	2.0	2.1
	100.0	100.0
Capital and reserves		
called-up share capital		
equity capital	2.6	2.5
non-equity capital	0.1	0.1
share premium	5.6	5.5
revaluation reserves	1.6	1.3
profit and loss account	27.0	26.9
associated undertakings' reserves	2.4	2.3
	39.3	38.6
Minority interests	5.2	5.0
Creditors: more than one year		
borrowings and finance leases	16.6	20.4
other creditors	0.5	0.5
provisions for liabilities and charges	5.3	4.7
	66.9	69.2
Creditors: less than one year		
borrowings and finance leases	13.4	12.7
other creditors	19.7	18.1
	100.0	100.0

retained earnings in the profit and loss account and the total borrowings and finance leases. These latter two sources being shown as the major ones for the company.

Two other forms of commitment are the other form of leasing – operating leases – and pension fund payments. The commitment to operating lease payments is shown in note 13 (a) to the financial statements on page (237) as totalling £30.2 million, which is less than 1 per cent of total assets and spread over a number of years. The pension fund payments are shown in note 6, page (228), which indicates the actuarial value of the assets in the funds exceed the accrued service liabilities. At present the costs are minimal and have been for the past five years and seem likely to remain that way in the short term.

The trend in funding ratios is given in Table 14.6 and from this several points emerge: the first is that well over 60 per cent of the assets are of a fixed nature and that these are all financed by long-term funds. The amount of long-term funds left to finance current assets is very small indicating a very aggressive funding policy by the company, a point reinforced by the low current ratio. The greater the proportion of funds in current liabilities the greater the financial risk from non-payment of debts on the due date. Unless the company wants to go out of business there is what might be termed an irreducible minima for both stock and debtors and these, it is argued, could or should be financed by long-term finance if the company is trying to match finance with the assets.

The long-term funds have increased over the five years with the gearing a little higher as the long-term debt, as a proportion of total long-term funds, increases marginally. The capital gearing is a little higher too so that the shareholders could benefit increasingly as turnover and profits improve. The increase in the dividend cover is because the annual dividend uplift has been made conservatively, because the profit growth has not been fast and the company needed funds for reinvestment. However, although the company may be geared up, financially and operationally, the chairman in his 1997 report is guardedly optimistic about BOC's future.

Sometimes companies announce their future financial plans in the annual report, though not in great detail. BOC have taken the opportunity to give further explanation to an announcement made earlier in the financial year that it intended to sell the healthcare business. The segmental information in the accounts and in the performance review help put it in the shop window for review by potential purchasers.

Investment

The next stage of the review examines the investment profile of the company and questions whether the company is making enough investments to ensure future profitability.

This is neither an easy question to answer nor is it easy to derive ratios and values which are of use in arriving at an answer. For example, how capital intensive an industry is the company in? What is the average age of its present assets? How does the annual amount of depreciation compare with the annual total new investment in fixed assets? Is there a change in the mixture of owning and hiring assets? Similarly, what investment is the company undertaking in its personnel?

Comparisons between capital expenditure and sales and the annual depreciation expenses are relatively straightforward to make. The sales turnover figure for 1997 can be found in Table 10.1, while the amount of depreciation written off can be found in note 7 on pages 230–1 along with the capital expenditure for the year. BOC's capital expenditure to sales ratio for 1997 is computed as follows:

$$\frac{\text{Capital expenditure}}{\text{Turnover}} \times 100 = \frac{675.8}{3,677.6} \times 100 = 18.4 \text{ per cent}$$

This percentage gives an indication of the level of capital expenditure undertaken to sustain the particular level of sales. Movements from the trend line should be particularly noted and investigated. An increasing trend line would indicate an increasing capitalization by the company and thus an increase in the fixed costs of the business. The capital expenditure to depreciation charge ratio for 1997 can be computed similarly:

$$\frac{\text{Capital expenditure}}{\text{Depreciation}} = \frac{675.8}{271.6} = 2.49 \text{ times}$$

(Note that in note 14(a) on the cash flow statement the figure of depreciation includes £4.9 million amortization of intangible assets listed in note 8 on page 231).

Both these ratios are best reviewed as part of a time series, so that they place in perspective the changes over the past twelve months. Some analysts perceive deprecation as the setting aside of profits for the replacement of the asset being depreciated, rather than considering it as a matching of expired cost against the turnover it has helped to earn. The ratio of capital expenditure to depreciation does give an indication of the replacement rate of new for old assets, though it makes no allowance for price changes or for corporate growth. To help with the latter, a further ratio of capital expenditure to total tangible fixed assets can be computed using the information in note 7, pages 230–1. If possible the gross book value of the tangible assets should be used, but, failing that, the net book value can be used.

The capital expenditure to fixed tangible assets ratio for BOC for 1997 is

$$\frac{\text{Capital expenditure}}{\text{Gross book value, tangible fixed assets}} \times 100 = \frac{675.8}{5,204.4} \times 100$$
$$= 13.0 \text{ per cent}$$

Thus the capital expenditure is replacing fixed assets at a rate of once every eight years (i.e. 100/13) approximately, assuming there is no inflation and they are all assets of the same type. Note 7 also provides information on the proportion of leased to owned assets used by the company. Using the net book values given for leased assets of £43.8 million, and net tangible fixed assets of £2,953.7 million, the ratio can be computed as follows:

$$\text{Leased to total tangible fixed assets 1997} = \frac{43.8}{2,953.7} \times 100 = 1.5 \text{ per cent}$$

This indicates that the company leases a very small percentage of its fixed tangible assets. As further evidence of the company's commitment to future capital expenditure, the amount of the company's actual commitments is also given in note 7. The amount committed at the end of 1997 of £389.8 million was greater than any previous year-end commitments of the past five years, which could be construed as a positive sign, particularly if reinforced by comments in the chairman's report.

With the increasing pace of technological advancement, machinery is seen to be replacing people in manufacturing industry. A ratio comparing capital expenditure with the average number of employees can be calculated to identify the level of new investment per employee. The average number of employees is given in note 6 as 40,733 for 1997. The ratio can be calculated as follows:

$$\text{Capital expenditure per employee 1997} = \frac{\text{£675.8 million}}{40,733} = \text{£16,591}$$

The level of capital expenditure when compared with the employment costs of the workforce is approximately 74 per cent, which should reinforce the view about the degree of importance of the level of capital expenditure of the company.

Again, a compilation of a trend series of the important ratios of BOC can be made and is given in Table 14.8.

Although the financial report does not provide statistics concerning the age of the company's fixed assets, it is possible to see that it is turning over its fixed assets once somewhere between every seven to eleven years. Given that many of the owned assets are land and buildings with a life well in excess of that, it would appear that BOC is investing heavily in its plant and equipment. More detailed ratios using the information in note 7 would reinforce that statement. As with the profitability ratios it is worth computing the capital expenditure ratios for the business and geographical segments. The five-year trend figures are shown in Table 14.9

The pattern of investment has changed dramatically over the past two years with a very significant upsurge in capital expenditure. The increase in the annual levels of expenditure are 60 per cent when compared to turnover, but, capital expenditure per employee, or total spend on capital expenditure are around 80 per cent or more higher than five years previously; that is a very considerable increase.

Several patterns emerge from Table 14.9 reinforcing what was stated by BOC in its performance review. In the business segments, gases and related products saw the large increase in capital expenditure in 1996 continue in 1997. This apparently is to continue in 1998, though more in the European region rather than in the Americas and Asia/Pacific.

Over the five years the largest effort has been placed in the three regions outside Europe, a more than doubling of investment effort. It also shows up the cut back in healthcare in the past year, perhaps not surprising if they are about to sell the division. By segmenting the data the analyst will get a more focused picture on the investment

Table 14.8   Trend of important ratios of the BOC Group plc – capital expenditure

	1993	1994	1995	1996	1997
Capital expenditure to turnover (%)	11.7	10.8	11.5	14.5	18.4
Capital expenditure to gross fixed assets (%)	9.0	8.5	8.9	11.0	13.0
Capital expenditure to depreciation (times)	1.59	1.45	1.62	2.05	2.49
Capital expenditure per employer (£'000)	9.36	9.05	10.30	13.39	16.59

Table 14.9   The BOC Group plc – trend of investment ratios by business segment and geographic region

	1993	1994	1995	1996	1997
Business segments					
Capital expenditure to turnover (%)					
Gases, etc.	14.4	13.8	16.6	22.4	26.5
Vacuum technology	7.9	11.5	5.1	6.1	6.1
Distribution	7.9	11.5	13.6	10.7	10.0
Healthcare	8.5	3.9	3.6	5.3	4.4
Capital expenditure to capital employed (%)					
Gases, etc.	14.2	14.2	16.6	21.6	24.1
Vacuum technology	14.4	21.3	11.2	15.5	12.8
Distribution	14.4	21.3	23.7	20.5	21.1
Healthcare	12.8	6.5	5.9	8.0	6.1
Capital expenditure per employee (£'000)					
Gases, etc.	12.7	12.8	16.5	23.4	27.4
Vacuum technology	5.0	7.7	6.8	9.0	7.7
Distribution	5.0	7.7	7.2	5.6	5.4
Healthcare	7.6	3.7	3.5	5.2	4.4
Geographic regions					
Capital expenditure to turnover (%)					
Europe	16.4	13.5	13.7	13.7	16.1
Americas	8.5	9.3	12.8	22.7	18.1
Africa	10.7	9.2	10.0	8.9	22.3
Asia/Pacific	14.7	14.1	15.5	19.8	28.5
Capital expenditure to capital employed (%)					
Europe	15.3	13.1	13.8	14.1	15.8
Americas	10.4	12.8	16.6	25.4	19.3
Africa	18.9	14.5	14.0	13.5	27.0
Asia/Pacific	15.8	16.0	17.9	23.0	30.8
Capital expenditure per employee (£'000)					
Europe	11.8	10.0	10.9	11.5	13.3
Americas	9.6	11.5	16.9	31.6	25.6
Africa	4.0	3.5	4.0	3.7	8.9
Asia/Pacific	16.2	16.9	21.0	28.2	37.8

patterns across both business sectors and regional markets which will help reflect more precisely the statements made in the directors' review.

Capital acquisitions ratio

A company's ability to obtain or maintain its competitive advantage is partially due to its capital assets. The company must therefore have the necessary cash-generating ability in order to finance the acquisition of these investments. For the majority of companies cash generated by profitable operations is the major source of funds for reinvestment in the company. A comparison of the cash spent on new assets, either for replacement or for expansion, can be made to the amount of cash left from operations after payment of interest, tax and dividends. It is not possible to break down investment activity into consistent categories when making an external review, though internally it is easier but not necessarily completely straightforward. The ratio is the proportion of cash received net from operations to amount invested:

$$\frac{\text{Net cash inflow from operations after servicing of finance and payment of taxes}}{\text{Net amount invested}}$$

The cash inflow and outflow figures can be taken from the cash flow statement (see page 115), with the numerator in 1997 derived from the net cash inflow from operations of £733.8 million less the net cash outflow on interest and dividends of £225.5 million and less the tax paid of £109.5 million. The net cash outflow on investing of £625.3 million provides the denominator. The percentage capital acquisitions ratio for 1997 is computed as

$$\text{Capital acquisitions ratio 1997} = \frac{733.8 - 225.5 - 109.5}{625.3} \times 100$$

$$= 63.8 \text{ per cent}$$

In 1997, 63.8 per cent of the new investment was self-financed with the balance coming either from a reduction in cash or cash equivalent assets, or financing and treasury activities. A five-year summary of the capital acquisitions ratio is as follows:

	1993	1994	1995	1996	1997
Capital acquisitions ratio (per cent)	65.6	98.7	88.2	60.3	63.8

Economic conditions will influence investment decisions and financing decisions and it is quite possible for this ratio to change considerably from one year to the next.

Capital market conditions may make the raising of new long-term funds much cheaper during some periods than during others. Thus a company may raise more capital than it needs for investment during a period. Conversely there may be market pressures that cause a company to make investments that require funding from short-term sources because there is no long-term capital available. For the first example the capital acquisition ratio may be low, while for the second the ratio could exceed 100 per cent.

Investment in employees

Companies are required by US and UK GAAP to provide some information about the pension schemes operated by the company and their net costs. In addition information is provided about the various share option schemes the company operates. (If all these options were exercised they could increase the nominal share capital by 4 per cent. Approximately two-thirds of the options are available for the executive minority, but in total the various schemes include over 15 per cent of the employees. This does help indicate some idea of the possible size of employee committment to the company.)

In total the annual pension and social security costs amount to approximately 12 per cent of the total employment costs. In turn the employment costs amount to 24.7 per cent of turnover – a ratio that has remained remarkably consistent over the past three years. Though note 6 also includes average employee numbers, year end total remuneration, etc., it only provides a partial indication of the investment the company is or is not putting into its workforce. Though one can calculate the average remuneration per employee from the statistics provided, it is not very helpful given the range of jobs and the diversity of the locations of those jobs geographically. Nevertheless some useful general measures have been computed earlier in the efficiency section (see page 134).

Management of financial risks

Companies are becoming more and more multinational in their operations and the financial market place is becoming larger, wider and more sophisticated in its products and operations. Thus the need to assess a company's management of, and ongoing position in, its financial risks increases in importance.

The main risk areas arise in the currency, interest rate and credit dealings. To these three could be added the use of financial derivatives. Currency risk can arise from outstanding and future transactions and from the translation of the foreign currency values of assets and liabilities into sterling.

The main reason why differential interest rates exist between countries is because the market expects the exchange rate between those countries' currencies to move and counter the differential. Thus it is always possible to borrow in the lower interest rate currency, convert, and invest at the higher rate and thus make a 'profit', this of course is shown in the profit and loss account. At the same time there will almost certainly be a reduction in the capital value, but this will be passed through the balance sheet via the total recognized gains and losses statement. Thus profits could have been bolstered at the expense of the shareholders' equity. This can be checked by calculating the average cost of net borrowings and comparing it with the rates due on the portfolio of loans outstanding. From note 3 (see page 218) we obtain net interest payable of £99.2 million with net borrowings and finance leases for 1997 and 1996 respectively of £1,375.3 million and £1,230.6 million. So the average cost of net borrowings per capitalized interest rate for 1997 is:

$$\text{Average cost of net borrowings 1997} = \frac{99.2}{\frac{1}{2}(1,375.3 + 1,230.6)} \times 100 = 7.6 \text{ per cent}$$

Comparing the average rate of 7.6 per cent and the rates quoted in note 3 (see page 220) for the outstanding loans, it can be seen that there is little difference between the two. Also compare the amount of the foreign currency net investment translation effect in the total recognised gains and losses with the size of the net borrowings. In 1997 the translation effect is a reduction of £89.8 million (6.5 per cent of net borrowings). Neither suggest the company is mismatching its currency and interest rate risks.

The extent of the use of hedging mechanisms is also important information, particularly if the risks are left uncovered. At the end of 1997 BOC had 14 interest rate swap agreements with notional principal amounts of £643.3 million, which is 13.1 per cent of the groups total assets, while at the same point in time BOC had 16 currency swap agreements outstanding with a notional value of £476.2 million, (9.7 per cent of total assets). In each case the amount and proportion has grown considerably from 1996.

Conclusions

To reach a conclusion, the analyst has to make an overall review and decide whether or not the company is in good financial health. Here then, it is necessary to pull together the answers to all the main questions of each stage. From this the main lines of business will have been identified and assessed, and decisions made as to what should happen in the future. By reviewing the SWOT analysis in the light of the profitability assessment, and the operating efficiency in conjunction with the forecast needs for investment and the implications for liquidity and finance, it is possible to provide a very full report, the nature and direction of which will be determined in some way by the needs of the individual for whom it is prepared.

15 Other uses of financial ratios

So far the use of ratios has been to provide the basis for a subjective assessment of a business either as a whole and/or for some specific part of it. This chapter will address the use of ratios in more objective analytical structures which aim to provide specific recommendations to decision makers. Some results from research have proved to have a more practical application than others. For example, financial ratios have been found useful in forecasting potential corporate bankruptcies and in classifying a prospective customer's credit rating. Research is still continuing into the use of financial ratios in models to identify potential takeover targets, or to value shares. Two areas where the application of straightforward statistical techniques to financial ratios have helped improve the quality of the general picture of a company have been time series analysis and line-of-business analysis.

Time series analysis

Time series analysis involves the calculation of the ratios of a company not just for the current or preceding year but for a longer period of time, which may be five, ten or twenty years or more. The objectives of such an analysis are first to provide a 'standard' against which the current performance and financial stability of a company or business unit might be compared and, second, to attempt to isolate trends over time that might enable future values of the ratios to be predicted.

When conducting a time series analysis, it is obviously important to ensure that there has been consistency in accounting practices; where changes have occurred, these must be calibrated before the analysis is undertaken. It is also possible that the reasons for changes over time in a particular variable, such as sales or profits, may be due to economy – or industry-wide factors outside the control of a particular company. Simply to compare one period with another without adjusting for these factors may be misleading.

Two examples of where accounting alternatives can cause sizeable inconsistencies over time are foreign-currency translation and exceptional items. Care must be taken to ensure that exceptional items are what they say they are and thus are excluded from the annual profit figures while cognizance must be given to the influence of the foreign currency translation which will vary annually, sometimes materially. Material changes and influences should be excluded.

Time series analysis utilizes any systematic patterns in the behaviour of a financial series, such as revenue, costs, or profits, over time to generate forecasts of future values for the variable. It can also be used in non-forecasting contexts where management is looking for explanations of the values found in a series, e.g. if investigating whether profits have been 'managed' over the years or to provide a statistical model for executive compensation plans.

The statistical techniques used in time series analysis involve the isolation of four separate components of trends:

1 the secular component (the regular movement in trends caused by factors whose influence tends to be in the same direction over a long period);
2 the seasonal component (the short-term movement in trends caused by seasonal variations);
3 the cyclical component (the movement in trends caused by medium- and long-term cyclical fluctuations);
4 the residual component (the irregular movements in trends caused by random and unpredictable events).

Having identified the components of trends affecting a time series of past ratios, it is possible, through the use of the mathematical technique of least-squares regression, to determine a trend line for each ratio under consideration. (The statistical technique is not discussed here; readers are referred elsewhere, e.g. Foster (1986) for an introduction to an in-depth review.) It is this trend line that determines the yardstick against which the ratios of the current year should be compared and it provides the starting point for assessing whether the performance of the current period might be thought 'good' or 'bad'. The trend line also provides a base for predicting future values of the ratios.

This kind of analysis is, with the advent of spreadsheets, now an inexpensive and relatively easy procedure to conduct. In the previous chapter, ratios were calculated for The BOC Group plc for the past five years and, though they were not subjected to a rigorous time series analysis, a broad trend with apparent deviations was obvious in a number of instances. This was sufficient to provide some valuable commonsense observations but for a more rigorous approach recourse to time series analysis is advocated.

Line-of-business analysis

When time series analysis is used for prediction purposes, the examination of segmental, or line-of-business, information is crucial. The information for share-trading and lending decisions is drawn not only from a company's annual report but also from many other sources – forecasts of growth in particular industries and countries, general economic trends, details of major contracts awarded, details of major customers, the introduction of new manufacturing processes, new products, competitors' activities, changes in legislation, changes in key personnel and so on. Much of this information is specific to particular lines of business or geographical locations. The overall performance of a diversified group of companies is obviously affected by the individual performances of specific segments, which will in turn be affected by the environment in which they operate. Any prediction of overall performance will therefore require segmental information, so that all the factors that might have an effect on the performance of individual segments may be taken into account. In the earlier chapters it was plain to see the big differences in the profit margins of the different segments of The BOC Group and of their different returns on capital employed (see Chapter 10 and Table 11.1).

It must be noted that firms have considerable discretion over the line of business reporting; how the separate activities are combined and then described, how the intra-group transfers are calculated or transfer prices set. Many companies are sensitive about the economic value of this information to competitors and to governments of countries in which they trade and in which they wish to minimize taxes. They are therefore not as full in their disclosures as they could be. They can ensure a lack of consistency over time in the way in which the constituent parts of a company are grouped together. Full and frank disclosure can provide a basis for very useful ratio analysis, especially when combined with the analysis of competing firms in similar areas of business. There is a substantial demand for information which compares the performance and financial position of different companies and there are several organizations which attempt to meet this demand by undertaking a cross-sectional ratio analysis.

Cross-sectional analysis – inter-firm comparison

Cross-sectional ratio analysis offers a further means of providing a 'standard' against which performance can be measured. A comparison of the ratios of a particular company, either with those of individual companies in the same industry or with some average of the group of companies in the industry, will be useful in assessing relative performance. Time series analysis using financial values or ratios has already been mentioned; it is used for comparing one entity at different point in time. Cross-sectional analysis compares different entities at the same points in time. To the extent that the investment decision facing shareholders and lenders involves choosing which companies to invest in, or which to lend to, the use of ratio analysis to compare the performance of different companies is helpful. A further example is the predictions of the financial distress of firms in the same or different industries. This we shall cover in more depth in the next section. There are, however, a number of problems associated with such inter-firm comparisons.

The first difficulty is in deciding on the appropriate industrial classification of a particular company. Many of the industrial groups contain companies that are surprisingly different. Moreover, diversified companies will, by definition, be involved in a range of quite different activities, each of which might belong to a different industrial classification. In the Stock Exchange industrial classification scheme, BOC is included in the 'general chemicals' sector, which places it among companies with which it has very little in common, such as ICI, Allied Colloids, British Tar Products and so on.

The second difficulty concerns the effects of corporate size. When comparing the results of individual companies, it is not sufficient merely to ensure that the companies operate in the same industry. They should also be more or less comparable in size. Even though one of the supposed benefits of ratio analysis is its ability to adjust for size differences, there are occasions when this breaks down. For example, many ratios make use of the annual sales figure. If company A has annual sales of £150 million and these represent the major part of the total industry sales, an increase of 10.0 per cent may require a significant effort. If company B has annual sales of just £1 million, an increase of 10.0 per cent may be achieved much more easily. A further difference caused by size is the degree of risk associated with the company. Large companies usually have better access to the capital markets than their smaller competitors and find it easier to raise long-term finance; during particularly difficult periods, such large companies might often be supported by governments. In contrast, small companies are often restricted to the relatively riskier short-term credit and overdraft sources. Large companies might also be expected to benefit from the use of more sophisticated technology and superior marketing channels.

A further difficulty facing inter-firm comparison is that ratio analysis by itself may fail to reflect the true position of the different companies. For instance, the ratios of company X may be superior in every way to those of company Y, or superior to the industry average. However, if nine-tenths of the output of company X is taken up by just one customer, it may be more risky than its comparators. As with time series analysis, cross-sectional ratio analysis must be supplemented with information drawn from a variety of other sources.

Perhaps the most serious obstacle to perfect inter-firm comparison is the existence of variations in accounting policies and practices. Even though there are standards for accounting reporting which were discussed in the early chapters, a wide range of permissible accounting treatments still exist for such items as depreciation, stock valuation, intangibles and the like. Such differences obviously affect the validity of the comparison exercise. The only way that this particular problem can be overcome is through a standardized comparison scheme. The Centre for Interfirm Comparison operates one such scheme and seeks to ensure that the figures supplied by participant companies are truly comparable by providing detailed instructions – about the definition of terms, valuation principles and so on. Only by pursuing such an approach is it possible to attribute differences in ratios solely to differences in operational performance and economic position, rather than to differences in accounting terminology and treatment. Unfortunately, the information and data produced by the Centre for Interfirm Comparison are available only to participating companies and not to all external users of company reports. Appendix B gives details of a number of sources of comparative statistics and data.

One example of the use of publicly available financial ratios is the information provided by FAME in Appendix B. Various consulting organizations make use of the financial values and ratios to build their own models from which they can then make recommendations to clients/public concerning the value of a particular company as a potential investment, or disinvestment. One such model that is cross-sectional is called market value added (MVA) which will be described briefly later in this chapter.

The prediction of corporate bankruptcy

An ability to predict the likelihood of the bankruptcy or failure of a company would be of obvious benefit to shareholders, lenders, suppliers and managers alike. Over the past forty years, a substantial amount of research has been undertaken on the extent to which ratio analysis might be useful in making such predictions. Much of the research effort has been based on US data, and the methodology generally adopted has involved the comparison of the ratios of failed companies for several years prior to failure with those of companies that did not fail.

The results of the research have been impressive, showing that significant differences were discernible between the ratios of failed and non-failed companies for up to five years before failure. Earlier research concentrated on the ability of a single ratio to predict failure – the 'univariate' approach – and perhaps the best known examples of the use of this approach are in the earlier work by Beaver (1966). He selected a sample of seventy-nine US companies that had either become bankrupt or had defaulted on the payment of interest or preference dividends. These he classified as failed companies; each failed company was then paired with a company from the same industry and of equivalent size that had not failed. For each of the pairs of companies, Beaver calculated thirty of the more conventional financial ratios for each of the five years prior to the demise of the failed company. He found that the mean ratios of the failed companies were substantially worse than those of the non-failed companies over the five-year period.

However, simply detecting differences in the mean values of ratios does not necessarily indicate predictive ability, and Beaver went on to test for that. He assumed that, for each pair of companies, the one with the poorer ratio would be the one most likely to fail, and made that the basis of his prediction. The prediction was compared with the actual outcome to determine the extent to which mis-classification occurred. Obviously, if this particular technique had no predictive ability at all, the classification would, at random, be correct for 50 per cent of the time and incorrect for 50 per cent of the time. Beaver found that, from the thirty ratios he used, a small number were particularly successful in predicting failure – success being measured in terms of the lowest number of incorrect classifications. The most successful of all was the cash-flow-total-debt ratio, with only 10 per cent of the companies incorrectly classified five years prior to failure. Somewhat surprisingly, the current ratio, which is often thought of as an important indicator of liquidity, was not a particularly good predictor: 20 per cent of the companies were incorrectly classified one year prior to failure and 31 per cent five years prior to failure.

An alternative to the univariate approach is the 'multivariate' approach which considers several different ratios simultaneously. The seminal research work on the use of multivariate models to predict failure or non-failure was carried out by Altman (1968) in the USA. He used the statistical technique of multiple discriminant analysis, which is designed to classify observations into distinct groupings depending on the characteristics of the observations. In Altman's case, the observations were individual companies and he was seeking to classify them as 'failed' or 'non-failed', depending on the various financial characteristics of each company (size, profitability, liquidity and so on). The use of multiple discriminant analysis facilitates a linear combination of the economic characteristics that best discriminate between failed and non-failed companies. This linear combination is known as a discriminant function and is of the form

$$Z = b_1X_1 + b_2X_2 + b_3X_3 + \ldots + b_nX_n$$

where X_1, X_2, X_3 etc. are the various financial ratios, b_1, b_2, b_3 etc. are the discriminant coefficients and Z is the discriminant score. It is the value of the discriminant score that is used to classify companies as either failed or non-failed.

Altman used the paired-sample method and selected thirty-three manufacturing companies that had failed and paired them with thirty-three manufacturing companies that had not failed. Size and industry were the criteria for pairing. For each company, he computed twenty-two accounting and non-accounting measures and then considered these in various combinations as predictors of failure. The following linear combination was found to be the best discriminator of the bankruptcy of a company, and it contained just five of the variables.

$$Z = 0.012X_1 + 0.014X_2 + 0.033X_3 + 0.006X_4 + 0.0099X_5$$

where X_1 is working capital/total assets, X_2 is retained earnings/total assets, X_3 is profit before interest and taxes/total assets, X_4 is market value of equity/ book value of total debt and X_5 is sales/total assets.

This model is applied in solvency evaluation by calculating each of those five ratios for the company under consideration, feeding them into the discriminant function and calculating the discriminant score (usually known simply as the Z score). The value of the computed Z score is compared with the cut-off point that best discriminated between failed and non-failed companies.

Space precludes too detailed a discussion on the conceptual underpinning of the various models which have in general been devised from the original Altmann approach. But it should be noted that the studies have pointed out that over a period of time, changes due to environmental changes do occur in the financial ratios. For example, levels of profitability and liquidity will tend to be lower during the downturn of the trade cycle. Thus lower ratios for a nevertheless successful company, when fed into the predictive model, could cause an erroneous prediction of failure, if the prediction model has been based on ratios achieved by companies during better economic times.

British research and commercial usage in this area has been spearheaded by Taffler with his first paper in 1977. Subsequently developing his model commercially, the company Syspas Ltd, computes a Z-score for each company in its population and then ranks all the quoted companies in order of their Z-score. The coefficient and ratios incorporated in Syspas's model, though not publicly available have been vigorously tested over time and have been found to be very robust. Only four variables are used. The ranking positions of the companies are placed into percentiles.

From their database Syspas are then able to identify the cut-off Z-score. If a company achieves a Z-value below this then it is deemed to be at risk. From this can be computed the percentage of companies with Z-scores below the cut-off, thus producing the quoted percentage of companies at risk. In 1977 there were approximately 11 per cent at risk, which increased with fluctuations to a peak of 29 per cent in 1992, whilst now it is around 22 per cent. Smith (1996) provides some good examples of how Syspas predicted the distress of Queens Moat Houses plc and Tiphook plc. An indication can be obtained of the industry average for the company, the percentage of companies at risk and the percentage point of the investigated company. Trends for each of the three variables can be portrayed graphically over time which will show off the relative position of the client company, the industry and the at-risk stage with the changes in those positions. This clearly is of help to analysts, managers, investors, etc. because of the objectivity it provides in support of the signals it gives. Appropriate action can be taken by the individual concerned.

The merits of not just concentrating on accounting data appealed to some, particularly if there was a possible use for commercial application. Argenti (1976), by combining quantitative and qualitative factors, developed a model which produced an A score based on both financial statement data and qualitative assessments of management performance. More recently this work, too, has been extended to examine these issues in relation to small UK firms (Keasey and Watson 1987).

So although any particular predictive model may never be applicable at all times and under all circumstances, the models that have been developed do appear to have had quite definite predictive ability. Because of the potential payoff from being able to develop a proven predictive model, research continues apace. Most of the published research results have involved a retrospective analysis, being based on past data for firms that actually failed, and are subject to statistical shortcomings. A complete issue of the *Journal of Business Finance and Accounting* (vol. 17, no. 1, Spring 1990) was given over to financial statement analysis. It did include articles on takeover predictions as well as articles considering the *ex ante* predictive approach, the case of current cost accounting based ratios and the use of other statistical techniques than Z scores. The individual bibliographies to each article, when combined, provide a very full list of works on the use of financial ratios for anyone who wishes to follow up an earlier work, or who perhaps doubts the statements made here.

The evidence is impressive and has helped in the identification of those crucial ratios that have a strong measure of predictive ability. Thus, although the role of financial ratio analysis in the prediction of future profits, dividends and share prices may be somewhat unclear, its importance in the prediction of future solvency seems much clearer. So much so that there are commercial services available for those wishing to use Z-score analysis. In Appendix B (see page 248) the Qui Score and rating for BOC is given which for 1997 was 64 but still stable. The Qui Score in 1995 was 64 and stable falling slightly to 61 and stable in 1996. FAME publish the Qui Score for each company, which is a measure of the likelihood of company failure in the twelve months following the date of calculation. There are five distinct bands identified, secure, stable, normal, unstable and high risk. A company score is compared with the band range and an interpretation of the company's risk factor made. In the case of BOC, falling in the stable range is interpreted as a 'company failure is a rare occurrence and will only come about if there are major company or marketplace changes.' In the case of BOC, the major change is the sale of the health care group, which can only help the company.

Loan and credit-rating models

To potential lenders, the prediction of the future solvency of an aspiring client is extremely important and the use of models such as the bankruptcy or distress models, as they are sometimes called, is a vital cog in the decision-making machine.

Each bank has its own lending evaluation model which it uses to produce an assessment of a potential borrower, which it then uses in conjunction with other pieces of subjective and objectively measured data to help prepare the information dossier prior to the loan decision. Foster (1986) has an interesting, if a little dated, chapter on the types of models used in the USA.

Prediction of takeover targets

The prediction of takeover targets is another area where there are potentially large rewards for the model builder who can accurately predict companies that become takeover targets which are then successfully acquired. At present the work of researchers can be placed into two parts, either classificatory or predictive.

An article by Palepu (1986) reports a study using classificatory analysis. He took two samples of firms from the manufacturing and mining sectors. The first was a group made up of the 163 companies already taken over during the 1971–9 period under study. They were known as the targets. A second control sample of 256 companies was randomly selected from these sectors.

The mean values for each sample for ten different variables were compared on a univariable basis. It highlighted that, on average, the targets:

■ had lower returns on the stock market over the four years prior to takeover;
■ exhibited lower sales growth and greater resource surpluses, e.g. cash-rich firms;
■ were not predominantly located in industries in which acquisitions had taken place in the previous year;
■ were smaller in book-asset size than the average control sample firm.

These findings from the univariate comparisons reinforced some of the views already held by city individuals drawn from their own personal experiences. The more sophisticated multivariate analysis was then undertaken and Palepu (1986) reported that the likelihood ratio index never rose above 12.45 per cent, even though it was statistically significant. The likelihood ratio index is a measure of the overall explanatory power of the multivariate model. Such a low explanatory power suggests that any attempt at building a takeover predictive model upon which trading rules could be based is probably going to be unsuccessful.

The rationale behind attempts to build a predictive model for trading purposes is self-evident, and a number of authors have tried. Rege (1984) calculated financial ratios for liquidity, leverage, dividend payout, total asset turnover and profitability. He used these ratios to see if he could differentiate between those companies that are likely to be taken over and those that are not. His study was based on Canadian firms. His variables were unable to isolate potential takeover targets as they could not distinguish between taken-over and non-taken-over firms. Others, such as Bartley and Boardman (1990), have been marginally more successful, but results and methods are not yet commercially viable. However, since the benefits from the derivation of a model that could predict takeover targets are considerable, work will go on. Like the work in building models to forecast companies in financial distress, work in this area will continue, using expanded databases, longer time series, different groups of financial ratios, different statistical tools or perhaps the introduction of non-financial values, until it is felt either that the end result is not achievable or that a workable trading model is designed. For example, recent work has focused on utilizing financial ratios in models to predict corporate divestments, MBO's and the 'liquidation/merger' alternative (see Peel (1990) for a review of these).

Equity valuation models

Just as companies and other members of the investment community are interested in developing models for identifying takeover targets, and other corporate options, they have, from a much earlier time, been involved with the development of equity share valuation models for use in the selection of shares for buying or selling.

Underlying the development of these models is the belief that the market is not completely efficient in its pricing of shares, thus enabling some traders to gain better than average returns. These models are part of the fundamental approach to investment appraisal and are usually based on the use of data from the financial statements. They change over time as their relative effectiveness and reliability diminish, being replaced by new and different versions. As the models become part of the public domain through marketing by City firms, their effectiveness tends to depreciate due to the increased buying and selling pressures of the market arising from the ever-widening public knowledge of the model.

As an example, it is worth mentioning one model since it does appear to have had some limited success in detecting over- or undervalued shares. It is a US model called Value Line. Value Line uses a combination of three criteria to measure a share's price and profit characteristics against those of comparable shares in its listing. It then ranks the share on an expected 'relative price performance in the next twelve months' using this combination. Thus investors can select shares in the different groups which meet their risk and return needs, where the expected return for the group is indicated by the model. The three criteria are the non-parametric value position, the earnings momentum and the earnings surprise factor. These three do involve some financial statement information, predominantly profits related.

Many of the recommendations made by analysts concerning the under- or over-valuation of shares will be based to a greater or lesser extent on methods or models which combine objectively and subjectively based information. Financial ratios will have been used to derive some of the objective and some of the subjective elements incorporated in the model. Precisely which ratios, or with what weighting or in which combinations, will be dependent upon whose model. But no matter which model or approach is adopted there is a need to understand the financial information and ratios that are used in them. Jim Slater is regarded by many as a stock market investment expert, thanks to the success of both his advice and his commercial activities. His method for identifying undervalued shares called 'the Zulu principle' still requires the 'analyst' to undertake some financial ratio analysis as part of the evaluation process (Slater 1992). The only certain thing is that no method yet has proved to be completely accurate in its predictions.

Asset-pricing models

A great amount of work by academics has been undertaken in empirically testing the asset-pricing models based on CAPM (capital asset pricing model) and APT (arbitrage pricing theory).

The two main parameters of interest are the beta (β) value of a security and the variances of its returns. The β value is a measure of a security's responsiveness to the movements of the market portfolio and is therefore a measure of the risk level of the security. It is also known as its systematic risk measure. β links the security's return with that of the market's risk premium over the risk-free rate through the expression

$$E(R_i) = R_f + \beta_i[E(R_m) - R_f]$$

where $E(R_i)$ is the expected return of the ith security, R_f, is the return on the risk-free asset and $E(R_m)$ is the expected return on the market portfolio, which is the combination of the assets available in the market.

The Risk Measurement Service (RMS) of London Business School publishes a quarterly listing of the β values for shares traded on the London Stock Exchange, along with other linked parameters for those shares. With the ever-increasing size of the databases available, empirical research has discovered various specific effects in market operations, e.g. the small-firm effect, the weekend/Monday effect and so on. Details of these relatively specific and discrete effects can be incorporated into earlier, more general models, thus improving the accuracy of the inferences that can be made from patterns of past share returns or information gleaned from financial statements.

The derivation of a company's cost of capital through the CAPM approach which combined with the use of data from the balance sheet and profit and loss account of a company have helped produce a successful business for an American firm, Stern Stewart. Their conceptual approach derives two things, market value added (MVA) and economic value added (EVA). The former compares the total market value of the capital components of a company with the book value of the same components, shares, retained earnings, debentures, loans etc. found in the balance sheet. The difference between the two totals being the market value added. Effectively, the larger the positive MVA the more highly regarded the company in the market place. The computation of an annual EVA for the companies indicates historic support (or otherwise) for the futuristic view of the company from the MVA computation. EVA is a form of residual income for a company derived by deducting from a company's after-tax profit the capital cost of servicing its total sources of finance (debt and equity). The cost of equity being derived from the CAPM model. Thus an annual value of EVA is computed indicating historically the performance of the company in creating economic value. It is of course quite possible for a company to have a strong MVA and a negative EVA for a year. The concepts are an evolution from the shareholder value analysis (SVA) initiated by Rappaport (1986). Commercial interests abound that attempt to use financial and economic concepts with or without data obtained from the corporate accounts.

As described in the earlier sections of this chapter, links are still being investigated and developed between financial statement information or financial ratios and models designed for either predictive or explanatory purposes. It is clear, though, that at present research in these areas still has not reached a stage where systematic trading rules, built on financial statement information, can be used profitably by the investing public. Nevertheless the work continues to improve both the quality of the information reported in the financial statements and the sophistication of the models into which it is incorporated.

Part Three

Appendices

Appendix A: Financial review of The BOC Group plc for the year ended 30 September 1997

Group five year record

Turnover

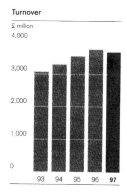

Profit before tax

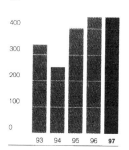

Profit and loss	1993 £ million	1994 £ million	1995 £ million	1996 £ million	1997 £ million
Turnover of subsidiary undertakings[1]	3,067.5	3,292.3	3,543.9	3,752.1	**3,677.7**
Operating profit before exceptional items[1]	420.8	435.4	496.4	539.4	**540.4**
Restructuring costs	–	(85.0)	–	–	–
Operating profit[1]	420.8	350.4	496.4	539.4	**540.4**
Loss on disposal of operations	–	(16.6)	–	–	–
Profit before interest	420.8	333.8	496.4	539.4	**540.4**
Interest (net)	(83.2)	(80.7)	(94.2)	(94.5)	**(95.2)**
Profit before tax	337.6	253.1	402.2	444.9	**445.2**
Tax on profit on ordinary activities	(115.4)	(121.7)	(128.6)	(137.9)	**(129.1)**
Profit after tax	222.2	131.4	273.6	307.0	**316.1**
Attributable to minority shareholders	(18.3)	(17.8)	(24.6)	(28.7)	**(28.5)**
Profit for the financial year	203.9	113.6	249.0	278.3	**287.6**
Earnings per 25p Ordinary share					
Net basis, undiluted:					
– on published profit	42.97p	23.82p	51.97p	57.74p	**59.31p**
– before exceptional items	42.97p	43.87p	51.97p	57.74p	**59.31p**
Ordinary dividend per share[2]					
Actual	23.2p	23.2p	24.8p	27.0p	**29.0p**
Adjusted for inflation	26.0p	25.5p	26.2p	28.0p	**29.0p**
Number of fully paid Ordinary shares in issue at the year end (million)	475.7	477.9	480.5	483.3	**487.1**

1. Continuing operations.
2. Dividends paid in the calendar year.

Balance sheet	1993 £ million	1994 £ million	1995 £ million	1996 £ million	**1997 £ million**
Employment of capital					
Fixed assets					
Tangible assets	2,295.5	2,374.3	2,561.7	2,747.6	**2,953.7**
Intangible assets	44.9	38.4	33.8	33.4	**28.8**
Investments	190.2	191.9	255.7	286.3	**319.5**
Working capital	375.6	360.9	390.3	496.9	**464.3**
	2,906.2	2,965.5	3,241.5	3,564.2	**3,766.3**
Capital employed[3]					
Shareholders' capital and reserves	1,488.8	1,509.8	1,655.6	1,818.7	**1,892.8**
Minority shareholders' interests	207.2	220.9	241.2	242.8	**245.0**
	1,696.0	1,730.7	1,896.8	2,061.5	**2,137.8**
Non current liabilities and provisions	245.0	271.4	278.4	272.1	**253.2**
Net borrowings and finance leases[4]	965.2	963.4	1,066.3	1,230.6	**1,375.3**
	2,906.2	2,965.5	3,241.5	3,564.2	**3,766.3**
Other selected financial information					
Total assets	3,785.4	3,910.1	4,362.4	4,636.0	**4,898.8**
Long-term liabilities	904.2	1,126.4	946.2	1,039.5	**1,254.4**
Capital expenditure	359.8	356.3	408.9	542.3	**675.8**
Depreciation and amortisation	229.5	249.8	256.5	268.7	**276.5**
Employees					
UK	10,665	10,956	11,361	11,555	**11,513**
Overseas	29,601	28,465	28,720	29,358	**29,861**
Continuing operations	40,266	39,421	40,081	40,913	**41,374**
Ratios					
Return on average capital employed[5]	15.7%	14.8%	16.0%	15.9%	**15.0%**
Debt/capital employed	33.2%	32.5%	32.9%	34.5%	**36.5%**
Debt/equity	56.9%	55.7%	56.2%	59.7%	**64.3%**

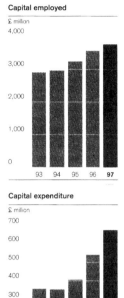

Capital employed

£ million

Capital expenditure

£ million

3. As defined in note 1b) to the financial statements.

4. Analysed for 1997 and 1996 in note 3c) to the financial statements.

5. Operating profit before exceptional items as a percentage of the average capital employed. For 1997 the average is calculated on a monthly basis.

Finance and treasury review

Financial indicators

The trends of financial indicators which, taken together, are a measure of performance and efficiency of the finance and tax structures in place, are:

	1997	1996	1995
Interest cover (times)	5.7	5.7	5.3
Debt/equity (%)	64.3	59.7	56.2
Debt/capital employed (%)	36.5	34.5	32.9
Average cost of net borrowings, before capitalised interest (%)	7.7	8.1	8.7
Average cost of net borrowings, after capitalised interest (%)	6.8	7.3	8.6
Group tax rate (%)	29	31	32

The ratios are commented on below in the appropriate section.

Financing

The Group has access to a range of funding: debt finance is raised by issuing bonds, commercial paper, other obligations to investors and through borrowings from banks.

As well as medium and long-term borrowings, the Group has substantial short-term borrowings, principally in the form of commercial paper and bank borrowings. It is the Group's policy that all outstanding commercial paper is fully backed by committed medium-term borrowing facilities. To achieve this, the Group maintains substantial medium-term committed facilities with a group of strong relationship banks.

Overall, net debt increased by £144.7 million as a result of a net cash outflow of £265.1 million offset mainly by a reduction in borrowings of £99.4 million due to exchange rate movements. In 1997, the Group has marginally increased the proportion of medium and longer-term debt principally through the issue of a £150 million loan note which matures in 2002. In 1996 the principal movements in financing were primarily due to Eurobond and guaranteed notes issues totalling £288.5 million, a net increase in commercial paper of £101.6 million, a decrease in cash of £30.6 million, offset by a repayment of guaranteed notes of £158.2 million, repayment of medium-term loans of £44.5 million and a favourable exchange rate movement of £24.6 million. The 1995 movement in borrowings was largely due to an increase in commercial paper issued of £66.1 million.

The gearing ratio (net debt including finance leases as a percentage of capital employed) was 36.5 per cent in 1997, compared with 34.5 per cent in 1996 and 32.9 per cent in 1995. The 1997 year end debt/equity ratio was 64.3 per cent, compared with 59.7 per cent in 1996 and 56.2 per cent in 1995.

The Group has access to a diverse range of debt finance which includes commercial paper, public bonds and bank borrowings which, it believes, will be available to meet long-term financing needs. The Group has sufficient facilities to cover likely borrowing needs. Management anticipates that capital expenditure in 1998 will be covered by cash inflow from operating activities.

Management of financial risks

The board of directors sets the treasury policies and objectives of the Group which include controls over the procedures used to manage currency, interest rate and credit risk. The approach to managing risk is set out below. This approach is expected to continue during the next financial year. On a day-to-day basis, group treasury carries out these policies, with regular review meetings with the group finance director. Specific and significant activities need approval from the finance committee, which consists of directors of the company.

Currency risk The Group faces currency risk principally on its net assets, most of which are in currencies other than sterling. Currency movements can therefore have a significant effect on the Group's balance sheet when translating these foreign currency assets into sterling. In order to reduce this effect the Group manages its borrowings, where practicable and cost effective, to hedge its foreign currency assets.

Where possible, hedging is done using direct borrowings in the same currency as the assets being hedged or through the use of other hedging methods such as currency swaps. Group borrowings are currently held in a wide range of currencies, and after swaps, 80 per cent of net

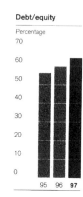

Debt/equity

Percentage

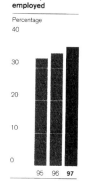

Debt/capital employed

Percentage

Interest cover

Times

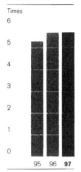

95 96 **97**

**Average cost of
net borrowings**[1]

Percentage

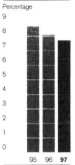

95 96 **97**

[1] Before capitalised interest

debt (1996: 80 per cent) is denominated in the principal currencies affecting the Group: US dollars, Australian dollars, Japanese yen, South African rand and sterling. The aggregate of the notional principal values of currency swaps was £476.2 million spread over a range of currencies. The combined market value of such swaps at 30 September 1997 was £477.5 million. No adjustment is made in the financial statements to reflect the market value of swaps.

The balance sheets of overseas operations are translated into sterling at the closing rates of exchange for the year and any exchange difference is dealt with as a movement in reserves. This is explained more fully in the accounting policy note on page 69. The profit and loss accounts of overseas businesses are translated at average rates of exchange and this translation impact directly affects the profit and loss account of the Group.

The Group manages its currency flows to minimise currency transaction exchange risk and forward contracts are used as appropriate to hedge net currency flows and selected individual transactions. A large proportion of the Group's foreign exchange cover is executed in the UK (which includes cover for exposures on net trade flows of the Group's companies in the US and certain other countries) and Australia. For these countries, the aggregate principal amount of forward cover outstanding at 30 September 1997 amounted to £189 million.

Interest rate risk In order to manage interest rate risk the Group maintains both floating rate and fixed rate debt. At present there is a 47:53 ratio. Underlying borrowings are arranged on both a fixed rate and a floating rate basis and, where appropriate, the Group uses interest rate swaps to vary this mix and to manage the Group's interest rate exposure.

The aggregate of the notional principal values of interest rate swaps and currency swaps, which also affect the floating rate/fixed rate mix, was £1,119.5 million at 30 September 1997. The combined market value of such swaps at 30 September 1997 was £1,129.6 million.

The Group does not undertake any trading activity in financial instruments nor does it enter into any leveraged derivative transactions.

Counterparty risk Cash deposits and financial instruments give rise to credit risk on the amounts due from counterparties. Credit risk is managed by limiting the aggregate amount and duration of exposure to any one counterparty depending upon their credit rating and by regular reviews of these ratings. The possibility of material loss arising in the event of non-performance by a counterparty is considered unlikely.

The currency and interest rate hedging profile of the Group's borrowings at 30 September 1997 is shown in note 3 to the financial statements. Further information on financial risk management is also given in note 3 to the financial statements.

Interest
The charge before deducting capitalised interest and before the Group's share of interest of associated undertakings was £99.2 million in 1997, which represented 7.7 per cent of average net borrowings during the year. After taking into account capitalised interest and associated undertakings the net interest charge was £95.2 million. Interest cover (the number of times that the net interest charge is covered by operating profit) remained at 5.7 times. The amount of interest capitalised during the year was £11.2 million (1996: £8.7 million, 1995: £3.2 million). After deducting capitalised interest, the interest charge, excluding associated undertakings, was £88.0 million which represents 6.8 per cent of net borrowings.

Debt maturity profile
The maturity profile of the Group's gross borrowings is as follows:

| | 1997 | | 1996 | |
	£m	%	£m	%
More than five years	**489.2**	**30.2**	460.7	33.1
Two to five years	**414.7**	**25.6**	272.5	19.6
One to two years	**97.3**	**6.0**	34.2	2.5
Within one year	**620.4**	**38.2**	623.1	44.8
Total	**1,621.6**		1,390.5	

A substantial proportion of the debt which matures within one year is commercial paper issued by various Group companies. The Group maintains US$420 million of committed multi-currency facilities with a group of relationship banks. These facilities mature in 2002 and provide back-up for the issue of commercial paper.

Inflation

Over the last three years, inflation has not had a material impact on the revenue or profit of the Group.

Taxation

The tax charge for 1997 of £129.1 million is calculated in accordance with UK accounting standards, including statement of standard accounting practice 15 on accounting for deferred taxation (SSAP15), under which provision is made for deferred taxes that are likely to become payable in the foreseeable future. Full provision for deferred taxes would have increased the charge by £20.3 million in 1997.

The tax charge in 1997 fell by two per cent to 29 per cent, after a reduction in 1996 of one per cent. The fall in the tax charge to 29 per cent was partly a result of the reduction in the UK corporation tax rate in the year from 33 per cent to 31 per cent and also to changes in country profit mix and increased capital expenditure. The Group pays corporation tax in the UK at an average marginal rate of 12 per cent due to advance corporation tax (ACT) on dividends. UK tax remained high due to the remittance of dividends but this was again largely offset by double tax relief and the use of surplus ACT. The company continues to utilise its ongoing surplus ACT. UK taxation is explained on page 104.

The Group pays federal alternative minimum tax (AMT) at the statutory rate of 20 per cent in the US. In the other principal subsidiaries, the tax rate is typically between 30 per cent and 50 per cent.

Contingencies

The Group monitors all contingent litigation liability including matters relating to the environment via a process of consultation and evaluation which includes senior management, internal and external legal advisers and internal and external technical advisers. This process results in conclusions with respect to potential exposure and provisions are made or adjusted accordingly by reference to accounting principles. Management believes that the Group has adequately provided for contingencies which are likely to become payable in the future. None of these contingencies is material to the Group's financial condition, results of operations or liquidity.

Legal proceedings

Group companies are parties to various legal proceedings, which are considered to constitute ordinary and routine litigation incidental to the business conducted by the relevant subsidiary or associated undertaking, including some in which claims for damages in large amounts have been asserted.

The outcome of litigation to which Group companies are party cannot be readily foreseen, but the directors believe that they will be disposed of without material effect on the Group's financial conditions, results of operations or liquidity.

Insurance

Operational management is responsible for managing business risks. Several Group departments advise management on different aspects of risk and monitor results. Insurance cover is held against major catastrophes. For any such event, the Group will bear an initial cost before external cover begins.

Accounting

For the first time, this report and accounts incorporates US reporting requirements following the Group's listing in September 1996 on the New York Stock Exchange.

The Group cash flow statement and supporting notes have been prepared based on the revised UK financial reporting standard 1 (FRS 1). Comparative figures have been restated to be consistent across three years.

The report of the management resources committee continues to follow the disclosure recommendations which have been issued on directors' remuneration. Where appropriate, in order to improve clarity, voluntary disclosures are also given.

As a global business the Group supports initiatives to harmonise accounting standards. Its own accounting policies are based on accounting principles generally accepted in the UK (UK GAAP) but the Group also considers the implications of US GAAP and international accounting standards. The Group plays an active part in accounting developments by responding to new proposals and by appropriate representation.

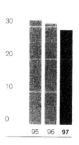

Group tax rate

Percentage

95 96 **97**

**Average exchange rates:
US dollar**

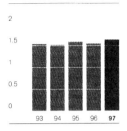

Australian dollar

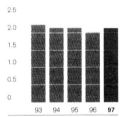

Japanese yen

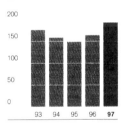

South African rand

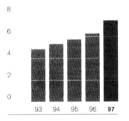

US GAAP

The financial statements of The BOC Group have been prepared in accordance with UK GAAP which differs in certain respects from US GAAP.

The US accounting information in note 16 to the financial statements gives a summary of the principal differences between the amounts determined in accordance with the Group's accounting policies (based on UK GAAP) and amounts determined in accordance with US GAAP together with the reconciliation of profit before tax and shareholders' funds from a UK GAAP basis to a US GAAP basis, and a movement in shareholders' funds on a US GAAP basis.

The profit before tax for the year ended 30 September 1997 under US GAAP was £416.3 million (1996: £427.1 million, 1995: £356.1 million), compared with profit before tax of £445.2 million in 1997 (1996: £444.9 million, 1995: £402.2 million) under UK GAAP. Shareholders' funds at 30 September 1997 were £1,827.9 million (1996: £1,816.2 million), compared to £1,892.8 million (1996: £1,818.7 million) under UK GAAP. The difference primarily results from the differing accounting treatment of pensions, goodwill, restructuring costs, investments, deferred taxes and fixed asset revaluations.

Exchange rates

The majority of the Group's operations are located outside the UK and operate in currencies other than sterling.

The effects of fluctuations in the relationship between the various currencies are extremely complex and variations in any particular direction may not have a consistent impact on the reported results. In 1997, sterling strengthened against the principal currencies affecting the Group (as shown below) by six per cent against the US dollar and Australian dollar, 18 per cent against the Japanese yen and 19 per cent against the South African rand. The impact of exchange rates on the 1997 results is considered in the performance review. Exchange rate movements were not significant in 1996 nor in 1995.

The rates of exchange to sterling for the currencies which have principally affected the Group's results over the last five years were:

	1997	1996	1995	1994	1993
US dollar					
At 30 September	**1.61**	1.56	1.58	1.58	1.51
Average for the year	**1.63**	1.54	1.58	1.51	1.53
Highest rate during year	**1.71**	1.59	1.64	1.58	1.78
Lowest rate during year	**1.56**	1.50	1.54	1.46	1.42
Australian dollar					
At 30 September	**2.22**	1.97	2.10	2.13	2.32
Average for the year	**2.12**	2.00	2.13	2.13	2.22
Highest rate during year	**2.29**	2.14	2.25	2.34	2.39
Lowest rate during year	**1.97**	1.89	1.99	2.03	2.03
Japanese yen					
At 30 September	**194.41**	173.28	156.13	156.08	160.00
Average for the year	**192.14**	163.38	147.99	157.79	175.63
Highest rate during year	**206.78**	173.28	161.01	168.77	208.25
Lowest rate during year	**173.38**	154.64	131.09	149.53	149.25
South African rand[1]					
At 30 September	**7.52**	7.09	5.78	6.73/5.62	6.59/5.20
Average for the year	**7.45**	6.25	5.71	6.86/5.30	7.09/4.82
Highest rate during year	**8.00**	7.09	5.90	7.95/5.73	8.21/5.29
Lowest rate during year	**7.01**	5.49	5.50	6.23/4.97	6.47/4.43

1. Since 1 January 1995, the South African rand has had only one accounting rate of exchange for conversion of foreign currency. Prior to then, two accounting rates of exchange were used: a financial and a commercial rate. For the translation of foreign currency, the Group applied the financial rate to balance sheet accounts and the commercial rate to profit and loss accounts. For 1993 and 1994 in the above table, the first rate of exchange given is the financial rate followed by the commercial rate.

On 21 November 1997, the latest practicable date for inclusion in this report and accounts, the rates of exchange to sterling for the principal currencies were as follows: US dollar was 1.69; Australian dollar was 2.41; Japanese yen was 212.56; South African rand was 8.16.

European Monetary Union

It seems probable that the single European currency (the Euro) will come into existence on 1 January 1999, but the British Government has indicated that the UK will not participate at that date.

While the UK accounts for the majority of BOC's turnover in Europe, its commercial operations in those countries which do participate will be affected. BOC has established a working party to examine what actions its businesses need to take to ensure a smooth transition to the new currency. Management believes that BOC's commercial operations can be adapted in the required timescales.

Principal operating companies

The following operating companies principally affect the amount of profit or assets of the Group:
* The BOC Group Inc, a wholly-owned Delaware corporation and a subsidiary of The BOC Group Inc, a wholly-owned Nevada corporation;
* BOC Limited, a wholly-owned English company;
* BOC Gases Australia Limited, a wholly-owned Australian company;
* BOC Distribution Services Ltd, a wholly-owned English company;
* Osaka Sanso Kogyo KK, a Japanese company, in which the Group's interest is just under 50 per cent;
* Ohmeda Inc, a wholly-owned Delaware corporation; and
* African Oxygen Limited, a South African company, in which the Group's shareholding is 57 per cent.

Supplier payment policy

The Group applies a policy of agreeing and clearly communicating the terms of payment as part of the commercial arrangement negotiated with suppliers and then paying according to those terms. In addition the UK-based businesses have committed to the CBI Prompt Payers Code since 1994. A copy of the code can be obtained from the CBI at Centre Point, 103 New Oxford Street, London WC1A 1DU.

For UK businesses, trade creditors as a proportion of amounts invoiced by suppliers represents 46 days at 30 September 1997.

Going concern

The directors are confident, after having made appropriate enquiries, that the Group has adequate resources for the foreseeable future. For this reason, they continue to adopt the going concern basis in preparing the accounts. Management believes that its current credit facilities provide sufficient working capital to meet the present requirements of its existing businesses and that the gearing ratio is appropriate given the nature of the Group's activities.

Corporate governance

The BOC Group is committed to business integrity, high ethical values and professionalism in all its activities. As an essential part of this commitment, the board supports the highest standards in corporate governance.

Board and committee structure

The board of The BOC Group plc is responsible for the Group's systems of corporate governance and is ultimately accountable for the Group's activities throughout the world. The board comprises the chairman, executive and non-executive directors.

The Group has long recognised the vital role that non-executive directors have in ensuring high governance standards and the BOC board has for many years had a significant non-executive element. The non-executive directors have full access to both management and the internal and external auditors and there is a formal procedure for directors to obtain independent professional advice in the furtherance of their duties should this be necessary.

The full board meets regularly throughout the year. It has a formal schedule of matters reserved to it but otherwise delegates specific responsibilities to committees. Details of committee members and the responsibilities of the board committees are on pages 9 to 11.

Directors

The directors holding office at the date of this report are named on page 9. Mr C P King was appointed a non-executive director on 13 November 1996. The other named directors held office throughout the year to 30 September 1997. Mr R Malpas and Lord Tugendhat retired as directors on 31 December 1996. At every annual general meeting one-third of the directors must retire by rotation and may be reappointed.

Officers

The officers of the company are the executives who currently serve on the executive management board as named on pages 12 and 13. This board was formed in July 1996 and all the officers served throughout the year ended 30 September 1997 except for Dr J Fairlie who was appointed on 17 January 1997.

Internal control

The board of directors has overall responsibility for the Group's system of internal control. The schedule of matters reserved to the board ensures that the directors maintain full and effective control over all significant strategic, financial, organisational and compliance issues.

The directors have delegated to executive management the establishment and implementation of a system of internal controls appropriate to the various business environments in which it operates. The Group operates under a system of controls which has been developed and refined over time to meet its current and future needs and which is communicated through various operating and procedural manuals. These include but are not limited to:

- The definition of the organisational structure and the appropriate delegation of authorities to operational management.
- Procedures for the review and authorisation of capital investments including post-acquisition reviews and appraisals.
- Strategic planning and the related annual planning and quarterly reforecasting process.
- The monthly reporting and review of financial results and other operating statistics as well as the Group's published quarterly financial statements which are based on a standardised reporting process.
- Accounting and financial reporting policies to ensure the consistency, integrity and accuracy of the Group's accounting records.
- Specific treasury policies and objectives and the on-going reporting and review of all significant transactions and financing operations.

The internal control system is monitored and supported by an internal audit function that operates on a global basis and reports to management and the audit committee on the Group's operations. The work of the internal auditors is focused on the areas of greatest risk to the Group determined on the basis of a risk management approach to audit. The external auditors are engaged to express an opinion on the Group report and accounts, which are prepared from the Group's accounting records and comply fully with UK generally accepted accounting principles. They independently and objectively review the performance of management in reporting operating results and financial condition. In coordination with the internal auditors they also review and test the system of internal financial control and the data contained in the report and accounts to the extent necessary for expressing their opinion.

The directors believe that the Group's system of internal financial control provides reasonable but not absolute assurance that assets are safeguarded, transactions are authorised and recorded properly and that material errors and irregularities are either prevented or would be detected within a timely period. Having reviewed its effectiveness, the directors are not aware of any significant weakness or deficiency in the Group's system of internal financial control during the period covered by this report and accounts.

Cadbury Code of Best Practice

In December 1992, the committee on the Financial Aspects of Corporate Governance (the Cadbury committee) published a Code of Best Practice. The board considers that throughout the financial year under review the company complied with the Code.

The directors' report on going concern is included in the finance and treasury review on page 49.

As recommended by the Cadbury committee and required by the London Stock Exchange, the company's auditors have considered the directors' Statement of Compliance in relation to those points of the Code which can be objectively verified. This report to the board is set out on page 52.

Corporate donations

During the year The BOC Group made donations of £1,179,000, including £612,000 donated to charities registered in the UK. The Group also spent £576,000 on projects identified by The BOC Foundation for the Environment. No political donations were made in the UK.

Traditionally, charitable and community projects funded by BOC have had strong synergies with our business activities, as, for example, in the field of research into respiratory illness supported by our 12-year association as founder sponsor of The British Lung Foundation.

However, this does not preclude involvement in other projects of benefit to the community, such as The BOC Covent Garden Festival which encourages young musicians and performers.

Meanwhile, at the local level, our businesses and operational sites are increasingly active in helping community and charitable projects, with our matched giving scheme yet again proving its worth as a way of channelling corporate funding to support the fund-raising efforts and initiatives of individual BOC employees.

Outside the UK, the development of community programmes is in the hands of our local companies. Each company is responsible for choosing which projects to support, and for providing the required funding. This devolved approach has resulted in a rich variety of programmes that are truly relevant to the communities in which BOC businesses operate around the world. Current examples range from welding schools in Poland and Russia where free training in basic gas welding is provided to young unemployed people, to mobile clinics providing basic, primary health care to people living in rural communities around Calcutta.

Since 1990 we have funded The BOC Foundation for the Environment, which supports projects which aim to demonstrate in a practical way how pollution can be reduced in the UK. More than 50 projects have been funded so far, focusing mainly on issues of waste management and water quality.

Annual General Meeting

The Annual General Meeting will be held at The Dorchester (Ballroom), Park Lane, London WIA 2HJ on Friday 16 January 1998 commencing at 11.00 am. The Notice of the Annual General Meeting, which includes explanations of all resolutions, is contained in a separate circular which has been sent to all shareholders.

Resolutions to receive the report and accounts and to re-elect Dr D Chatterji, Mr A E Isaac, Mr D G John and Mr J H Macdonald will be put to shareholders. All four directors retire by rotation and are willing to be reappointed.

Dr D Chatterji, Mr A E Isaac and Mr D G John have service or appointment contracts terminable by the company on not more than two years' notice and by the individual director on six months' notice. Mr J H Macdonald does not have a service contract.

The auditors, Coopers & Lybrand, retire in accordance with Section 385 of the Companies Act 1985. A resolution for their reappointment will be proposed at the Annual General Meeting.

Other resolutions to be put to shareholders seek approval for the following:

a) renewal of the authority for the directors to allot shares
b) renewal of the authority for the directors to allot shares for cash other than to existing shareholders in proportion to their holdings
c) renewal of the authority to offer scrip dividends
d) reduction of capital by cancellation and repayment of the three classes of Preference shares and amendment to the Memorandum and Articles of Association to remove references to the three classes of Preference shares
e) granting of general authority for the company to purchase its own shares up to a maximum of ten per cent of issued share capital

The report of the directors has been approved by the board and signed on its behalf by:

Gloria J Stuart Secretary
Windlesham, 28 November 1997

Report of the auditors to The BOC Group plc
on the statement of compliance with the Code of Best Practice

In addition to our audit of the financial statements, we have reviewed the directors' statement on page 51 concerning the company's compliance with the paragraphs of the Cadbury Code of Best Practice which the London Stock Exchange has specified for our review and the directors' adoption of the going concern basis in preparing the financial statements. The objective of our review is to draw attention to non-compliance with Listings Rules 12.43(j) and 12.43 (v).

We carried out our review in accordance with guidance issued by the Auditing Practices Board. That guidance does not require us to perform the additional work necessary to, and we do not, express any opinion on the effectiveness of either the company's system of internal financial control or its corporate governance procedures, nor on the ability of the company to continue in operational existence.

Opinion
With respect to the directors' statements on internal financial control on page 50 and going concern on page 49, in our opinion the directors have provided the disclosures required by the Listing Rules referred to above and such statements are not inconsistent with the information of which we are aware from our audit work on the financial statements.

Based on enquiry of certain directors and officers of the company and examination of relevant documents, in our opinion the directors' statement on compliance with the Code appropriately reflects the company's compliance with the other aspects of the Code specified for our review by Listing Rule 12.43(j).

Coopers & Lybrand
Chartered accountants
London, 28 November 1997

Report of the management resources committee

The committee

The board of The BOC Group has recognised for a very long time the need for employment conditions and remuneration practices that reward and motivate the company's senior executives around the world in line with prevailing market conditions and the interests of our shareholders. In 1980, BOC was one of the first companies in Britain to establish a board committee, the management resources committee (MRC), to review and set executive employment conditions and remuneration. It comprises all of the board's non-executive directors and meets at least six times a year. Neither the chairman nor any executive director sits on the committee, although the chief executive and the chairman are brought in from time to time for discussions on senior executive remuneration.

The main function of the committee is to set the company's overall policy on executive employment conditions and remuneration, and to decide the specific remuneration, benefits and terms of employment for each executive director, including the chief executive and a number of other senior executives.

The committee also determines the remuneration of the chairman. The remuneration of other non-executive directors is determined by the board as a whole, based on outside advice and a review of current practices in other companies.

Remuneration policy

Our remuneration policy for senior executives reflects the global and competitive nature of our businesses. BOC is one of only a handful of truly global companies based in the UK. We manufacture in some 60 countries and sell our products in many more. Our technology, developed in many different parts of the world, is exploited on every continent. BOC's most senior executives all have significant international business experience. Our executive remuneration policy objectives are:

- to ensure that individual rewards and incentives are directly aligned with the performance of the company and the interests of the shareholders; and
- to maintain a competitive programme which enables the company to attract and retain the highest calibre executives.

Basic conditions and contracts of employment are fairly standard and are described below. However, to determine the elements and levels of remuneration appropriate to an individual executive, the committee draws on a wide variety of data. This includes professional advice from outside the company, and a number of national and international surveys on executive pay and conditions. Size, complexity, competitiveness, international spread and key financial ratios form the basis of these survey comparisons. Another key factor in determining an executive's remuneration is of course individual performance.

The typical elements of the remuneration 'package' for BOC's executive directors and other senior executives are: basic salary, allowances and benefits, the possibility of an annual 'variable compensation' bonus based on performance, participation in a long-term incentive plan relating to share price performance, and pension benefits.

Taking all of this into account, a high performing executive in BOC can expect to be in the top 50 per cent, and in exceptional cases in the top 25 per cent, of the range for comparable jobs in other companies.

Basic salary and benefits

Salaries are reviewed annually in the context of individual and business performance, external salary surveys and internal BOC relativities. Remuneration for executives in those of our businesses outside the UK is normally denominated in the local currency. Overseas allowances are paid to certain executives whilst on international assignment.

Variable compensation

As part of the overall objective to provide a competitive senior management reward programme, the Group operates a variable compensation award plan. This plan establishes a clear link between the success of the business and an individual's annual bonus. Furthermore, the plan ensures that the individual's personal objectives derive from BOC's strategic priorities.

The level of payments depends upon the performance of the Group, its constituent businesses and the individual concerned. Targets are set annually by the committee and include financial and other strategic objectives.

The measures for 1997 were internal financial targets for earnings growth and return on capital employed. Both the targets and actual performance are expressed at constant exchange rates to avoid undue benefit or penalty from the translation impact of currency movements. The individual's personal performance against strategic business goals was also a key component in the calculation.

For 1997, bonus awards for executive directors were made to reflect performance against the above criteria. Bonus scales are reviewed from time to time by the committee to take account of prevailing market practices.

Annual bonus awards are included in the directors' remuneration for the year. The table on page 57 shows the bonus earned in 1997 and payable in 1998.

Long-term incentives

The board firmly believes that long-term incentive programmes increase the focus of our key managers on sustaining company performance and provide a strong incentive for retaining and attracting high calibre individuals.

Since 1995, BOC has operated a share option programme for senior executives, including executive directors, which utilises both newly issued shares and purchased shares. Under the terms of all the grants made since 1995 no exercise can be made by any executive unless BOC's share price outperforms the FTSE 100 index. Performance preconditions will always form a part of our executive share option programme.

In 1997, the MRC conducted a full review of its long-term incentive policy, having particular regard to the prevalence of new long-term incentive plans being introduced in a number of UK companies. After careful consideration, the MRC has decided that the existing share option programme remains the most appropriate way to align senior executive remuneration with shareholder interests.

The option programme enables executives to participate in share price growth. The options have a ten year life and the earliest that they can be exercised is three years from the date of grant. They provide a long-term incentive to achieve company performance that is directly linked with the fortunes of BOC shareholders. Grants of share options are at the market price of the company's shares at the time of grant. They are not issued at a discount to the market.

The grant policy adopted by the company for the executive directors is an annual grant based on a multiple of between one and two times the average salary of this group of individuals. Deviations from this policy are made from time to time to reflect promotions, position in the marketplace and performance.

BOC executives have also, in the past, received awards under a share incentive unit plan which is described more fully on page 61.

Retirement benefits

BOC has a number of different retirement programmes appropriate to the different countries in which we operate. Pension entitlements for our executives vary according to local competitive market practices, length of service and age. Details of individual arrangements for executive directors are given on page 58.

To supplement their company pensions US executives may make additional provision for their retirement by participating in the company sponsored Savings Investment Plan, which is available to all employees. In this plan their contribution of up to six per cent of salary is matched by a 50 per cent company contribution to a maximum of three per cent of salary. Any contribution above six per cent is not matched.

Service contracts

All executive directors have terms of service which can be terminated by the company on not more than two years' notice, and by the individual director on six months' notice. This is in line with current market practice. It provides directors with a reasonable degree of security, thus enabling them to concentrate on the challenges involved in securing the long-term future of the Group.

The management resources committee considers carefully any arrangements for early termination to ensure that failure is not 'rewarded'.

Directors' individual remuneration

Details of the directors' individual remuneration, share options, share incentive units and other share holdings are given on pages 57 to 61.

Compliance

The company has complied with Section A of the best practice provisions annexed to the Listing Rules of the London Stock Exchange and the management resources committee confirms that it has given full consideration to section B of these provisions in framing its remuneration policy.

Craig Tedmon Chairman
Management resources committee
Windlesham, 28 November 1997

Remuneration and interests

a) Directors' remuneration	1997	1996
i) Charged against profit in the year	£'000	£'000
Salaries and benefits	**2,139**	2,444
Annual bonuses – paid in the year[1]	**–**	850
– payable[1]	**803**	713
Fees to non-executive directors	**148**	157
Amounts paid to a third party for a non-executive director's services	**28**	25
	3,118	4,189
Company pension contributions to money purchase schemes	**34**	33
Company pension contributions to defined benefit schemes	**632**	500
Company pension contributions overprovided in previous years	**–**	(467)
Provision for share incentive scheme[2]	**1,675**	1,722
Payments to former directors and their dependants[3] – pensions	**174**	303
– other	**303**	290
	5,936	6,570

The retirement benefits accruing to each of the directors are described on page 58.

1. For the year ended 30 September 1996, profit was charged with the bonus payable in addition to the bonus paid in respect of the previous year. Thereafter the bonus charged is in respect of the bonus for the year.

2. Provisions are made for payments which may be made to directors or former directors under the share incentive unit scheme. Provisions are charged to operating profit over the period before the payments are determined, or entitlement arises, and are based on expected increases in the company's share price. The amount provided at 30 September 1997 was £7.4 million (1996: £12.3 million). This year, payments totalling £7.2 million were made to past directors (1996: £2.6 million), which were provided for in previous years.

3. This represents pensions and other payments to former directors and/or their dependants which were not provided for in previous years. Total pension payments to former directors made in the year and previously provided for were nil (1996: £3.0 million).

4. The aggregate remuneration charged against profit for directors and members of the executive management board in the year was £9.3 million. Remuneration of members of the executive management board other than directors is given in b) on page 59.

| ii) Individual remuneration | Year ended 30 September 1997 | | | | 1996 |
	Basic salary/fees £'000	Allowances and benefits[1] £'000	Bonus payable[2] £'000	Total remun- eration £'000	Total remuneration £'000
Chairman					
D G John[3]	349	65	–	414	316
Executive directors					
Dr D Chatterji	225	18	111	354	357
S Ghasemi[4]	260	15	156	431	353
A E Isaac	252	78	140	470	365
F D Rosenkranz	439	20	255	714	623
Dr R G Stoll	319	99	141	559	603
Non-executive directors					
D E Baird	25	–	–	25	25
R F Chase[5]	28	–	–	28	25
H C Groome	25	–	–	25	6
C P King	22	–	–	22	–
J H Macdonald	30	–	–	30	30
Dr C S Tedmon	30	–	–	30	29
Directors who retired during the year[6]					
R Malpas	8	–	–	8	30
Lord Tugendhat	8	–	–	8	30
Total	**2,020**	**295**	**803**	**3,118**	**2,792**

1. Includes overseas and relocation expenses.

2. The bonus is that payable for the year ended 30 September 1997.

3. 1996 includes fees paid prior to his appointment as chairman.

4. Mr Ghasemi was appointed to the board on 10 July 1996. The remuneration for 1996 is his total remuneration for the year.

5. Paid to Mr Chase's employers.

6. Directors who also served during the year but ceased to be directors prior to 30 September 1997.

Mr John was appointed chairman on 19 January 1996. His remuneration for 1996 from that date was £308,500. Provision for his pension in the year was £161,000 (1996: £67,000). He does not participate in the variable compensation plan.

Mr Rosenkranz was the highest paid director in 1997 with remuneration as shown above. Contributions for his pension amounted to £50,000 (1996: £90,000).

Dr Stoll has a relocation loan with the overseas Group subsidiary which employs him. This loan was made to him as part of his joining arrangements in 1991, prior to his appointment as a director. It is repayable over the next four years and the balance at 30 September 1997 was £93,000.

Non-executive directors do not participate in the Group's incentive programmes, nor is their remuneration pensionable. They are paid at the rate of £25,000 per annum, plus a further fee of £5,000 where they act as chairman of a board committee.

iii) Pensions

Dr D Chatterji, age 53: Pension is covered under the US cash balance retirement plan and the US senior executive pension plan, which, in combination, entitle Dr Chatterji to a lump sum benefit on retirement at age 60 equivalent to a pension of approximately 32 per cent of final base salary.

S Ghasemi, age 53: Pension is covered under the US cash balance retirement plan and the US senior executive pension plan, which, in combination, entitle Mr Ghasemi to a lump sum benefit on retirement at age 60 equivalent to a pension of approximately 38 per cent of final base salary.

A E Isaac, age 56: Pension to contractual retirement age 60 is being funded in the UK through a combination of tax-approved personal pension plan and funded unapproved retirement benefit scheme, which is underpinned by a guarantee for which provision is being made in the accounts.

D G John, age 59: Pension to contractual retirement age 65 is a defined benefit unfunded arrangement for which provision is being made in the accounts.

F D Rosenkranz, age 52: Pension benefits are funded under the UK senior executive pension scheme. On retirement at age 60, he will be entitled to a pension of two-thirds of his final 12 months' salary.

Dr R G Stoll, age 55: Pension is covered under the US cash balance retirement plan and a contractual retirement commitment. On retirement at 62, he will be entitled to a pension of up to 50 per cent of the three year average base salary.

| | | Defined benefit plans | | | | Defined contribution plans |
| | | Deferred benefit at 30 September 1997 | | Increase in year net of inflation £'000 | Increase in transfer value less members contributions £'000 | Company contributions in year £'000 |
		Pension £'000	Lump sum £'000			
UK-based directors						
A E Isaac	1997	–	599	197	147	–
	1996	–	394	198	128	–
D G John	1997	18	–	10	143	–
	1996	8	–	8	100	–
F D Rosenkranz	1997	222	–	28	351	–
	1996	190	–	73	793	–
US-based directors						
Dr D Chatterji	1997	–	307	134	134	10
	1996	–	170	31	31	10
S Ghasemi	1997	–	359	190	190	11
	1996	–	167	31	31	10
Dr R G Stoll	1997	64	–	14	164	14
	1996	51	–	13	125	14

The transfer value equivalent excludes directors' contributions and has been calculated in accordance with Actuarial Guidance Note GN11.

b) Executive officers

The aggregate remuneration of members of the executive management board, other than directors, for services in all capacities during 1997 was as follows:

Charged against profit in the year	1997 £'000
Salaries and benefits	**1,940**
Annual bonuses	**764**
Provision for share incentive scheme	**334**
Company pension contributions	**304**
	3,342

Members of the executive management board, other than directors, had the following aggregate beneficial interests in the company's securities: 38,156 Ordinary shares; 1,394,373 share options; and rights to 375,000 share incentive units.

c) Directors' interests

i) Directors' interests at 30 September 1997

The directors of the company and their families had the following beneficial interests in the company's securities and rights under the share incentive scheme:

	At 30 September 1997			At 1 October 1996		
	Ordinary shares	Share options	Share incentive units	Ordinary shares	Share options	Share incentive units
D E Baird	**5,000**	**–**	**–**	5,000	–	–
R F Chase	**2,097**	**–**	**–**	2,036	–	–
Dr D Chatterji	**2,108**	**222,713**	**155,000**	2,108	172,713	205,000
S Ghasemi	**515**	**290,000**	**30,000**	500	240,000	30,000
H C Groome	**900**	**–**	**–**	500	–	–
A E Isaac	**700**	**197,357**	**45,000**	700	147,357	45,000
D G John	**1,484**	**225,000**	**–**	548	150,000	–
C P King	**1,000**	**–**	**–**	–	–	–
J H Macdonald	**1,228**	**–**	**–**	1,192	–	–
F D Rosenkranz	**31,797**	**496,508**	**200,000**	29,566	372,835	215,000
Dr R G Stoll	**500**	**215,000**	**142,500**	500	215,000	142,500
Dr C S Tedmon	**6,850**	**–**	**–**	6,646	–	–

There has been no change in the interest of any of the directors between 1 October 1997 and 17 November 1997. Options are granted over Ordinary shares of 25p each under senior executive and general employee share option schemes.

Apart from the above and service agreements, no director has had any material interest in any contract with the company or its subsidiaries requiring disclosure under the Companies Act 1985.

The aggregate beneficial interests in the company's securities of both directors and members of the executive management board was 92,335 Ordinary shares and 3,040,951 share options.

ii) Directors' interests – average prices and movements

The movements in the numbers and weighted average price of directors' share options and share incentive units are shown below. To recognise the different nature of the options and incentive units, they are shown separately, together with a description of the terms under which they may be exercised. The company's Register of Directors' Interests which is available for inspection in accordance with the Companies Act 1985, contains full details of directors' shareholdings and options. The Ordinary share price at 30 September 1997 was 1,101p and during the year ranged from a high of 1,172p to a low of 828p.

| | Exercised during the year | | | | Grants during the year | |
Share options – movements	Number	Weighted average exercise price (pence)	Weighted average market price at date of exercise (pence)	Gain on exercise £'000	Number	Weighted average price (pence)
Dr D Chatterji	–	–	–	–	50,000	980
S Ghasemi	–	–	–	–	50,000	980
A E Isaac	–	–	–	–	50,000	980
D G John	–	–	–	–	75,000	980
F D Rosenkranz	1,327	565	1,011	6	125,000	980
Dr R G Stoll	50,000	638	994	178	50,000	980

The total gains made by directors on options exercised during the year was £184,000 (1996: £225,000).

| | Rights at 30 September 1997 | | | | |
| | Currently exercisable* | | Not yet exercisable | | |
Share options – year end	Number	Weighted average price (pence)	Number	Weighted average price (pence)	Number with performance condition attached
Dr D Chatterji	70,000	662	152,713	870	150,000
S Ghasemi	90,000	580	200,000	883	200,000
A E Isaac	–	–	197,357	837	150,000
D G John	–	–	225,000	939	225,000
F D Rosenkranz	70,000	662	426,508	913	425,000
Dr R G Stoll	65,000	638	150,000	874	150,000

*No performance condition attached.

Options granted up to 1994 are not normally exercisable until they have been held for four years. Grants thereafter are not normally exercisable until a performance condition has been met and they have been held for three years. No directors' options lapsed during the year.

Share incentive units	Cash on deposit at 1 October 1996 £'000	Gain converted to cash in year[1] £'000	Paid in year £'000	At 30 September 1997		
				Cash on deposit and not yet paid £'000	Units not yet converted	
					Number of units	Weighted average price (pence)
Current directors:						
Dr D Chatterji	46	262	(47)	261	155,000	577
S Ghasemi	–	–	–	–	30,000	677
A E Isaac	–	–	–	–	45,000	716
F D Rosenkranz	–	73	(73)	–	200,000	555
Dr R G Stoll	289	16	(73)	232	142,500	655
Former directors:						
P G Bosonnet	–	511	–	511	–	–
A P Dyer	253	678	(265)	666	650,000	605
R V Giordano	6,830	106	(6,936)	–	–	–
P J-J Rich	–	676	–	676	175,000	536

1. The amounts shown as converted to cash in the year include interest earned from the date of conversion.

The share incentive unit plan provides for cash payments to executives based on increases in the share price over a period of up to eight years from the time of grant. Grants under the plan were made between 1989 and 1995 to supplement or substitute for grants under the share option schemes. No grants have been made since 1995.

Executives may elect to convert share incentive units to cash provided that the units have been held for three years. The fixed cash sum, determined by reference to the share price on the date of election over and above the original grant price, will earn interest at one per cent above the Midland Bank base rate. A full cash payment can only be received by an executive after eight years but limited early payments may be made in certain circumstances between the fourth and eighth years, at the discretion of the management resources committee. The plan includes significant forfeiture penalties in the event that an executive leaves the company other than on retirement before the expiration of the eight year period.

On normal retirement, or earlier at the discretion of the management resources committee, an executive will normally continue to participate in the scheme so long as he observes a non-compete covenant in favour of the company. Full payment will be made at the eighth anniversary or earlier at the discretion of the management resources committee.

Former directors were granted their share incentive units when they were executive directors of the company.

Responsibility of the directors
For preparation of the financial statements

Company law requires the directors to prepare financial statements for each financial year which give a true and fair view of the state of affairs of the company and of the Group at the end of the year and of the profit or loss for the year. In preparing those financial statements, the directors are required to:

- select suitable accounting policies and then apply them consistently;
- make judgements and estimates that are reasonable and prudent;
- state whether applicable accounting standards have been followed, subject to any material departures disclosed and explained in the financial statements;
- prepare the financial statements on the going concern basis unless it is inappropriate to presume that the Group will continue in business.

The directors confirm that the financial statements comply with the above requirements.

The directors are responsible for keeping proper accounting records which disclose with reasonable accuracy at any time the financial position of the company and enable them to ensure that the financial statements comply with the Companies Act 1985. The directors also have general responsibility for taking reasonable steps to safeguard the assets of the Group and to prevent and detect fraud and other irregularities.

Report of the auditors
To the members of The BOC Group plc

We have audited the financial statements on pages 64 to 99. We have also examined the amounts disclosed relating to remuneration, share options and long term incentive scheme interests of the directors which form part of the report of the management resources committee on pages 56 to 61.

Respective responsibilities of directors and auditors
The consolidated financial statements are the responsibility of the company's directors. It is our responsibility to form an independent opinion, based on our audit, on those statements and to report our opinion to you.

Basis of opinion
We conducted our audit in accordance with generally accepted auditing standards in the UK which are substantially the same as those generally accepted in the US. An audit includes examination, on a test basis, of evidence relevant to the amounts and disclosures in the financial statements. It also includes an assessment of the significant estimates and judgements made by the directors in the preparation of the financial statements and of whether the accounting policies are appropriate to the company's circumstances, consistently applied and adequately disclosed.

We planned and performed our audit so as to obtain all the information and explanations which we considered necessary in order to provide us with sufficient evidence to give reasonable assurance that the financial statements are free from material misstatement, whether caused by fraud or other irregularity or error. In forming our opinion we also evaluated the overall adequacy of the presentation of information in the financial statements.

Opinion
In our opinion, the financial statements referred to above: a) give a true and fair view of the state of affairs of the company and of the Group at 30 September 1997 and of the profit, total recognised gains and losses and cash flows of the Group for the year then ended and have been properly prepared in accordance with the Companies Act 1985; b) present fairly, in all material respects, the consolidated financial position of the Group at 30 September 1997 and 1996 and the consolidated results of its operations and cash flows for each of the three years in the period ended 30 September 1997, in conformity with UK generally accepted accounting principles. These differ in certain respects from those generally accepted in the US. The effects of the major differences in the determination of profit before tax and shareholders' funds are shown in note 16 to the financial statements.

Coopers & Lybrand
Chartered accountants and registered auditors
London, 28 November 1997

Group profit and loss account
Years ended 30 September

	Notes	**1997** **£ million**	1996 £ million	1995 £ million
Turnover				
Continuing operations		**3,929.9**	4,014.4	3,704.8
Acquisitions		**33.7**	5.1	47.1
Turnover, including share of associated				
undertakings	1(a)	**3,963.6**	4,019.5	3,751.9
Less associated undertakings' turnover		**285.9**	267.4	208.0
Turnover of subsidiary undertakings		**3,677.7**	3,752.1	3,543.9
Cost of sales	2(a)	**(2,105.5)**	(2,115.5)	(1,986.6)
Gross profit		**1,572.2**	1,636.6	1,557.3
Net operating expenses	2(a)	**(1,093.4)**	(1,154.7)	(1,106.3)
Operating profit				
Continuing operations		**478.5**	481.7	447.7
Acquisitions		**0.3**	0.2	3.3
Profit of subsidiary undertakings		**478.8**	481.9	451.0
Share of profit of associated undertakings		**61.6**	57.5	45.4
Operating profit	1(b)	**540.4**	539.4	496.4
Interest (net)	3(a)	**(95.2)**	(94.5)	(94.2)
Profit on ordinary activities before tax		**445.2**	444.9	402.2
Tax on profit on ordinary activities	4(a)	**(129.1)**	(137.9)	(128.6)
Profit on ordinary activities after tax		**316.1**	307.0	273.6
Minority interests		**(28.5)**	(28.7)	(24.6)
Profit for the financial year		**287.6**	278.3	249.0
Dividends including non-equity	12(a)	**(140.4)**	(130.1)	(118.8)
Surplus for the financial year		**147.2**	148.2	130.2
Earnings per 25p Ordinary share, net basis, undiluted	2(c)	**59.31p**	57.74p	51.97p

Group balance sheet
At 30 September

	Notes	1997 £ million	1996 £ million
Fixed assets			
Tangible assets	7	**2,953.7**	2,747.6
Intangible assets	8	**28.8**	33.4
Investment in own shares	9	**24.0**	22.6
Other investments	9	**295.5**	263.7
		3,302.0	3,067.3
Current assets			
Stocks	10(a)	**354.3**	403.4
Debtors due within one year	10(b)	**901.7**	906.1
Investments		**16.7**	7.7
Deposits and cash due within one year	10(c)	**222.2**	155.8
Assets due beyond one year	10(d)	**101.9**	95.7
Current assets		**1,596.8**	1,568.7
Current liabilities			
Creditors: amounts due within one year			
Borrowings and finance leases	10(e)	**(620.4)**	(623.1)
Other creditors	10(f)	**(886.2)**	(911.9)
Current liabilities		**(1,506.6)**	(1,535.0)
Net current assets		**90.2**	33.7
Total assets *less* current liabilities		**3,392.2**	3,101.0
Long-term liabilities			
Creditors: amounts due beyond one year			
Borrowings and finance leases	11(a)	**(1,001.2)**	(767.4)
Other creditors		**(23.5)**	(26.3)
Provisions for liabilities and charges	11(b)	**(229.7)**	(245.8)
		(1,254.4)	(1,039.5)
Total net assets		**2,137.8**	2,061.5
Capital and reserves			
Called up share capital			
– equity capital	12(b)	**121.8**	120.8
– non-equity capital	12(b)	**2.5**	2.5
Share premium account	12(c)	**272.4**	259.4
Revaluation reserves	12(c)	**63.8**	71.9
Profit and loss account	12(c)	**1,320.7**	1,252.5
Associated undertakings' reserves	12(c)	**111.6**	111.6
Shareholders' funds		**1,892.8**	1,818.7
Minority shareholders' interests		**245.0**	242.8
Total capital and reserves		**2,137.8**	2,061.5

The financial statements were approved by the board of directors on 28 November 1997 and are signed on its behalf by:

Danny Rosenkranz Director   **J Howard Macdonald** Director

Group cash flow statement
Years ended 30 September

	Notes	**1997** **£ million**	1996 £ million	1995 £ million
Net cash inflow from operating activities	14(a)	**733.8**	625.1	647.4
Returns on investments and servicing of finance				
Interest paid		**(113.3)**	(108.9)	(107.8)
Interest received		**15.9**	23.5	14.4
Dividends paid to minorities in subsidiaries		**(6.3)**	(5.9)	(9.3)
Interest element of finance lease rental payments		**(0.2)**	(0.4)	(0.7)
Preference dividends paid		**(0.1)**	(0.1)	(0.1)
Returns on investments and servicing of finance		**(104.0)**	(91.8)	(103.5)
Tax paid		**(109.5)**	(115.8)	(105.8)
Capital expenditure and financial investment				
Purchases of tangible fixed assets		**(650.8)**	(533.6)	(407.4)
Sales of tangible fixed assets		**34.5**	47.1	36.7
Purchases of current asset investments		**(9.0)**	(4.7)	–
Capital expenditure and financial investment		**(625.3)**	(491.2)	(370.7)
Acquisitions and disposals				
Acquisitions of businesses	15(a)	**(31.7)**	(25.8)	(49.9)
Net cash/(overdrafts) acquired with subsidiaries		**0.5**	0.2	(11.8)
Disposals of businesses	15(a)	**23.8**	13.8	28.7
Net overdrafts disposed of with subsidiaries		**–**	2.0	–
Investments in associated undertakings		**(26.3)**	(12.1)	(2.5)
Acquisitions of intangibles		**(1.2)**	(3.9)	–
Purchases of trade investments		**(13.4)**	(4.9)	(11.8)
Sales of other investments		**9.7**	17.0	9.9
Acquisitions and disposals		**(38.6)**	(13.7)	(37.4)
Equity dividends paid		**(121.5)**	(121.1)	(111.3)
Net cash outflow before use of liquid resources and financing		**(265.1)**	(208.5)	(81.3)
Management of liquid resources				
Net (purchase)/sale of short-term investments		**(62.3)**	(19.8)	0.2
Financing				
Issue of shares		**22.1**	20.7	7.6
Increase in debt	14(d)	**342.1**	182.2	103.3
Net cash inflow from financing		**364.2**	202.9	110.9
Increase/(decrease) in cash		**36.8**	(25.4)	29.8

A reconciliation of the increase/(decrease) in cash to the movement in net debt in the year is given in note 14b).

Total recognised gains and losses
Years ended 30 September

	Notes	**1997** **£ million**	1996 £ million	1995 £ million
Parent[1]		**365.9**	38.8	145.6
Subsidiary undertakings		**(95.3)**	235.6	88.3
Associated undertakings		**17.0**	24.8	16.1
Goodwill written off on disposal of subsidiary undertakings	15(b)	**–**	(20.9)	(1.0)
Profit for the financial year		**287.6**	278.3	249.0
Unrealised deficit on revaluations		**–**	(0.7)	(1.3)
Exchange translation effect on:				
– results for the year		**(4.0)**	(3.2)	(0.3)
– foreign currency net investments		**(89.8)**	(13.7)	20.7
Total recognised gains and losses for the year	12(c)	**193.8**	260.7	268.1

1. In accordance with the concession granted under the Companies Act 1985, the profit and loss account of The BOC Group plc has not been presented separately in these financial statements.

2. Profit attributable to the parent company includes dividends received from subsidiary and associated undertakings, often through intermediate holding companies. These dividends may include the distribution of earnings of previous periods. As a result, the relationship of profit between parent, subsidiary and associated undertakings may show fluctuations from year to year.

Movement in shareholders' funds
Years ended 30 September

	1997 **£ million**	1996 £ million	1995 £ million
Profit for the financial year	**287.6**	278.3	249.0
Dividends	**(140.4)**	(130.1)	(118.8)
	147.2	148.2	130.2
Other recognised gains and losses	**(93.8)**	(17.6)	19.1
Goodwill:			
– taken to reserves on acquisitions	**(9.2)**	(6.8)	(19.5)
– reversal of write-off through profit and loss account on disposals	**–**	20.9	1.0
Shares issued	**11.1**	9.6	7.6
Scrip dividends	**18.8**	8.8	7.4
Net increase in shareholders' funds for the year	**74.1**	163.1	145.8
Shareholders' funds at 1 October	**1,818.7**	1,655.6	1,509.8
Shareholders' funds at 30 September	**1,892.8**	1,818.7	1,655.6

Balance sheet of The BOC Group plc
At 30 September

	Notes	1997 £ million	1996 £ million
Fixed assets			
Tangible assets	7(d)	**29.1**	29.5
Investments	9(d)	**1,878.7**	1,580.5
		1,907.8	1,610.0
Current assets			
Debtors due within one year	10(b)	**155.2**	24.9
Deposits and cash	10(c)	**34.3**	9.8
Assets due beyond one year	10(d)	**43.5**	48.8
Current assets		**233.0**	83.5
Current liabilities			
Creditors: amounts due within one year			
Borrowings and finance leases	10(e)	**(147.1)**	(99.0)
Other creditors	10(f)	**(66.1)**	(66.4)
Current liabilities		**(213.2)**	(165.4)
Net current assets/(liabilities)		**19.8**	(81.9)
Total assets *less* current liabilities		**1,927.6**	1,528.1
Long-term liabilities			
Creditors: amounts due beyond one year			
Borrowings and finance leases	11(a)	**(499.2)**	(353.2)
Other creditors		**(4.8)**	(6.7)
		(504.0)	(359.9)
Total net assets		**1,423.6**	1,168.2
Capital and reserves			
Called up share capital			
– equity capital	12(b)	**121.8**	120.8
– non-equity capital	12(b)	**2.5**	2.5
Share premium account	12(d)	**272.4**	259.4
Other reserves	12(d)	**9.4**	9.4
Profit and loss account	12(d)	**1,017.5**	776.1
Total capital and reserves		**1,423.6**	1,168.2

The financial statements were approved by the board of directors on 28 November 1997 and are signed on its behalf by:

Danny Rosenkranz Director   **J Howard Macdonald** Director

Accounting policies

General
- **Accounting convention** These accounts are based on the historical cost accounting convention including the revaluation of certain land and buildings and comply with all applicable UK accounting standards.

  UK accounting standards differ in certain respects from those generally accepted in the US and the major effects of these differences in the determination of profit before tax and shareholders' funds are shown in note 16 to the financial statements. Disclosure requirements of both the UK and US are incorporated throughout the notes to these financial statements.

- **Basis of consolidation** The Group accounts include the accounts of the parent undertaking and of all subsidiary and associated undertakings.

  Acquisitions are included from the date of acquisition. Goodwill on acquisitions, being the excess of the fair value of the purchase price over the fair value of net assets acquired, is taken to reserves.

  Results of businesses discontinued are included in the results for the year up to the date of relinquishing control and analysed as discontinued operations; prior years' analyses are restated to reflect those businesses as discontinued. Profit or loss on disposal of businesses includes the surplus over net asset value and the write-off of related goodwill. There is a corresponding credit to reserves for the goodwill which had already been taken to reserves on acquisition.

- **Exchange** Profit and loss and other period statements of the Group's overseas operations are translated at average rates of exchange. Assets and liabilities denominated in foreign currencies are translated at the rates of exchange ruling at the financial year end. Assets or liabilities swapped into other currencies are accounted for in those currencies.

  Exchange differences are dealt with as a movement in reserves where they arise from the translation of the opening net assets of overseas operations, the retranslation of retained earnings of overseas operations from average to closing rates of exchange and the translation or conversion of foreign currency borrowings taken to hedge overseas assets.

  All other exchange differences, both realised and unrealised, are taken to the profit and loss account. The principal exchange rates affecting the Group are shown on page 48.

Turnover
Turnover is based on the invoiced value of sales and includes the sales value of long-term contracts appropriate to the state of completion. It excludes sales between Group undertakings, VAT and similar sales-based taxes.

Operating profit
Operating profit reflects the results of the activities of the various businesses which constituted the Group during the year.
- Revenue expenditure on research and development is written off when incurred.
- The results of certain subsidiary and associated undertakings operating in countries subject to hyperinflation are adjusted to reflect the falling value of monetary assets and liabilities.

Retirement benefits
The regular cost of providing benefits is charged to operating profit over the employees' service lives on the basis of a constant percentage of earnings. Variations from regular cost, arising from periodic actuarial valuations, are allocated to operating profit over the expected remaining service lives of current employees on the basis of a constant percentage of current and estimated future earnings.

Tangible fixed assets

No depreciation is charged on freehold land or construction in progress. Depreciation is charged on all other fixed assets on the straight line basis over the effective lives except for certain tonnage plants where depreciation is calculated on an annuity basis over the life of the contract.

Straight line depreciation rates vary according to the class of asset, but are typically:

	per annum
Freehold property	2%- 4%
Leasehold property (or at higher rates based on the life of the lease)	2%- 4%
Plant and machinery	7%-10%
Cylinders	4%-10%
Motor vehicles	7%-20%
Computer hardware and major software	25%

- Land and buildings are revalued periodically. The basis of valuation for non-specialised property is existing use value, and for specialised property is depreciated replacement cost.
- Interest costs on major fixed asset additions are capitalised during the construction period and written off as part of the total cost.
- Where finance leases have been entered into, the obligations to the lessor are shown as part of borrowings and the rights in the corresponding assets are treated in the same way as owned fixed assets.

Intangible fixed assets

Material intangibles acquired, such as patents and trademarks, are capitalised and written off over their effective economic lives.

Stocks

Stocks and work in progress are valued at the lower of cost and net realisable value. Cost where appropriate includes a proportion of overhead expenses. Work in progress is stated at cost less progress payments received or receivable. Cost is arrived at principally on the average and 'first-in, first-out' (FIFO) basis.

Deferred tax

Deferred tax is provided on the liability method in respect of:
- the excess of capital allowances over historical cost depreciation and
- other timing differences and exposures

where, in the opinion of the directors, the potential tax liability is likely to become payable in the foreseeable future.

Financial derivatives

Interest rate and currency swaps are used only as balance sheet hedging instruments and included in net borrowings. Cash flows are shown as part of 'returns on investments and servicing of finance'. Exchange differences arising on the notional principal of these swaps during their life and at termination or maturity are dealt with as a movement on reserves, as described above (see Exchange). Forward contracts are used to hedge currency flows and are not included in the financial statements until realised.

No adjustment is made in the financial statements to account for derivatives at market value but appropriate disclosure is made in the notes to the financial statements, based on relevant guidance from both UK and US accounting and regulatory bodies.

The Group's approach to the use of derivatives in the management of risk is outlined in the finance and treasury review.

Notes to the financial statements

1. Segmental information

a) Turnover

	Gases and related products £ million	Vacuum technology £ million	Distribution services £ million	Health care £ million	Total by origin £ million	Total by destination £ million
1997						
Europe	**659.3**	**109.4**	**287.9**	**161.3**	**1,217.9**	**1,058.7**
Americas	**805.0**	**202.6**	–	**262.9**	**1,270.5**	**1,484.0**
Africa	**341.0**	–	–	–	**341.0**	**341.0**
Asia/Pacific	**1,024.6**	**55.0**	**1.4**	**53.2**	**1,134.2**	**1,079.9**
Turnover[1]	**2,829.9**	**367.0**	**289.3**	**477.4**	**3,963.6**	**3,963.6**
1996						
Europe	642.9	122.9	282.5	181.0	1,229.3	1,150.3
Americas	754.7	211.1	–	259.5	1,225.3	1,217.7
Africa	354.4	–	–	–	354.4	360.5
Asia/Pacific	1,062.2	82.9	–	65.4	1,210.5	1,291.0
Turnover[1]	2,814.2	416.9	282.5	505.9	4,019.5	4,019.5
1995						
Europe	589.5	96.7	263.2	180.6	1,130.0	1,083.7
Americas	696.5	170.9	–	278.5	1,145.9	1,113.0
Africa	337.0	–	–	–	337.0	341.4
Asia/Pacific	1,009.1	61.7	–	68.2	1,139.0	1,213.8
Turnover[1]	2,632.1	329.3	263.2	527.3	3,751.9	3,751.9

b) Business analysis

	Gases and related products £ million	Vacuum technology £ million	Distribution services £ million	Health care £ million	Corporate £ million	Total £ million
1997						
Operating profit[1]	**415.6**	**53.1**	**31.9**	**44.5**	**(4.7)**	**540.4**
Capital employed[2]	**3,109.2**	**175.1**	**137.5**	**344.5**	–	**3,766.3**
Capital expenditure[3]	**749.4**	**22.5**	**29.0**	**21.0**	**3.4**	**825.3**
Depreciation and amortisation	**216.5**	**12.8**	**22.7**	**21.1**	**3.4**	**276.5**
1996						
Operating profit[1]	408.3	62.4	27.9	53.1	(12.3)	539.4
Capital employed[2]	2,929.0	163.4	147.0	331.7	(6.9)	3,564.2
Capital expenditure[3]	631.5	25.4	30.1	26.6	4.1	717.7
Depreciation and amortisation	209.0	10.5	22.9	24.5	1.8	268.7
1995						
Operating profit[1]	374.2	46.6	23.9	59.8	(8.1)	496.4
Capital employed[2]	2,633.9	149.4	150.8	322.4	(15.0)	3,241.5
Capital expenditure[3]	438.2	16.8	35.8	19.1	2.5	512.4
Depreciation and amortisation	197.3	9.0	22.3	25.7	2.2	256.5

1. Gases and related products includes Group share of associated undertakings' turnover of £285.9 million (1996: £267.4 million, 1995: £208.0 million) and Group share of operating profit of associated undertakings of £60.8 million (1996: £57.5 million, 1995: £45.4 million).

2. Capital employed comprises the capital and reserves of the Group, its long-term liabilities and all current borrowings net of cash and deposits.

3. Includes capital expenditure of associated undertakings of £149.5 million (1996: £175.4 million, 1995: £103.5 million) mainly in gases and related products and Asia/Pacific region. Partners in associated undertakings account for £84.0 million (1996: £97.3 million, 1995: £60.0 million) with the Group share accounting for £65.5 million (1996: £78.1 million, 1995: £43.5 million).

1. Segmental information continued
c) Regional analysis

	Europe £ million	Americas £ million	Africa £ million	Asia/Pacific £ million	Total £ million
1997					
Operating profit	**228.1**	**88.7**	**63.3**	**160.3**	**540.4**
Capital employed[2]	**1,239.3**	**1,194.7**	**282.0**	**1,050.3**	**3,766.3**
Capital expenditure[3]	**195.7**	**230.5**	**76.0**	**323.1**	**825.3**
1996					
Operating profit	202.0	113.6	66.0	157.8	539.4
Capital employed[2]	1,193.1	1,095.6	232.7	1,042.8	3,564.2
Capital expenditure[3]	167.8	278.4	31.5	240.0	717.7
1995					
Operating profit	167.0	119.1	62.0	148.3	496.4
Capital employed[2]	1,123.8	885.6	241.1	991.0	3,241.5
Capital expenditure[3]	155.1	146.6	33.7	177.0	512.4

d) Significant country analysis

	UK 1997 £ million	1996 £ million	1995 £ million	US 1997 £ million	1996 £ million	1995 £ million
Turnover	**903.0**	898.0	826.4	**1,159.0**	1,117.5	1,059.7
Operating profit	**190.6**	175.4	156.4	**66.3**	79.7	87.7
Capital employed[2]	**988.7**	933.0	903.5	**1,038.8**	926.2	736.1
Capital expenditure[3]	**158.1**	130.0	124.8	**181.5**	229.7	134.0

2, 3. For footnotes see page 71.

2. Profit and loss
a) Analysis of costs

	Continuing operations £ million	Acquisitions £ million	1997 Total £ million	1996 Total £ million	1995 Total £ million
Cost of sales	**(2,079.9)**	**(25.6)**	**(2,105.5)**	(2,115.5)	(1,986.6)
Distribution costs	**(305.2)**	**–**	**(305.2)**	(310.8)	(314.7)
Administrative expenses	**(705.6)**	**(7.8)**	**(713.4)**	(749.8)	(709.9)
Research and development	**(80.6)**	**–**	**(80.6)**	(98.5)	(91.5)
Income from other fixed asset investments	**5.8**	**–**	**5.8**	4.4	9.8
Net operating expenses	**(1,085.6)**	**(7.8)**	**(1,093.4)**	(1,154.7)	(1,106.3)

b) Fees to auditors

	1997 £ million	1996 £ million	1995 £ million
Audit fees (Parent: £0.2 million, 1996: £0.2 million, 1995: £0.2 million)	**1.9**	1.8	1.8
Other fees – UK	**0.6**	0.8	0.3
– rest of world	**0.4**	0.5	0.7
	2.9	3.1	2.8

2. Profit and loss continued
c) Earnings per share
i) Earnings

	1997 £ million	1996 £ million	1995 £ million
Amounts used in computing the earnings per share			
Profit for the financial year	**287.6**	278.3	249.0
Less Preference dividend	**0.1**	0.1	0.1
Earnings attributable to Ordinary shareholders	**287.5**	278.2	248.9

	1997 million	1996 million	1995 million
ii) Average number of 25p Ordinary shares			
Undiluted	**484.8**	481.9	479.0

3. Treasury information
a) Interest (net)

	1997 £ million	1996 £ million	1995 £ million
On borrowings totally repayable within five years	**77.2**	81.3	80.5
On all other borrowings	**35.7**	32.6	36.0
	112.9	113.9	116.5
Interest receivable	**(13.7)**	(17.8)	(25.1)
Interest payable (net)	**99.2**	96.1	91.4
Share of interest of associated undertakings	**7.2**	7.1	6.0
Interest capitalised	**(11.2)**	(8.7)	(3.2)
Interest (net)	**95.2**	94.5	94.2
Interest payable on finance leases	**0.4**	0.7	0.9
Interest payable on borrowings repayable by instalments	**21.3**	15.0	17.2

b) Currency, interest rate and counterparty exposure
The Group's approach to managing currency and interest rate risk and its use of swaps in that process is described in the finance and treasury review.

Interest rate swaps
At 30 September 1997, the Group had entered into 14 interest rate swap agreements with notional principal amounts of £643.3 million (1996: £538.2 million). The swaps' underlying currencies are sterling, US dollars, Japanese yen, Australian dollars and Deutschmarks and have maturity dates of between six months and nine years from 30 September 1997. The following table shows the weighted average interest rates payable and receivable on interest rate swaps at 30 September:

	1997	1996
Average receivable swap rate	**6.55%**	6.28%
Average payable swap rate	**6.32%**	5.96%

The weighted average receivable/payable swap interest rate is calculated by applying the notional swap interest received or paid, using rates applicable at year end, to the notional principal of outstanding swaps at the year end.

Of the notional principal amounts of £643.3 million (1996: £538.2 million), £74.0 million (1996: £135.7 million) is repayable within one year and the repayment profile of the remaining £569.3 million (1996: £402.5 million) is shown in note 3 c) ii).

3. Treasury information continued
Currency swaps
At 30 September 1997, the Group had entered into 16 currency swap agreements with notional
principal amounts of £476.2 million (1996: £323.0 million). The maturity dates range between
five months and seven years from 30 September 1997. The following table illustrates the impact of
the currency swaps on the Group's net debt:

	Capital employed £ million	Gross borrowings £ million	Cash and investments £ million	Net hedges £ million	Adjusted net borrowings £ million
Sterling	1,000.2	(414.0)	58.2	120.8	(235.0)
US dollar	1,063.0	(506.8)	32.7	(70.5)	(544.6)
Australian dollar	242.0	(208.5)	21.6	85.5	(101.4)
South African rand	250.4	(72.8)	2.6	–	(70.2)
Japanese yen	307.2	(65.9)	12.4	(90.1)	(143.6)
Canadian dollar	59.6	(27.7)	1.5	–	(26.2)
Deutschmark	36.6	(70.6)	9.6	45.7	(15.3)
Thai baht	74.6	(47.5)	–	–	(47.5)
Other	732.7	(207.8)	107.7	(91.4)	(191.5)
Total	3,766.3	(1,621.6)	246.3	–	(1,375.3)

The hedges shown above are currency swaps. The average receivable interest rate on these was
6.18 per cent and the average payable interest rate was 5.12 per cent.
  The currency and interest rate exposure of the net borrowings of the Group at 30 September
1997, after taking into account interest rate and currency swaps entered into by the Group, is given
in the table below.

	Fixed rate £ million	Floating rate £ million	1997 Total £ million	1996 Total £ million
Sterling	158.3	76.7	235.0	131.1
US dollar	283.3	261.3	544.6	525.7
Australian dollar	21.1	80.3	101.4	118.2
South African rand	37.0	33.2	70.2	59.2
Japanese yen	118.8	24.8	143.6	145.3
Canadian dollar	1.1	25.1	26.2	28.2
Deutschmark	23.8	(8.5)	15.3	73.0
Thai baht	13.5	34.0	47.5	41.8
Others	67.8	123.7	191.5	108.1
	724.7	650.6	1,375.3	1,230.6

Counterparty risk
The Group is exposed to credit-related losses in the event of non-performance by counterparties
to financial instruments, but does not expect any counterparties to fail to meet their obligations.
There are procedures and policies in place limiting the Group's exposure to concentrations of credit
or country risk.

3. Treasury information continued
c) Borrowings and finance leases
i) Analysis

	Group 1997 £ million	Group 1996 £ million	Parent 1997 £ million	Parent 1996 £ million
Secured				
Industrial Revenue Bond 2008	2.2	2.2	–	–
Finance leases	4.7	6.6	–	–
Other secured borrowings	108.8	77.8	–	–
Unsecured				
12¼% Unsecured Loan Stock 2012/2017	100.0	100.0	100.0	100.0
7¼% Notes 2002	150.0	–	150.0	–
5⅞% Notes 2001	124.2	128.2	124.2	128.2
7.45% Guaranteed Notes 2006	155.2	160.3	–	–
7% Guaranteed Bonds 1997	–	96.2	–	–
Pollution Control and Industrial Bonds 1995/2012	43.1	44.4	–	–
European Investment Bank loans 1996/2003	85.5	59.6	–	–
6.75% Bonds 2004	125.0	125.0	125.0	125.0
Medium-term loans 1999	45.0	50.7	–	–
Commercial paper	391.6	253.6	32.4	–
Other borrowings	286.3	285.9	114.7	99.0
Total borrowings and finance leases	1,621.6	1,390.5	646.3	452.2
Less: Cash and deposits – due within one year	222.2	155.8	34.3	9.8
— due beyond the year	24.1	4.1	–	–
Net borrowings and finance leases	1,375.3	1,230.6	612.0	442.4

A reconciliation of net cash flow to the movement in net debt is given in note 14b).

ii) Maturity

	Group 1997 £ million	Group 1996 £ million	Parent 1997 £ million	Parent 1996 £ million
Long and medium-term bank loans				
Repayable – beyond five years	4.7	11.4	–	–
— two to five years	56.4	102.6	–	–
— one to two years	72.3	26.0	–	–
Loans other than from banks				
Repayable – beyond five years	481.2	445.4	225.0	225.0
— two to five years	357.8	169.3	274.2	128.2
— one to two years	24.7	7.5	–	–
Finance leases				
Repayable beyond one year	4.1	5.2	–	–
Borrowings and finance leases (note 11)	1,001.2	767.4	499.2	353.2
Short-term – repayable within one year				
Bank loans and overdrafts	219.0	264.2	113.5	95.1
Loans other than from banks	400.8	357.5	33.6	3.9
Finance leases	0.6	1.4	–	–
Total borrowings and finance leases	1,621.6	1,390.5	646.3	452.2
Less: Cash and deposits				
Repayable – within one year	222.2	155.8	34.3	9.8
— beyond one year	24.1	4.1	–	–
Net borrowings and finance leases	1,375.3	1,230.6	612.0	442.4
Of the borrowings shown above, the following are repayable by instalments				
Due wholly or in part after five years	85.8	61.8	–	–
Instalments falling due after five years	52.3	17.8	–	–

3. Treasury information continued

	Interest rate swaps		Borrowings and finance leases	
	1997 **£ million**	1996 £ million	**1997** **£ million**	1996 £ million
Repayment profile of interest rate swaps, borrowings and finance leases:				
Long-term repayable – beyond five years	**155.3**	285.3	**489.2**	460.7
Medium-term repayable – four to five years	**306.0**	1.6	**192.3**	23.7
– three to four years	**1.5**	15.9	**180.0**	151.4
– two to three years	**76.4**	21.7	**42.4**	97.4
– one to two years	**30.1**	78.0	**97.3**	34.2
	569.3	402.5	**1,001.2**	767.4

iii) Short term interest rates

The average interest rate on commercial paper at 30 September 1997 was 5.1 per cent and on other short-term borrowings was 9.1 per cent.

iv) Facilities

The Group maintains a number of short and medium-term committed lines of credit. The main medium-term facilities are multi-currency agreements with a group of relationship banks, under which the Group may borrow up to US$420 million (1996: US$420 million) for general corporate purposes. These facilities mature in 2002 and were undrawn both at 30 September 1997 and 30 September 1996.

	1997		1996	
	Carrying amount £ million	**Fair value £ million**	Carrying amount £ million	Fair value £ million
d) Fair value of financial instruments				
Short and long-term borrowings and swap agreements[1]	**(1,399.4)**	**(1,433.8)**	(1,234.7)	(1,242.6)
Long-term investments[2]	**36.9**	**115.7**	44.1	162.1
Long-term receivables[3]	**38.6**	**38.7**	33.4	32.3
Cumulative Preference shares	**(2.5)**	**(1.7)**	(2.5)	(1.5)
Foreign exchange contracts	**–**	**(0.2)**	–	0.6

1. Short and long-term borrowings and swap agreements:
   For borrowings not at fixed rates of interest, it is assumed that the carrying amount is approximately equal to the fair value. For borrowings at fixed rates of interest, the payments which the Group is committed to make have been discounted at the short-term variable rates for each currency at 30 September 1997. Quoted market prices have been used in the calculations for publicly traded debt wherever possible. The fair value of currency and interest rate swap agreements entered into in connection with long-term borrowings is the estimated amount the Group would receive or pay to terminate the agreements.

2. Long-term investments:
   The fair value has been based on quoted market prices where available or the carrying amount.

3. Long-term receivables:
   For material items, the fair value is estimated based on the discounted future cash flows. For other items, the carrying value is deemed to be approximately equal to the fair value.

4. Tax
a) Tax on profit on ordinary activities

	1997 **£ million**	1996 £ million	1995 £ million
Payable in the UK			
Corporation tax at 31%/33%[1] (1996: 33%, 1995: 33%)	**89.8**	108.9	91.0
Advance corporation tax (ACT)	**(4.0)**	(11.2)	(7.7)
Double tax relief	**(30.0)**	(44.1)	(39.0)
	55.8	53.6	44.3
Payable overseas			
US – Federal alternative minimum tax at 20%	**1.8**	3.7	7.5
– State and local taxes	**2.6**	3.0	6.7
Australia at 36% (1996: 36%, 1995: 33%)	**14.6**	13.6	13.3
South Africa at 35% (1996: 35%, 1995: 35%)	**9.2**	14.8	17.3
Other countries	**36.3**	37.0	29.7
	64.5	72.1	74.5
Provision for deferred tax – overseas	**(0.1)**	1.8	2.1
Tax charge arising in associated undertakings	**8.9**	10.4	7.7
	129.1	137.9	128.6

b) Deferred tax
i) Deferred tax UK GAAP

	Provision £ million	Full potential liability £ million
Analysis		
Arising from accelerated depreciation allowances[2]	36.0	345.2
Other timing differences	0.3	(5.5)
Tax losses available	(1.5)	(34.7)
ACT available for offset	–	(15.9)
	34.8	289.1
Movement during the year		
At 1 October 1996	41.7	285.6
Exchange adjustment	(2.6)	(13.3)
Arising during the year[3]	(0.1)	20.2
Transfers to current tax	(4.5)	(4.5)
Other movements	0.3	1.1
At 30 September 1997	**34.8**	**289.1**

1. The UK corporation tax rate was reduced from 33 per cent to 31 per cent on 1 April 1997.

2. In the event that revalued assets were to be entirely disposed of at their book value, additional tax on such disposals would be approximately £6.2 million (1996: £6.7 million, 1995: £6.1 million).

3. If provisions for deferred tax were made on the basis of the full potential liability (excluding the amount in respect of revalued assets) the tax charge for the year would be £149.4 million (1996: £199.8 million, 1995: £143.2 million).

4. Tax continued
ii) Deferred tax US GAAP
For US GAAP reporting, the Group follows SFAS 109, Accounting for Income Taxes, in respect of deferred taxation. SFAS 109 requires deferred tax to be fully provided on all temporary differences.
   The table below provides a reconciliation of full potential deferred taxes from a UK GAAP basis to a US GAAP basis at 30 September 1997.

	Full liability UK GAAP £ million	Adjustments to US GAAP £ million	Full liability US GAAP £ million
Accelerated capital allowances	345.2	(2.1)	343.1
Other temporary differences	(5.5)	43.4	37.9
Advance corporation tax available for offset	(15.9)	–	(15.9)
Tax losses and other credits available	(34.7)	(46.9)	(81.6)
Valuation allowance	–	46.9	46.9
	289.1	41.3	330.4

Movement during the year	
At 1 October 1996	339.1
Exchange adjustment	(13.3)
Arising during the year	21.5
Transfers to current tax	(4.5)
Other movements	(12.4)
At 30 September 1997	**330.4**

The components of deferred tax assets/(liabilities) at 30 September 1997 were:

	1997 £ million	1996 £ million
Long-term		
Asset	**148.2**	158.5
Liability	**(506.0)**	(537.1)
Net liability	**(357.8)**	(378.6)
Short-term		
Asset	**46.4**	55.3
Liability	**(19.0)**	(15.8)
Net asset	**27.4**	39.5
Total deferred tax assets	**194.6**	213.8
Total deferred tax liabilities	**(525.0)**	(552.9)
	(330.4)	(339.1)

4. Tax continued
c) Reconciliation of effective tax rate
The table set out below provides a reconciliation between the UK corporation tax rate and the Group's effective tax rate, computed by taking the various elements of the tax reconciliation as a percentage of profit before taxes.

	1997 **%**	1996 %	1995 %
UK corporation tax rate[1]	**32.0**	33.0	33.0
Difference in tax rates of overseas subsidiaries and associates	**1.7**	1.6	0.9
Excess of tax depreciation over book depreciation	**(2.5)**	(1.2)	(1.7)
Advance corporation tax	**(0.9)**	(2.5)	(1.9)
State and local taxes	**0.4**	0.7	1.7
Utilisation of brought forward losses	**(0.8)**	–	–
Other items with less than a 5% net effect	**(0.9)**	(0.6)	–
Effective Group tax rate	**29.0**	31.0	32.0

1.   The UK corporation tax rate was reduced from 33 per cent to 31 per cent on 1 April 1997.

d) Unused tax credits
UK corporation tax is payable to the Inland Revenue, in advance of the normal due date for the payment of the liability, in respect of dividends paid to shareholders. Such payments are referred to as advance corporation tax (ACT). Although ACT is available for offset without time limit against corporation tax, the Group has written off any ACT paid in the year which exceeds the maximum amount offsettable for that year and included it as part of the tax charge. The ACT carried forward for tax purposes at 30 September 1997 amounted to approximately £15.9 million, and this will be available for offset against any future liability to corporation tax.

On a consolidated basis, the Group has net operating loss carryforwards of £119.9 million, of which £112.6 million are provided for by a valuation allowance. A valuation allowance is provided when it is more likely than not that some or all of the losses will not be realised. If not offset against taxable income, these losses will expire as follows:

Year	Net operating loss £ million
1998	19.5
1999	4.1
2000	3.4
2001	2.0
2002	4.1
Thereafter, or no expiry date	86.8

4. Tax continued

For US Federal tax purposes, the Group has investment tax credit and general business carryforwards of approximately £32.2 million, which are available to reduce income taxes otherwise payable; however, if not used, the credits will expire as follows:

Year	Investment tax and general business credits £ million
1998	0.4
1999	10.3
2000	4.6
2001	2.3
2002	1.9
Thereafter	12.7

In addition, the Group has alternative minimum tax credits for US Federal income tax purposes of approximately £43.5 million which can be carried forward to reduce regular tax liabilities of future years. There is no expiration date on these credits.

Investment tax credits are accounted for by the flow-through method whereby they reduce income taxes currently payable and the provision for income taxes in the period the assets giving rise to such credits are placed in service. Deferred tax assets, subject to the need for a valuation allowance, are recognised to the extent that the investment tax credits are not currently utilised.

5. Directors

Directors' remuneration and interests are given in the report of the management resources committee.

6. Employees
a) Number of employees by business

	1997 Year end	1997 Average	1996 Year end	1996 Average
Gases and related products	27,954	27,411	27,368	26,966
Vacuum technology	2,923	2,922	2,979	2,822
Distribution services	5,523	5,401	5,559	5,370
Health care	4,696	4,730	4,754	5,090
Corporate	278	269	253	247
	41,374	40,733	40,913	40,495

b) Number of employees by region

	1997 Year end	1997 Average	1996 Year end	1996 Average
Europe	15,008	14,680	14,692	14,594
Americas	9,103	8,986	8,939	8,797
Africa	8,640	8,524	8,633	8,600
Asia/Pacific	8,623	8,543	8,649	8,504
	41,374	40,733	40,913	40,495

c) Employment costs

	1997 £ million	1996 £ million	1995 £ million
Wages and salaries	799.9	805.9	764.8
Social security costs	95.4	96.7	92.8
Other pension costs	13.9	14.4	17.8
	909.2	917.0	875.4

6. Employees continued
d) Option and incentive schemes
BOC operates a share option programme for both executives and employees. The features of these
are given in the report of the management resources committee and the employees report.

i) Summary of movements in share options	Employee options and rights million	Executive options and rights million	Long-term share incentive units million
1994/95			
Outstanding at 1 October 1994	7.2	10.3	5.9
Granted	1.3	3.0	–
Exercised	(1.1)	(1.2)	(0.4)
Lapsed	(0.7)	(0.5)	–
Outstanding at 30 September 1995	6.7	11.6	5.5
Exercisable at 30 September 1995	0.3	2.8	4.1
Option price range at 30 September 1995	369p-699p	389p-786p	458p-742p
Option price range for exercised options	351p-699p	389p-627p	463p-536p
1995/96			
Granted	1.4	3.7	–
Exercised	(1.0)	(1.7)	(2.5)
Lapsed	(0.5)	(1.2)	(0.1)
Outstanding at 30 September 1996	6.6	12.4	2.9
Exercisable at 30 September 1996	0.1	2.8	2.0
Option price range at 30 September 1996	478p-827p	389p-930p	458p-742p
Option price range for exercised options	369p-827p	389p-742p	458p-742p
1996/97			
Granted	1.4	3.2	–
Exercised	(1.1)	(1.6)	(0.8)
Lapsed	(0.5)	(0.7)	–
Outstanding at 30 September 1997	**6.4**	**13.3**	**2.1**
Exercisable at 30 September 1997	**0.2**	**2.9**	**2.0**
Option price range at 30 September 1997	**479p-882p**	**389p-1,119p**	**458p-742p**
Option price range for exercised options	**478p-827p**	**389p-742p**	**458p-742p**
Number of participants	**5,960**	**459**	**21**

ii) Weighted average exercise price	Employee options and rights pence	Executive options and rights pence	Long-term share incentive units pence
Outstanding at 1 October 1996	652	733	588
Granted	882	981	–
Exercised	550	634	532
Lapsed	696	807	677
Outstanding at 30 September 1997	**712**	**800**	**608**

6. Employees continued

iii) Analysis of share options outstanding at
30 September 1997

	Date of grant	Number of shares	Weighted average option price pence	Normal exercisable date
Employee share options				
	1991	358,420	479	1998
	1992	531,170	569	1997-1998
	1993	47,800	634	1999
	1994	1,073,551	662	1998-2000
	1995	1,848,317	635	1999-2002
	1996	1,200,969	827	2001-2003
	1997	1,392,670	882	2001-2004
Executive share options and rights				
	1988	35,000	389	1992-1998
	1989	294,135	463	1993-1999
	1990	419,118	536	1994-2000
	1991	367,988	532	1995-2001
	1992	766,000	629	1995-2002
	1993	1,052,600	742	1997-2003
	1994	1,759,000	677	1998-2004
	1995	2,301,000	722	1998-2005
	1996	3,214,000	914	1999-2006
	1997	3,064,500	981	2000-2007
Long-term share incentive units				
	1990	100,000	491	1992-1997
	1991	483,750	486	1993-1999
	1992	405,000	597	1994-2000
	1993	292,500	742	1996-2001
	1994	755,000	650	1996-2002
	1995	45,000	716	1997-2002

The company applies APB Opinion 25, Accounting for Stock Issued to Employees and related interpretations in accounting for its plans. By applying this statement the employee share schemes are deemed non-compensatory and therefore do not result in an expense for financial reporting purposes. Under the executive schemes, grants of share options are at the market price of the company's shares at the time of grant, hence no discount or compensation arises. Accordingly, there is no compensation cost to the Group.

If compensation cost for the Group's share option plans had been determined based on the fair value at the grant dates for awards under those plans consistent with the method of US SFAS 123, Accounting for Stock Based Compensation, the Group's profit before tax would be charged with an additional cost of £6.9 million (1996: £3.2 million). The impact on earnings per share for 1997 and 1996 is not material.

The Black Scholes model was used to measure the compensation expense under US SFAS 123, with assumptions used for grants in 1996 and 1997 of exercise prices equal to the stock price at grant dates, dividend yield of 3.5 per cent, expected volatility of 16.6 per cent, an 8.0 per cent weighted average interest rate based on UK Gilts on the date of grant with a maturity equal to the expected term and an expected term of between 5 to 6.5 years.

6. Employees continued
e) Retirement benefits
i) Pensions – UK GAAP

The Group operates a number of pension schemes throughout the world. The majority of the schemes are self administered and the schemes' assets are held independently of the Group's finances. Pension costs are assessed in accordance with the advice of independent professionally qualified actuaries.

The principal schemes are of the defined benefit type. In the UK and Australia they are based on final salary, in the US on annual salary and in South Africa on the final 24 months' salary. On the advice of respective actuaries, Group funding is suspended and is unlikely to be required during the next financial year. For the UK schemes, the surplus of assets over liabilities indicated at the formal valuation resulted in a pension credit over the year. In the light of the abolition of the dividend tax credit on UK equity shares, as a prudent measure, the surplus has been reassessed and no pension credit taken for the final two quarters of the year. The cost for the year was:

	1997 £ million	1996 £ million	1995 £ million
Principal schemes			
Regular pension cost	**42.4**	34.8	33.1
Variations from regular cost	**(34.2)**	(34.5)	(29.4)
Interest	**(1.7)**	(1.5)	(1.3)
Other schemes	**4.3**	12.6	13.0
Net pension cost	**10.8**	11.4	15.4

The results of the most recent valuations of the principal schemes were:

	UK[3]	US	Australia	South Africa[4]
Valuation data				
Date of latest valuation or review	31 March	1 January	31 December	30 June
	1996	1996	1994	1997
Market value of investments (£ million)	961	264	100	124
Level of funding[1]	126%	129%	141%	135%
Method used	Projected	Projected	Projected	Projected
	Unit	Unit	Unit	Unit
Main assumptions for UK accounting purposes				
Rate of price inflation	4.5%	6.0%	6.0%	12.5%
Return on investments	5.0%	3.0%	3.5%	3.25%
Increase in earnings[2]	2.0%	0.8%	1.5%	1.1%
Main assumptions for US accounting purposes				
Discount rate	7.7%	6.5%	8.5%	15%
Return on assets	8.2%	9.0%	10.5%	15%
Compensation increase	5.6%	4.0%	5.5%	13.8%

1. The actuarial value of assets expressed as a percentage of the accrued service liabilities.

2. Above price inflation.

3. The UK fund valuation is produced using a discounted cash flow method. This is based on the investment income expected to be earned on a notional portfolio of UK equities assuming dividend growth of five per cent per annum.

4. South Africa is included as a principal scheme for the first time in 1997. It has not been included as a principal scheme in the 1996 or 1995 disclosures for both UK and US GAAP.

6. Employees continued

ii) Pensions – US GAAP

The principal schemes are those described in ei). At 30 September 1997 approximately 82 per cent of plan assets of the principal schemes were held in equity securities, with the remainder primarily in fixed income securities.

The pension cost under US GAAP has been calculated for the principal schemes in accordance with SFAS 87 using the assumptions shown in ei). The difference between the net credits is shown in the reconciliation of net income between UK GAAP and US GAAP in note 16. The pension credits for the principal schemes on a US GAAP basis were as follows:

	Years ended 30 September		
	1997 **£ million**	1996 £ million	1995 £ million
Service cost	**39.5**	33.5	30.7
Interest cost	**89.1**	78.5	72.6
Actual returns on assets	**(270.5)**	(224.1)	(141.1)
Net amortisation	**144.3**	106.4	35.9
Curtailment gain	**–**	–	(0.9)
Net periodic pension cost/(credit)	**2.4**	(5.7)	(2.8)

The following table shows the plans' funded status and the prepaid pension cost used to determine the adjustment required to bring the UK GAAP shareholders' funds to a US GAAP basis (see note 16):

	1997 **£ million**	1996 £ million
Projected benefit obligation	**(1,186.7)**	(979.0)
Plan assets at fair value	**1,716.1**	1,409.4
Plan assets in excess of projected benefits obligation	**529.4**	430.4
Unrecognised net asset	**(119.7)**	(110.9)
Unrecognised prior service costs	**33.3**	21.2
Unrecognised net gain	**(322.1)**	(221.9)
Prepaid pension cost at 30 September	**120.9**	118.8

iii) Other retirement costs

In the US the Group provides post-retirement benefits to former employees. These costs are accounted for on a basis similar to pensions. The cost for the year was:

	1997 **£ million**	1996 £ million	1995 £ million
Regular cost	**1.3**	1.4	1.5
Variations from regular cost	**(1.1)**	(1.0)	(0.9)
Interest	**2.2**	2.3	2.5
Curtailment gain	**–**	–	(2.4)
	2.4	2.7	0.7

7. Fixed assets – tangible assets

a) Group summary

	Land and buildings[1] £ million	Plant machinery and vehicles £ million	Cylinders £ million	Construction in progress £ million	Total £ million
Gross book value					
At 1 October 1996	718.5	3,405.4	517.1	270.0	4,911.0
Exchange adjustment	(41.9)	(188.1)	(23.1)	(29.7)	(282.8)
Capital expenditure[2]	28.1	354.0	59.8	233.9	675.8
Disposals	(7.6)	(87.4)	(9.7)	–	(104.7)
Transfers	–	64.0	4.3	(68.3)	–
Acquisitions and disposals of businesses	5.9	(2.9)	1.8	0.3	5.1
At 30 September 1997	**703.0**	**3,545.0**	**550.2**	**406.2**	**5,204.4**
Depreciation					
At 1 October 1996	179.5	1,801.0	182.9	–	2,163.4
Exchange adjustment	(9.1)	(94.3)	(7.1)	–	(110.5)
Provided during the year	21.2	222.7	27.7	–	271.6
Disposals	(2.4)	(63.6)	(8.1)	–	(74.1)
Transfers	–	(3.1)	3.1	–	–
Acquisitions and disposals of businesses	2.1	(1.8)	–	–	0.3
At 30 September 1997	**191.3**	**1,860.9**	**198.5**	**–**	**2,250.7**
Net book value at 30 September 1997[3]					
Owned assets	480.0	1,678.1	345.6	406.2	2,909.9
Leased assets	31.7	6.0	6.1	–	43.8
	511.7	**1,684.1**	**351.7**	**406.2**	**2,953.7**

1. Net book value of land and buildings at cost was £424.9 million (1996: £436.9 million).

2. Capital expenditure including associated undertakings is given in note 1.

3. Net book value includes net interest capitalised of £52.1 million (1996: £49.8 million).

b) Depreciation and operating lease rentals

	1997 £ million	1996 £ million	1995 £ million
Additional depreciation on revaluations included above	0.7	0.8	0.8
Depreciation on leased assets included above	3.6	3.9	5.2
Amortisation of capitalised interest included above	5.4	4.6	4.5
Operating lease rentals			
– hire of plant and machinery	8.3	7.6	9.1
– property rent	34.1	36.7	38.0
– other	18.6	16.1	16.1

c) Properties

The BOC Group has numerous manufacturing, distribution and office facilities which are located in some 60 countries. At 30 September 1997, the Group's investment in property, plant and equipment, comprising land and buildings, plant, machinery, vehicles and gas cylinders was located geographically as follows:

	£ million	%
Europe (mainly the UK)	1,062.2	36
Americas (mainly the US)	928.0	31
Africa	229.9	8
Asia/Pacific	733.6	25
	2,953.7	100

The above amounts are stated at cost net of accumulated depreciation, except in the case of certain land and buildings which are included at a valuation.

7. Fixed assets – tangible assets continued

d) Parent summary

	Land and buildings £ million	Plant machinery and vehicles £ million	Construction in progress £ million	Total £ million
Gross book value				
At 1 October 1996	34.3	13.1	0.5	47.9
Capital expenditure	–	3.1	0.1	3.2
Disposals	–	(2.6)	–	(2.6)
At 30 September 1997	**34.3**	**13.6**	**0.6**	**48.5**
Depreciation				
At 1 October 1996	10.4	8.0	–	18.4
Provided during the year	1.0	1.2	–	2.2
Disposals	–	(1.2)	–	(1.2)
At 30 September 1997	**11.4**	**8.0**	**–**	**19.4**
Net book value				
At 30 September 1997	**22.9**	**5.6**	**0.6**	**29.1**

e) Net book value of land and buildings at 30 September 1997

	Group £ million	Parent £ million
Freehold property	480.0	22.9
Leasehold property – long-term	26.1	–
– short-term	5.6	–
	511.7	22.9

f) Capital commitments

	Group 1997 £ million	1996 £ million	Parent 1997 £ million	1996 £ million
Against which orders had been placed	**236.5**	149.4	–	0.8
Authorised but not committed	**153.3**	78.3	–	–
	389.8	227.7	–	0.8

Included in capital commitments is £122.9 million (1996: £57.9 million) committed to other Group companies.

g) Asset revaluations

No properties were revalued during 1997. The net book value of properties revalued in 1996 was £7.3 million and earlier years, £273.5 million. Properties not revalued were £230.9 million.

8. Fixed assets – intangible assets

	£ million
Gross book value	
At 1 October 1996	50.4
Exchange adjustment	(1.4)
Acquired during the year	1.2
At 30 September 1997	**50.2**
Amortisation	
At 1 October 1996	17.0
Exchange adjustment	(0.5)
Provided during the year	4.9
At 30 September 1997	**21.4**
Net book value	
At 30 September 1997	**28.8**

9. Fixed assets – investments

a) Group

	Associated undertakings Group share of net assets £ million	Group loans £ million	Other investments at cost £ million	Own shares at cost £ million	Provisions £ million	Total £ million
At 1 October 1996	209.6	22.0	32.3	22.6	(0.2)	286.3
Exchange adjustment	(21.9)	(2.4)	(3.0)	–	–	(27.3)
Acquisitions/additions	28.6	1.2	12.8	4.1	(1.2)	45.5
Disposals	–	–	(4.0)	(2.7)	–	(6.7)
Increase in net assets	21.6	–	–	–	–	21.6
Other	0.3	(0.4)	0.1	–	0.1	0.1
At 30 September 1997	**238.2**	**20.4**	**38.2**	**24.0**	**(1.3)**	**319.5**

i) Associated undertakings

The cost of investment in associated undertakings was £122.7 million (1996: £107.5 million) and the attributable profit before tax was £54.4 million (1996: £50.4 million, 1995: £39.4 million).

ii) Own shares

For share-based incentive schemes which do not use new issue shares, options are satisfied by the transfer of shares held in trust for the purpose. At 30 September 1997, options over 4.1 million shares were outstanding under these schemes, for which 3.9 million shares in the company were held pending exercise.

Loans and advances for the purchase of shares in trust have been made either by the company or its subsidiaries. If the value of shares in trust is insufficient to cover the loans, the company and subsidiaries will bear any loss. The company also bears administrative costs on an accruals basis.

Deposits of £3.9 million are currently held in trust by The BOC Group Qualifying Employee Share Ownership Trust 1997. These deposits are included as part of the Group's net borrowings in accordance with UITF Abstract 13.

Based on the company's share price at 30 September 1997 of 1,101p, the market value of own shares held in trust was £42.9 million. This compares with the acquisition cost shown above. During the year scrip dividends of 0.1 million shares were taken on 3.8 million shares.

Own shares are shown as fixed asset investments for accounting purposes, in accordance with FRS 5 and UITF Abstract 13. Information on share option schemes appears in the report of the management resources committee and notes 6 and 12.

b) Valuation

	1997 £ million	1996 £ million
Listed on stock exchanges overseas	**37.2**	41.8
Unlisted – equity at directors' valuation	**253.1**	214.4
– other at directors' valuation	**29.2**	30.1
Total book value	**319.5**	286.3
Market value of listed investments	**115.7**	159.8

c) Income

	1997 £ million	1996 £ million	1995 £ million
Listed securities	**5.7**	1.8	6.5
Unlisted securities	**19.6**	17.2	17.4
	25.3	19.0	23.9
Less: Dividends receivable from associated undertakings	**19.5**	14.6	14.1
Income from other fixed asset investments	**5.8**	4.4	9.8

9. Fixed assets – investments continued

d) Parent

	Cost £ million	Amounts owing £ million	Provisions £ million	Total £ million
Investments (subsidiary and associated undertakings)				
At 1 October 1996	751.0	842.1	(12.6)	1,580.5
Net movements	72.8	225.4	–	298.2
At 30 September 1997	**823.8**	**1,067.5**	**(12.6)**	**1,878.7**

All of the investments were unlisted.

10. Net current assets/(liabilities)

a) Stocks

	Group 1997 £ million	1996 £ million
Raw materials	**92.3**	106.7
Work in progress	**73.0**	91.8
Gases and other finished goods	**193.9**	213.3
Payments on account	**(4.9)**	(8.4)
	354.3	403.4

Amounts relating to long-term contracts included in work in progress were £5.5 million (1996: £4.0 million).

There were no stocks held in the balance sheet of The BOC Group plc at either 30 September 1997 or 30 September 1996.

	Group 1997 £ million	1996 £ million	Parent 1997 £ million	1996 £ million
b) Debtors due within one year				
Trade debtors	**702.8**	703.3	**–**	–
Current accounts with subsidiary and associated undertakings	**–**	–	**120.1**	11.3
Other debtors	**158.6**	166.1	**14.2**	11.1
Prepayments and accrued income	**40.3**	36.7	**20.9**	2.5
	901.7	906.1	**155.2**	24.9
c) Deposits and cash due within one year				
Deposits	**100.0**	74.9	**34.3**	9.8
Cash at bank and in hand	**122.2**	80.9	**–**	–
	222.2	155.8	**34.3**	9.8
d) Assets due beyond one year				
Pensions prepayment	**53.0**	50.7	**43.2**	38.8
Deposits	**24.1**	4.1	**–**	–
Other debtors	**24.8**	40.9	**0.3**	10.0
	101.9	95.7	**43.5**	48.8

10. Net current assets/(liabilities) continued

e) Borrowings and finance leases[1]

	Group		Parent	
	1997 **£ million**	1996 £ million	**1997** **£ million**	1996 £ million
Bank loans and overdrafts	**219.0**	264.2	**113.5**	95.1
Loans other than from banks	**400.8**	357.5	**33.6**	3.9
Finance leases	**0.6**	1.4	**–**	–
	620.4	623.1	**147.1**	99.0

f) Other creditors

	Group		Parent	
Deposits and advance payments by customers	**73.3**	74.8	**–**	–
Trade creditors	**332.6**	346.7	**–**	–
Amounts due to subsidiary and associated undertakings	**–**	–	**7.3**	32.8
Payroll and other taxes, including social security	**33.8**	36.6	**0.2**	0.2
Taxation – UK	**65.6**	62.2	**15.3**	13.4
– Overseas	**50.3**	42.6	**–**	–
Other creditors	**212.2**	236.0	**33.1**	13.4
Accruals and deferred income	**118.4**	113.0	**10.2**	6.6
	886.2	911.9	**66.1**	66.4

11. Long-term liabilities

a) Borrowings and finance leases[1]

	Group		Parent	
	1997 **£ million**	1996 £ million	**1997** **£ million**	1996 £ million
Loans other than from banks	**863.7**	622.2	**499.2**	353.2
Bank loans	**133.4**	140.0	**–**	–
Finance leases	**4.1**	5.2	**–**	–
	1,001.2	767.4	**499.2**	353.2

b) Provisions for liabilities and charges	At 1 October 1996 £ million	Exchange adjustment £ million	Provided in the year £ million	Other movements £ million	At **30 September** **1997** **£ million**
Deferred tax	41.7	(2.6)	(0.1)	(4.2)	**34.8**
Retirement and other employee costs	113.0	(5.6)	6.4	(0.2)	**113.6**
Uninsured losses	31.7	(0.2)	1.3	–	**32.8**
Executive share incentive units	13.1	(0.3)	5.2	(4.7)	**13.3**
Other	46.3	(1.3)	(11.2)	1.4	**35.2**
	245.8	(10.0)	1.6	(7.7)	**229.7**

1. Details of borrowings and finance leases are given in note 3.

12. Dividends and equity
a) Dividends, including non-equity

	1997 pence	Per share 1996 pence	1995 pence	1997 £ million	1996 £ million	1995 £ million
Ordinary						
First interim, paid February	**14.5**	13.5	12.4	**70.1**	64.9	59.3
Second interim, paid August	**14.5**	13.5	12.4	**70.2**	65.1	59.4
	29.0	27.0	24.8	**140.3**	130.0	118.7
Preference						
Paid 30 June and 31 December				**0.1**	0.1	0.1
				140.4	130.1	118.8

b) Share capital
i) Analysis at 30 September

	Number of shares 1997 million	1996 million	1997 £ million	1996 £ million
Equity Capital:				
Ordinary shares of 25p each	**487.1**	483.3	**121.8**	120.8
4.55% Cumulative Preference shares of £1 each	**0.5**	0.5	**0.5**	0.5
3.5% Cumulative 2nd Preference shares of £1 each	**1.0**	1.0	**1.0**	1.0
2.8% Cumulative 2nd Preference shares of £1 each	**1.0**	1.0	**1.0**	1.0
			124.3	123.3
Issued and called up, fully paid, share capital				
Unissued capital unclassified shares of 25p each	**102.9**	106.7	**25.7**	26.7
Authorised			**150.0**	150.0

ii) Share issues

	Number millions
Issues of Ordinary shares of 25p each during the year were:	
Under the savings related share option scheme	1.0
Under the senior executives share option scheme	0.8
As scrip instead of cash dividends	2.0

12. Dividends and equity continued

c) Group reserves

	Share premium account £ million	Revaluation reserve £ million	Profit and loss account £ million	Associated undertakings' reserves £ million
At 1 October 1996	259.4	71.9	1,252.5	111.6
Total recognised gains and losses for the year	–	(4.7)	198.2	0.3
Goodwill:				
– taken to reserves on acquisitions	–	–	(8.9)	(0.3)
Reserves reclassified	–	(3.4)	3.4	–
Dividends	–	–	(140.4)	–
Premium on share issues (net)	13.0	–	(2.9)	–
Scrip dividends	–	–	18.8	–
At 30 September 1997	**272.4**	**63.8**	**1,320.7**	**111.6**

The undistributed profits of Group undertakings may be liable to overseas and/or UK tax (after allowing for double tax relief) if distributed as dividends.

There are no material exchange control restrictions on the remittance of funds to the UK.

Goodwill written off against reserves in respect of continuing businesses amounts to £315.0 million (1996: £330.2 million).

At 30 September 1997, in accordance with the Group's accounting policy, unrealised exchange losses (net of gains) on net borrowings at 30 September 1997 included in reserves amounted to £7.8 million (1996: £3.1 million).

Non-equity shareholders' interests in the share capital and reserves of the Group are limited to the nominal value of the Preference shares.

d) Parent reserves

	Share premium account £ million	Other reserves £ million	Profit and loss account £ million
At 1 October 1996	259.4	9.4	776.1
Profit for the financial year	–	–	365.9
Dividends	–	–	(140.4)
Premium on share issues (net)	13.0	–	(2.9)
Scrip dividends	–	–	18.8
At 30 September 1997	**272.4**	**9.4**	**1,017.5**

The premium on share issues represents amounts paid to The BOC Group plc for the issue of shares under the Group's share option schemes. Employees paid £10.1 million. The Group paid the balance of £2.9 million to a qualifying share ownership trust (Quest).

13. Commitments and contingent liabilities

a) Annual operating lease commitments

	Property leases £ million	Other operating leases £ million
Within one year	4.5	2.8
Between one and two years	3.1	3.5
Between two and five years	5.7	5.2
Over five years	5.1	0.3
	18.4	11.8

	Operating leases £ million
Rentals are due under operating leases from 1 October 1997 to completion as follows:	
Year to 30 September 1998	30.2
Year to 30 September 1999	21.4
Year to 30 September 2000	16.2
Year to 30 September 2001	10.3
Year to 30 September 2002	8.4
Thereafter	32.3
	118.8

b) Contingent liabilities, legal proceedings and bank guarantees

	Group £ million	Parent £ million
Guarantees of associated undertakings' borrowings	–	2.4
Guarantees of wholly-owned subsidiaries' borrowings	–	791.6
Other guarantees and contingent liabilities	34.9	–

Various Group undertakings are parties to legal actions and claims which arise in the ordinary course of business, some of which are for substantial amounts. While the outcome of some of these matters cannot readily be foreseen, the directors believe that they will be disposed of without material effect on the net asset position as shown in these financial statements.

The Group is committed to make future purchases under take-or-pay contracts. Obligations under such contracts in effect at 30 September 1997 are as follows:

Year ending 30 September	£ million
1998	60.9
1999	48.4
2000	49.0
2001	63.0
2002	47.7
	269.0

For the years ended 30 September 1997, 1996 and 1995 total purchases made relating to these contracts amounted to £54.7 million, £54.6 million and £54.9 million, respectively.

14. Cash flow
a) Net cash inflow from operating activities

	1997 £ million	1996 £ million	1995 £ million
Operating profit	**540.4**	539.4	496.4
Depreciation and amortisation	**276.5**	268.7	256.5
Operating profit of associated undertakings	**(61.6)**	(57.5)	(45.4)
Dividends from associated undertakings	**19.5**	14.6	14.6
Change in stocks	**29.0**	(52.4)	(36.9)
Change in debtors	**(60.3)**	(71.9)	(124.2)
Change in creditors	**23.5**	23.3	123.8
Exceptional cash flows	**(11.4)**	(19.5)	(28.1)
Other	**(21.8)**	(19.6)	(9.3)
Net cash inflow from operating activities	**733.8**	625.1	647.4

b) Reconciliation of net cash flow to movement in net debt

	1997	1996	1995
Decrease/(increase) in cash	**(36.8)**	25.4	(29.8)
Increase in debt (see note 14d))	**342.1**	182.2	103.3
Decrease/(increase) in liquid resources	**(62.3)**	(19.8)	0.2
Change in net debt resulting from cash flows	**243.0**	187.8	73.7
Borrowings assumed at acquisition	**0.9**	1.0	9.2
Borrowings transferred out on disposal	**–**	(0.2)	–
Inception of finance leases	**0.2**	0.3	–
Exchange adjustment	**(99.4)**	(24.6)	20.0
Movement in net debt in the year	**144.7**	164.3	102.9
Net debt at 1 October	**1,230.6**	1,066.3	963.4
Net debt at 30 September	**1,375.3**	1,230.6	1,066.3

c) Analysis of net debt

	At 1 October 1996 £ million	Cash flow £ million	Acquisitions/ disposals (excluding cash and overdrafts) £ million	Other non-cash changes £ million	Exchange adjustment £ million	At 30 September 1997 £ million
Deposits and cash due within one year	155.8	82.0	0.1	–	(15.7)	**222.2**
Deposits due beyond one year	4.1	20.4	–	–	(0.4)	**24.1**
	159.9	102.4	0.1	–	(16.1)	**246.3**
Borrowings and finance leases due within one year	(623.1)	(65.2)	–	–	67.9	**(620.4)**
Borrowings and finance leases due beyond one year	(767.4)	(280.2)	(1.0)	(0.2)	47.6	**(1,001.2)**
Net borrowings and finance leases	(1,230.6)	(243.0)	(0.9)	(0.2)	99.4	**(1,375.3)**

14. Cash flow continued
d) Increase in debt

	1997 £ million	1996 £ million	1995 £ million
Issue of 7¼% Notes 2002	150.0	–	–
Secured loans 1998/2005	45.9	–	–
European Investment Bank loans 1997/2003	42.4	–	–
Issue of 5⅞% Notes 2001	–	128.2	–
Issue of 7.45% Guaranteed Notes 2006	–	160.3	–
Repayment of 8.73% Guaranteed Notes 1996	–	(158.2)	–
Repayment of 7% Guaranteed Bonds 1997	(96.2)	–	–
Repayment of medium-term loans 1998/99	–	(50.0)	–
Net issues of commercial paper	159.5	95.2	66.1
Other (net)	40.5	6.7	37.2
Increase in debt	342.1	182.2	103.3

e) Consolidated cash flow statement: US format

	1997 £ million	1996 £ million	1995 £ million
Net cash provided by operating activities	526.7	423.5	447.5
Net cash used by investing activities	(663.9)	(504.9)	(408.1)
Net cash provided by financing activities	224.2	73.8	8.3
Net increase/(decrease) in cash and cash equivalents	87.0	(7.6)	47.7
Cash and cash equivalents at 1 October	140.5	140.6	96.5
Exchange adjustment	(14.6)	7.5	(3.6)
Cash and cash equivalents at 30 September	212.9	140.5	140.6

The Group cash flow statement on page 66 has been prepared in accordance with the revised UK financial reporting standard 1 (FRS 1), the objectives and principles of which are similar to those set out in US accounting principle SFAS 95, Statement of Cash Flows. The principal differences between the standards relate to classification of items within the cash flow statement and with regard to the definition of cash and cash equivalents.

Under FRS 1, cash flows are presented separately for: a) operating activities; b) returns on investments and servicing of finance; c) tax paid; d) capital expenditure and financial investment; e) acquisitions and disposals; f) equity dividends paid; g) management of liquid resources; and h) financing. Under SFAS 95, however, only three categories of cash flow activity are reported: a) operating activities; b) investing activities; and c) financing activities. Cash flows from returns on investments and servicing of finance (excluding preference dividends and dividends paid to minorities) and tax paid under FRS 1 would be included in operating activities under SFAS 95; capital expenditure and acquisitions and disposals would be included in investing activities under SFAS 95; equity dividends would be included as a financing activity under SFAS 95.

Under FRS 1, cash is defined as cash in hand and deposits repayable on demand with any qualifying financial institution, less overdrafts from any qualifying financial institution repayable on demand. Under SFAS 95, cash is defined as cash in hand and deposits but also includes cash equivalents which are short-term, highly liquid investments. Generally only investments with original maturities of three months or less come within this definition.

Set out above, for illustrative purposes, is a summary consolidated statement of cash flows under SFAS 95.

15. Acquisitions and disposals
a) Cash flow and fair values

	1997		1996		1995	
	Acquisitions £ million	Disposals £ million	Acquisitions £ million	Disposals £ million	Acquisitions £ million	Disposals £ million
Cash flow arising on the acquisition and disposal of businesses						
Tangible fixed assets	(10.1)	5.3	(7.7)	11.3	(32.2)	4.3
Associated undertakings and other fixed asset investments	(4.4)	0.1	(6.2)	0.3	(23.2)	1.9
Stocks	(6.2)	1.8	(1.1)	2.3	(1.2)	6.0
Debtors	(10.4)	–	(1.5)	12.4	(16.1)	7.5
Creditors including taxation	8.0	0.3	0.7	(11.5)	15.3	(0.2)
Cash	(0.5)	–	(0.2)		–	–
Borrowings	0.9	–	1.0	(2.2)	21.0	–
Minorities	1.6	–	(1.5)	–	0.1	–
Net assets (acquired) and disposed of	(21.1)	7.5	(16.5)	12.6	(36.3)	19.5
Goodwill on acquisitions	(9.2)	–	(6.8)	–	(18.6)	–
Surplus over book value on disposals	–	6.4	–	21.7	–	9.2
(Acquisition)/disposal price	(30.3)	13.9	(23.3)	34.3	(54.9)	28.7
Deferred payments	(1.4)	9.9	(2.5)	(20.5)	5.0	–
	(31.7)	23.8	(25.8)	13.8	(49.9)	28.7

In 1997 the Group acquired the Systems Chemistry business for £12.8 million. This will form part of the BOC Edwards organisation. There were no other material acquisitions or disposals during the year.

In 1996, the Group disposed of Delta Biotechnology Ltd. In 1995, BOC Distribution Services acquired TLO in France and London Cargo Group in the UK, and in Chile, the Group acquired a 41 per cent interest in Indura. In 1995, there were several disposals which included the Medical Engineering Systems business of Ohmeda and a retail gases operation in the US.

No significant fair value adjustments were made in 1997, 1996 or 1995.

b) Profit and loss on disposal and closure of businesses
In accordance with Group accounting policy, goodwill paid on acquisition of a business is written off as part of the profit or loss on disposal. During the year there was no goodwill written off on disposals (1996: £20.9 million, 1995: £1.0 million).

Group undertakings

A list of the Group's major operating undertakings, certain financing undertakings and undertakings in which the Group has a material interest is detailed below. All holdings shown are Ordinary shares. Undertakings are held either by The BOC Group plc or through other operating undertakings or through undertakings formed for the convenient holding of shares in certain subsidiary or associated undertakings. The Group holding percentages shown below represent the ultimate interest of The BOC Group plc. All companies are incorporated and registered in the country in which they operate as listed below.

	Group holding %		Group holding %
Aruba		**Fiji**	
BOC Gases Aruba NV	100	BOC Gases Fiji Ltd	88
Australia		**Finland**	
BOC Cargo Services Australia Pty Ltd	100	BOC Ohmeda Oy	100
BOC Gases Australia Ltd[3]	100	**France**	
South Pacific BOC Ramp Services		BOC Gaz SA	100
Australia Pty Ltd	50	Cryostar-France SA	100
Elgas Ltd	50	Edwards SA	100
Bangladesh		Ohmeda SA	100
BOC Bangladesh Ltd	60	Transports Logistique Organisation SA	100
Belgium		**Germany**	
BOC Cylinder Gas NV	100	BOC Gase GmbH	100
BOC NV	100	Edwards Hochvakuum GmbH	100
		Ohmeda GmbH & Co KG[2]	50
Bermuda		**Hong Kong**	
Priestley Insurance Company Ltd	100	The BOC Group Ltd	100
Brazil		Hong Kong Oxygen & Acetylene Co Ltd	50
BOC do Brasil Ltda	100	**India**	
Brunei		BOC India Ltd	55
Brunei Oxygen Sdn Bhd	25	**Indonesia**	
Canada		PT BOC Gases Indonesia	98
BOC Canada Ltd	100	PT Gresik Gases Indonesia	90
Chile		**Ireland**	
Indura S.A., Industria y Comercio	41	BOC Gases Ireland Ltd	100
Colombia		**Italy**	
Gases Industriales de Colombia SA	50	Edwards Alto Vuoto SpA	100
		Ohmeda SpA	100
Czech Republic		**Japan**	
BOC Logistic s.r.o.	100	BOC Japan Ltd	100
Denmark		Edwards Japan Ltd	90
BOC Ohmeda A/S	100	Ohmeda Ltd	100
England		Osaka Sanso Kogyo Ltd[2]	50
BOC Distribution Services Ltd	100	**Kenya**	
BOC Holdings[1,3]	100	BOC Kenya Ltd	65
BOC Ltd	100	**Korea**	
BOC Netherlands Holdings Ltd	100	BOC Distribution Korea Ltd	100
BOC Overseas Finance Ltd	100	Songwon Edwards Ltd	90
BOC Technologies Ltd	100	BOC Gases Korea Co Ltd	100
Edwards High Vacuum International Ltd	100		
London Cargo Group Ltd	100		
Ohmeda[1]	100		

	Group holding %
Malawi	
Industrial Gases Ltd[2]	44
Malaysia	
Malaysian Oxygen Bhd	28
Mauritius	
Les Gaz Industriels Ltée	20
Namibia	
IGL Properties (Pty) Ltd	57
Netherlands	
BOC Edwards Calumatic BV	100
BOC Gas BV	100
Kroeze Distributie BV	100
Ohmeda BV	100
Netherlands Antilles	
BOC Gases Curaçao NV	100
New Zealand	
BOC Gases New Zealand Ltd	100
Nigeria	
Industrial Gases plc	60
Norway	
Odda Smelteverk A/S	100
Pakistan	
BOC Pakistan Ltd	60
Papua New Guinea	
BOC Gases Papua New Guinea Pty Ltd	74
Peoples' Republic of China	
BOC Gases (North) Co Ltd	100
BOC Gases (Shanghai) Corporation Ltd	100
BOC Gases (Wuhan) Co Ltd	100
BOC Keppel Gases (Suzhou) Co Ltd	55
BOC Tisco Gases Co Ltd	50
Fushun BOC Industrial Gases Co Ltd	50
Shanghai BOC Industrial Gases Co Ltd	50
Shenyang BOC Gases Ltd	50
Tianjin BOC Industrial Gases Co Ltd	70
Philippines	
Consolidated Industrial Gases Inc	40
Southern Industrial Gases Philippines Inc	40
Poland	
BOC Gazy Sp. z o.o.	89
Puerto Rico	
Ohmeda Caribe, Inc	100

	Group holding %
Russia	
Volgograd Oxygen Factory AOOT	77
Singapore	
Ohmeda (Singapore) Pte Ltd	100
Singapore Oxygen Air Liquide Pte Ltd	50
Solomon Islands	
BOC Gases Solomon Islands Ltd	100
South Africa	
African Oxygen Ltd[3]	57
Afrox Ltd	57
Amalgamated Medical Services Ltd	57
Spain	
Ohmeda SA	100
Sweden	
BOC Ohmeda AB	100
Switzerland	
BOC AG	100
Taiwan	
BOC Lienhwa Industrial Gases Co Ltd	50
Thailand	
Thai Industrial Gases Public Co Ltd[2,3]	45
Turkey	
Birlesik Oksijen Sanayi AS	50
US	
The BOC Group, Inc[3]	100
BOC, Inc	100
Ohmeda, Inc	100
Ohmeda Medical Devices Division, Inc	100
Ohmeda Pharmaceutical Products Division, Inc	100
Venezuela	
BOC Gases de Venezuela, C.A.[3]	100
Vietnam	
North Vietnam Industrial Gases Ltd	50
Western Samoa	
BOC Gases (Western Samoa) Ltd	64
Zimbabwe	
BOC Zimbabwe (Pvt) Ltd	100

1. Unlimited companies having share capitals with registered offices at the same address as The BOC Group plc.
2. Consolidated as subsidiary undertakings because of dominant influence or indirect control through another partly-owned Group subsidiary. Other undertakings listed above owned 50 per cent or less are accounted for as associated undertakings.
3. Group undertakings which made acquisitions or investments during the year.

Appendix B: Sources of comparative statistics and data

The leading organization producing comparative statistics and data is the Centre for Interfirm Comparison (a non-profit undertaking jointly established by the British Institute of Management and the British Productivity Council). The Centre's main activity is the conduct of inter-firm comparisons as a service to management; it also advises on the use of management ratios within companies. It carries out comparative surveys and research activities in the field of performance assessment. For further information contact the Centre for Interfirm Comparison, Capital House, 48 Andover Road, Winchester, Hampshire SO23 7BH (telephone 01962 844144).

One of the principal commercial organizations producing individual business ratio reports and financial surveys for each of a wide range of industrial sectors is ICC Information Ltd. The reports present details of profitability, liquidity and efficiency ratios for the main companies operating in each industry. For further information contact ICC Information Ltd, ICC Field House, 72 Oldfield Road, Hampton, Middlesex TW12 2HQ (0181 481 8800).

Other companies active in the field of comparative information provision include the following: Datastream ICV, Monmouth House, 58–64 City Road, London EC1Y 2AL (0171 253 3000); Extel Financial Ltd, 13–17 Epworth Street, London EC2A 4DL (0171 251 3333); Jordan and Sons Ltd, 21 St Thomas Street, Bristol, Avon BS1 6JS (0117 923 0600); Dunn and Bradstreet Ltd, Holmers Farm Way, High Wycombe, Buckinghamshire HP12 4UL (01494 422000); Standard and Poor Compustat, Wimbledon Bridge House, 1 Hartfield Road, Wimbledon, London SW19 3RU (0181 543 2555); Syspas Ltd, Dyers' Hall, 11–13 Dowgate Hill, London EC4R 2SU (0171 236 1024).

In addition to these services, there are several annual or regular directories and yearbooks that contain valuable financial, organizational and statistical data on relevant companies. The *Times 1000* is an annual publication giving details of the turnover and capital employed, profit margin and return on total capital employed ratios (in addition to a considerable amount of other information) for each of the 1,000 largest British industrial and commercial companies, and for a wide range of financial institutions. The *Stock Exchange Official Year Book* is an annual publication giving full corporate and financial information on all companies listed on the Stock Exchange, including a summarized balance sheet and capital formation details for each company. The

Institute of Chartered Accountants in England and Wales issues *Financial Reporting*, an annual survey of published accounts which reports the results of detailed analyses of the reporting practices of a sample of 300 large industrial and commercial companies.

Government statistical bulletins and digests are useful sources of aggregated financial and performance data. The Office of National Statistics produces a monthly digest of financial information entitled *Financial Statistics*.

Finally, the directories, yearbooks and member publications of professional associations and trade bodies frequently provide financial and organizational information on their members and their activities. There are a considerable number of national and international directories and guides listing 'key' or sizeable enterprises; these entries are usually restricted to basic organizational and product information, but they form useful starting points for identifying appropriate companies and their activities.

In terms of examining the actual published annual reports and accounts of individual companies, a number of the largest municipal libraries throughout the UK maintain up-to-date collections of annual reports and accounts. The Guildhall Library in London has perhaps the largest accessible collection of such reports and accounts, while many university and business school libraries possess selective collections. For a considerable number of companies, key financial and operational data are available on a variety of computer tapes and information systems as, for example, the London Business School's or the Manchester Business School's computerized company records. The London Business School issues the quarterly *Risk Measurement Service* report, which details selected investment data for all quoted companies and provides risk measures for each company.

There are three major sources of computer-based financial information, FAME, Datastream and Extel. A copy of the FAME print-out for BOC is included in this appendix. This provides standard information about the company, name, address, SIC codes, etc., with five years figures for the profit and loss account, balance sheet, and the most recent cash flow statement. A selection of important ratios for the past five years is given including some trend ratios. A credit score and rating is given which is provided by Qui Score. Further information concerning directors, subsidiaries, etc. is provided by FAME but is not included here for space reasons. (The FAME print-out is provided by courtesy of Jordans Ltd.)

BOC GROUP PLC(THE)

R/O Address	: CHERTSEY ROAD		JW Company
	WINDLESHAM	Registered No	: 00022096
	SURREY	Type of company	Public, Not Quoted
	GU20 6HJ	Date of Incorporation	: 1/26/86
R/O Phone	: 01276 - 477222	Accounting Ref.Date	: 9/30
R/O Post Code	: GU20	Accounts Type	: Full
		Company Status	: Live

Latest Turnover	: 3,677,700 th GBP	Number of Holdings : 0	
Latest No of Employees	: 40,733	Number of Subsid. : 51	

Activities :   Holding company, whose subsidiaries are involved in production of gases and
related products; health care and vacuum technology

1992 SIC UK codes	: **Primary Code**	: 2411 - Manufacture of industrial gases
	Secondary Code(s)	: 2411, 2442, 2912
1981 SIC UK codes	: **Primary Code**	: 2511 - Inorganic chemicals except industrial gases
	Secondary Code(s)	: 25110, 25670, 25700, 32893, 34350, 37100, 37201, 61800, 83962

PROFILE

	9/97 12 Months th GBP Cons.	9/96 12 Months th GBP Cons.	9/95 12 Months th GBP Cons.	9/94 12 Months th GBP Cons.	9/93 12 Months th GBP Cons.	Average 5 Years th GBP
Turnover	3,677,700	3,752,100	3,543,900	3,292,300	3,235,500	3,500,300
Profit (Loss) before Tax	445,200	444,900	402,200	253,100	337,600	376,600
Net Tangible Assets (Liab.)	3,363,400	3,067,600	2,809,200	2,818,700	2,555,300	2,922,840
Shareholder Funds	1,892,800	1,818,700	1,655,600	1,509,800	1,488,800	1,673,140
Profit Margin (%)	12.11	11.86	11.35	7.69	10.43	10.69
Return on Shareholder Funds (%)	23.52	24.46	24.29	16.76	22.68	22.34
Return on Capital Employed (%)	13.12	14.35	14.15	8.86	12.98	12.69
Liquidity Ratio	0.82	0.76	0.76	0.93	0.79	0.81
Gearing (%)	111.99	104.77	107.30	105.66	106.56	107.25
Number of Employees	40,733	40,495	39,680	39,421	40,266	40,119

PROFIT & LOSS ACCOUNT

	9/97 12 Months th GBP Cons.	9/96 12 Months th GBP Cons.	9/95 12 Months th GBP Cons.	9/94 12 Months th GBP Cons.	9/93 12 Months th GBP Cons.	Average 5 Years th GBP
Turnover	3,677,700	3,752,100	3,543,900	3,292,300	3,235,500	3,500,300
UK Turnover						
Export Turnover						
Cost of Sales	-2,105,500	-2,115,500	-1,986,600	-1,882,500		-2,022,525
Total Expenses						
Gross Profit	1,572,200	1,636,600	1,557,300	1,409,800		1,543,975
Depreciation	-3,600	-268,700	-256,500			-176,266
Other Expenses	-1,028,200	-886,000	-804,400	-1,076,000		-948,650
Operating Profit	540,400	481,900	496,400	333,800		463,125
Other Income	24,900	84,000	25,100	20,600		38,650
Exceptional Items	0	0	0	0		
Profit (Loss) before Interest	565,300	565,900	521,500	354,400	420,800	485,580
Interest Paid	-120,100	-121,000	-119,300	-101,300	-83,200	-108,980
Profit (Loss) before Tax	445,200	444,900	402,200	253,100	337,600	376,600
Taxation	-129,100	-137,900	-128,600	-121,700	-115,400	-126,540
Profit (Loss) after Tax	316,100	307,000	273,600	131,400	222,200	250,060
Extraordinary Items	-28,500	-28,700	-24,600	-17,800	-18,300	-23,580
Profit (Loss) for Period	287,600	278,300	249,000	113,600	203,900	226,480
Dividends	-140,400	-130,100	-118,800	-110,600	-110,100	-122,000
Retained Profit(Loss)	147,200	148,200	130,200	3,000	93,800	104,480
Discontinued Operations						
Audit Fee	2,900	1,800	2,000	2,000	2,000	2,140
Remuneration	909,200	917,000	875,400	854,300	822,400	875,660
Directors' Remuneration		6,570	6,000			6,285
Highest Paid Director			1,000			1,000
Number of Employees	40,733	40,495	39,680	39,421	40,266	40,119

BALANCE SHEET

	9/97 12 Months th GBP Cons.	9/96 12 Months th GBP Cons.	9/95 12 Months th GBP Cons.	9/94 12 Months th GBP Cons.	9/93 12 Months th GBP Cons.	Average 5 Years th GBP
Fixed Assets						
Tangible Assets	2,953,700	2,747,600	2,561,700	2,374,300	2,295,500	2,586,560
Land & Building	917,900	539,000	551,200			669,366
Fixtures & Fittings	351,700	604,300	508,500			488,166
Plant & Vehicles	1,684,100	1,604,300	1,502,000			1,596,800
Intangible Assets	28,800	33,400	33,800	38,400	44,900	35,860
Investm. & Other Fixed Assets	319,500	286,300	255,700	191,900	190,200	248,720
Fixed Assets	3,302,000	3,067,300	2,851,200	2,604,600	2,530,600	2,871,140
Current Assets						
Stock & W.I.P.	354,300	403,400	363,500	328,100	317,800	353,420
Stock	281,300	311,600	285,900			292,933
W.I.P.	73,000	91,800	77,600			80,800
Trade Debtors	702,800	703,300	722,200	617,200	678,500	684,800
Bank & Deposits	222,200	155,800	183,800	132,800	258,500	190,620
Other Current Assets	317,500	306,200	241,700	227,400	0	218,560
Group Loans (asset)	0	0	0		0	0
Directors Loans (asset)	0	0	0		0	0
Other Debtors	183,400	202,800	150,700		0	134,225
Investm. & Other Cur. Assets	134,100	103,400	91,000		0	82,125
Current Assets	1,596,800	1,568,700	1,511,200	1,305,500	1,254,800	1,447,400
Current Liabilities						
Trade Creditors	-332,600	-346,700	-360,200	-323,200	-558,100	-384,160
Short Term Loans & Overdrafts	-620,400	-623,100	-589,000	-247,900	-475,000	-511,080
Bank Overdrafts	-619,800	-264,200	-262,800			-382,266
Group Loans (short t.)	0	0	0			0
Director Loans (long t.)	0	0	0			0
Hire Purch. & Leas. (short t.)	-600	-1,400	-1,800			-1,266
Hire Purchase (short t.)		0	0			0
Leasing (short t.)		-1,400	-1,800			-1,600
Other Short Term Loans	0	-357,500	-324,400			-227,300
Total Other Current Liabilities	-553,600	-565,200	-570,200	-481,900	-152,100	-464,600
Corporation Tax	0	-104,800	-93,600			-66,133
Dividends	0	0	0			0
Accruals & Def. Inc. (sh. t.)	-118,400	-113,000	-92,200			-107,866
Social Securities & V.A.T.	-149,700	-36,600	-41,900			-76,066
Other Current Liabilities	-285,500	-310,800	-342,500			-312,933
Current Liabilities	-1,506,600	-1,535,000	-1,519,400	-1,053,000	-1,185,200	-1,359,840
Net Current Assets (Liab.)	90,200	33,700	-8,200	252,500	69,600	87,560
Net Tangible Assets (Liab.)	3,363,400	3,067,600	2,809,200	2,818,700	2,555,300	2,922,840
Working Capital	724,500	760,000	725,500	622,100	438,200	654,060
Total Assets	4,898,800	4,636,000	4,362,400	3,910,100	3,785,400	4,318,540
Total Assets less Cur. Liab.	3,392,200	3,101,000	2,843,000	2,857,100	2,600,200	2,958,700
Long Term Liabilities						
Long Term Debt	-1,001,200	-767,400	-667,800	-855,000	-659,200	-790,120
Group Loans (long t.)	-997,100	0	0			-332,366
Director Loans (long t.)	0	0	0			0
Hire Purch. Leas. (long t.)	-4,100	-5,200	-6,100			-5,133
Hire Purchase (long t.)		0	0			0
Leasing (long t.)		-5,200	-6,100			-5,650
Other Long Term Loans	0	-762,200	-661,700			-474,633
Total Other Long Term Liab.	-498,200	-514,900	-519,600	-492,300	-452,200	-495,440
Accruals & Def. Inc. (l. t.)	0	0	0			0
Other Long Term Liab.	-268,500	0	-31,000			-99,833
Provisions for Other Liab.	-229,700	-514,900	-488,600			-411,066
Deferred Tax		-41,700	-42,000			-41,850
Other Provisions		-473,200	-446,600			-459,900
Long Term Liabilities	-1,499,400	-1,282,300	-1,187,400	-1,347,300	-1,111,400	-1,285,560
Total Assets less Liabilities	1,892,800	1,818,700	1,655,600	1,509,800	1,488,800	1,673,140
Shareholders Funds						
Issued Capital	124,300	123,300	122,600	119,500	121,400	122,220
Total Reserves	1,768,500	1,695,400	1,533,000	1,390,300	1,367,400	1,550,920
Share Premium Account	272,400	259,400	250,500	0		195,575
Revaluation Reserves	63,800	71,900	77,200	0		53,225
Profit (Loss) Account	1,320,700	1,252,500	1,117,800	993,200		1,171,050
Other Reserves	111,600	111,600	87,500	397,100		176,950
Shareholders Funds	1,892,800	1,818,700	1,655,600	1,509,800	1,488,800	1,673,140

CASH FLOW STATEMENT

	9/97 12 Months th GBP Cons.	9/96 12 Months th GBP Cons.	9/95 12 Months th GBP Cons.	9/94 12 Months th GBP Cons.	9/93 12 Months th GBP Cons.	Average 5 Years th GBP
Net Cash In(Out)flow Operat. Activ.	733,800					733,800
Net Cash In(Out)flow Ret. on Invest.	-104,000					-104,000
Taxation	-109,500					-109,500
Net Cash Out(In)flow Investing Activ.						
Capital Expenditure & Financial Investment	-625,300					-625,300
Acquisition & Disposal	-38,600					-38,600
Equity Dividends Paid	-121,500					-121,500
Management of Liquid Resources	-62,300					-62,300
Net Cash Out(In)flow from Financing	364,200					364,200
Increase(Decrease) Cash & Equiv.	36,800					36,800

FINANCIAL RATIOS

	9/97	9/96	9/95	9/94	9/93	Average
Current Ratio	1.06	1.02	0.99	1.24	1.06	1.07
Liquidity Ratio	0.82	0.76	0.76	0.93	0.79	0.81
Shareholders Liquidity Ratio	1.26	1.42	1.39	1.12	1.34	1.31
Solvency Ratio (%)	38.64	39.23	37.95	38.61	39.33	38.75
Asset Cover	4.89	6.04	6.53	4.57	5.74	5.56
Gearing (%)	111.99	104.77	107.30	105.66	106.56	107.25
Shareholders Funds per Empl. (Unit)	46,468	44,912	41,724	38,299	36,974	41,675
Working Capital per Employee (Unit)	17,787	18,768	18,284	15,781	10,883	16,300
Total Assets per Employee (Unit)	120,266	114,483	109,940	99,188	94,010	107,577

FINANCIAL TRENDS (%)

	1997 - 96	1996 - 95	1995 - 94	1994 - 93
Fixed Assets	7.65	7.58	9.47	2.92
Current Assets	1.79	3.80	15.76	4.04
Stock	-12.17	10.98	10.79	3.24
Debtors	-0.07	-2.62	17.01	-9.03
Total Assets	5.67	6.27	11.57	3.29
Current Liabilities	-1.85	1.03	44.29	-11.15
Creditors	-4.07	-3.75	11.45	-42.09
Loans/Overdraft	-0.43	5.79	137.60	-47.81
Long Term Liabilities	16.93	7.99	-11.87	21.23

FINANCIAL CHANGES (th GBP)

	1997 - 96	1996 - 95	1995 - 94	1994 - 93
Fixed Assets	234,700	216,100	246,600	74,000
Current Assets	28,100	57,500	205,700	50,700
Stock	-49,100	39,900	35,400	10,300
Debtors	-500	-18,900	105,000	-61,300
Total Assets	262,800	273,600	452,300	124,700
Current Liabilities	-28,400	15,600	466,400	-132,200
Creditors	-14,100	-13,500	37,000	-234,900
Loans/Overdraft	-2,700	34,100	341,100	-227,100
Long Term Liabilities	217,100	94,900	-159,900	235,900

PROFITABILITY RATIOS

	9/97	9/96	9/95	9/94	9/93	Average
Profit Margin (%)	12.11	11.86	11.35	7.69	10.43	10.69
Return on Shareholder Funds (%)	23.52	24.46	24.29	16.76	22.68	22.34
Return on Capital Employed (%)	13.12	14.35	14.15	8.86	12.98	12.69
Return on Total Assets (%)	9.09	9.60	9.22	6.47	8.92	8.66
Interest Cover	4.71	4.68	4.37	3.50	5.06	4.46
Stock Turnover	10.38	9.30	9.75	10.03	10.18	9.93
Debtors Turnover	5.23	5.33	4.91	5.33	4.77	5.12
Debtor Collection (days)	69.75	68.42	74.38	68.43	76.54	71.50
Creditors Payment (days)	33.01	33.73	37.10	35.83	62.96	40.53
Net Assets Turnover	1.08	1.21	1.25	1.15	1.24	1.19
Fixed Assets Turnover	1.11	1.22	1.24	1.26	1.28	1.22
Salaries/Turnover (%)	24.72	24.44	24.70	25.95	25.42	25.05
Turnover per Employee (Unit)	90,288	92,656	89,312	83,516	80,353	87,225
Average Remun. per Year (Unit)	22,321	22,645	22,061	21,671	20,424	21,825
Profit per Employee (Unit)	10,930	10,987	10,136	6,420	8,384	9,371

PROFITABILITY TRENDS (%)

	1997 - 96	1996 - 95	1995 - 94	1994 - 93
Turnover	-1.98	5.87	7.64	1.76
Profit before Taxation	0.07	10.62	58.91	-25.03
Interest Paid	-0.74	1.42	17.77	21.75
Number of Employees	0.59	2.05	0.66	-2.10

PROFITABILITY CHANGES

	1997 - 96	1996 - 95	1995 - 94	1994 - 93
Turnover (th GBP)	-74,400	208,200	251,600	56,800
Profit before Taxation (th GBP)	300	42,700	149,100	-84,500
Interest Paid (th GBP)	900	-1,700	-18,000	-18,100
Number of Employees	238	815	259	-845

Credit Score & Rating

Current QuiScore	(Year ending 9/97)	64	Stable
Previous Period's QuiScore	(Year ending 9/96)	61	Stable

QuiRating (£)   100,000

The calculations are based on accounts for relevant periods.
The QuiScore and QuiRating have been devised by Qui Credit assesment Ltd.
They must be interpreted and used in the light of the information provided by Qui Credit Assesment Ltd.

	9/97 12 Months th GBP Cons.	9/96 12 Months th GBP Cons.	9/95 12 Months th GBP Cons.	9/94 12 Months th GBP Cons.	9/93 12 Months th GBP Cons.	Average 5 Years th GBP
Turnover	3,677,700	3,752,100	3,543,900	3,292,300	3,235,500	3,500,300
Profit (Loss) before Tax	445,200	444,900	402,200	253,100	337,600	376,600
Net Tangible Assets (Liab.)	3,363,400	3,067,600	2,809,200	2,818,700	2,555,300	2,922,840
Shareholder Funds	1,892,800	1,818,700	1,655,600	1,509,800	1,488,800	1,673,140

Directors

D.E. Baird CHAIRMAN	4/7/97
Mr D.G. John CHAIRMAN	4/7/97
R.F. Chase MANAGING DIRECTOR	4/7/97
F.D. Rosenkranz CHIEF EXECUTIVE	4/7/97
A.E. Isaac FINANCE DIRECTOR	4/7/97
D. Chatterji DIRECTOR	4/7/97
H.C. Groome DIRECTOR	4/7/97
Mr C.P. King DIRECTOR	4/7/97
J.H. Macdonald DIRECTOR	4/7/97
C.S. Tedmon DIRECTOR	4/7/97
G.J. Stuart COMPANY SECRETARY Company Secretary	4/7/97
S. Ghasemi PRESIDENT	4/7/97
Dr R.G. Stoll PRESIDENT	4/7/97

Appendix C: Glossary of accounting terms

accounting concepts	The assumptions underlying the preparation of financial statements. The basic assumptions of going concern, accruals, consistency and prudence are included in this glossary.
accounting period	The period for which accounts are prepared, usually one year.
accounting policies	The specific accounting methods used by a business organization when preparing its accounts.
accounts payable	Alternative expression for *creditors*, i.e. amounts owing by a business to suppliers of goods and services.
accounts receivable	Alternative expression for *debtors*, i.e. amounts owing to a business by customers who have not yet paid for goods or services received.
accruals	The accounting concept which requires that revenues and expenses are recognized in the *accounting period* in which they are earned or incurred rather than in the period in which they are received or paid.
advance corporation tax (ACT)	The tax a company is required to pay to the Inland Revenue when it pays a dividend. The amount paid can usually be set off against the total liability to corporation tax for the year.
amortization	Alternative expression for *depreciation*, particularly that due mainly to the passage of time.
annual report	A report sent annually to the shareholders of a

company. It contains the financial statements and explanatory notes, the report of the auditors, the chairman's statement and the directors' report.

asset	Any property or rights owned by a company that have expected future economic benefits.
associated company	A company over which another company or group of companies has a significant influence. An associated company is essentially the same as a *related company*. A company will normally be assumed to be an associated/related company if between 20 per cent and 50 per cent of its ordinary share capital is owned by another company or group of companies.
bad debt	An amount owing from *debtors* which is not expected to be received.
capital employed	Usually refers to the total of the funds invested by shareholders plus the long-term debt.
capital expenditure	Expenditure on fixed assets.
cash flow	The receipts of cash by and payment of cash from a business.
cash flow statement	A financial statement that reports the cash receipts and cash payments of an accounting period. Financial Reporting Standard No. 1 requires all companies to publish a cash flow statement.
close company	A UK company which is controlled by not more than five shareholders or their families or partners.
consistency	The accounting concept that a company should use the same accounting policies over time.
consolidated accounts	A set of financial statements which combine the accounts of a *parent company* and its *subsidiaries* as if they were a single entity.
contingencies	Conditions (usually liabilities) that are known at the date of balance sheet, but of which the future outcome (i.e. the amount of the liability) is not known for certain.
corporation tax	The tax that is payable by companies.
cost of sales/cost of goods sold	The costs of making the products that have been sold in a period (usually consists of raw material, labour and production overhead).

creditors	Amounts owing by a business to suppliers of goods and services.
current assets	Assets which are already in the form of cash or are expected to be converted into cash within one year from the date of the balance sheet.
current cost accounting	A system of accounting which adjusts for changing prices.
current liabilities	Amounts which a company owes which are expected to be paid within one year from the date of the balance sheet. (Also referred to as 'Creditors: amounts falling due within one year'.)
debentures	Long-term loans which are usually secured on the assets of a company.
debtors	Amounts owing to a business from customers.
deferred asset	An amount owed to a company that is not expected to be received within one year from the date of the balance sheet.
deferred taxation	An estimate of the tax liability payable at some future date that is due to timing differences in the accounting treatment and taxation treatment of some types of income and expenditure. For example, the depreciation allowed for tax purposes (*capital allowances*) will usually be greater than the depreciation used for accounting purposes in the early years of an asset's life, but the situation will be reversed in later years.
depreciation	A charge against the profit of an *accounting period* to represent the estimated proportion of the cost of a fixed asset which has been consumed (whether through use, obsolescence or the passage of time) during that period.
dividend	The amount distributed to shareholders out of the profits of a company. Large companies will normally pay an interim dividend part way through the financial year, with a final dividend paid after the end of the financial year when it has been approved by the shareholders.
equity method	A method of accounting for investments in *associated companies*.
equity share capital	An alternative expression for the normal type of ownership finance, i.e. ordinary shares. It is defined as any issued share capital which has

unlimited rights to participate in either the distribution of dividends or capital.

exceptional items

Items appearing in the profit and loss account that arise within the ordinary course of business, but are of unusual size.

extraordinary items

Items of income and expenditure which are significant in amount and which are outside the normal activities of a business.

fixed assets

Assets such as land, buildings and machines which are intended for use on a continuing basis by the business rather than for sale.

gearing

The proportion of the *capital employed* of a company that is financed by lenders rather than shareholders.

going concern

An accounting concept which assumes that a business will continue in operation for the foreseeable future.

goodwill

The amount paid for a business which exceeds the fair value of the assets acquired.

gross profit

The difference between the value of sales and the *cost of sales*.

group accounts

The financial statements of a group of companies. These are usually presented in the form of *consolidated accounts*.

historical cost accounting

The conventional system of accounting under which assets are recorded at the original cost of acquiring or producing them.

holding company

A company which owns or controls other companies. (Control can occur through the ownership of 50 per cent of the voting rights or through the exercise of a dominant influence.)

inflation accounting

A system of accounting which, unlike *historical cost accounting*, takes account of changing prices.

insolvency

This occurs when a business is unable to pay debts as they fall due.

intangible assets

Assets such as *goodwill*, patents, trademarks, etc. which have no physical or tangible form.

interim report

A half-yearly or quarterly report issued by a company to its shareholders. *Listed companies* are required to publish an interim report.

issued share capital	The amount of the share capital of a company that has been issued to shareholders.
liabilities	The amounts owing by a company.
liquidity	The ability of a company to meet its immediate liabilities.
listed company	A public company listed or quoted on a stock exchange.
listed investments	Investments which are listed or quoted on a stock exchange.
loan capital	Alternative name for debt capital, i.e. the amounts borrowed by a company as a long-term source of finance.
mainstream corporation tax	The amount of a company's total liability to corporation tax for a year that has not previously been paid as *advance corporation tax*.
materiality	An accounting concept which states that the normal rules of accounting concerning valuation or disclosure need only be applied to amounts that are significant or important.
minority interests	The share capital of a subsidiary company that is not held by the *parent* company. When consolidated accounts are prepared, 100 per cent of the assets, liabilities, revenues and expenses of all subsidiaries are normally included. However, not all subsidiaries are 100 per cent owned and in such cases a minority of the shares will be left in the ownership of what are known as minority shareholders. The interests of these minority shareholders in the capital of the group (i.e. the minority interests) are shown separately in the consolidated balance sheet.
net current assets	An alternative name for *working capital*, i.e. the current assets less current liabilities of a company.
net realizable value	The amount at which an asset could be sold less the costs incurred in its sale.
net assets	The total of all the assets less liabilities to outsiders. This is equal to the *shareholders' funds*.
off balance sheet financing	Financing operations in such a way that some or all of the finance does not appear as a balance sheet item.

operating profit	Profit before the deduction of interest and tax.
ordinary shares	Shares which entitle the owners to share in the profits remaining after deducting loan interest, taxation and *preference share* dividends.
parent company	Similar to a *holding company*, i.e. a company which owns, or has effective control over the activities of, another company (its subsidiary).
post balance sheet events	Events occurring after the date of the balance sheet but before the accounts are issued. These can be events that require adjustment of the financial statements ('adjusting events') and events that require disclosure but do not require adjustment to the financial statements ('non-adjusting events').
preference shares	Shares which normally have preference over *ordinary* shares for payment of dividends and for repayment of capital if a company is wound up. Preference shares are usually entitled to a fixed rate of dividend.
private company	A company that is not allowed to issue shares or loan stock to the public.
profit	The excess of the revenues earned in a period over the costs incurred in earning them.
provision	An amount charged against profit to provide for an expected liability or loss even though the amount or date of the liability or loss is uncertain.
prudence	An accounting concept which requires that provisions be made for all known liabilities or losses when calculating profit but that any gains or revenues should only be included when realized in cash or near cash (e.g. debtors).
public company	A company whose shares and loan stock may be publicly traded. A public company must have 'public limited company' (or plc) as part of its name.
registrar of companies	A government official who is responsible for collecting and arranging public access to the annual reports of all companies.
related companies	The Companies Act term for what are essentially *associated companies*.
replacement cost accounting	A system of accounting in which assets (and related expenses such as depreciation) are valued

at what it would cost to replace them.

reserves	Reserves consist of the accumulated profits that have been retained by a company, plus any surplus from the revaluation of assets, plus any share premium. Reserves belong to shareholders and are part of *shareholders' funds*.
retained profits	Profits that have not been paid out as dividends to shareholders, but retained for further investment by the company.
revaluation reserve	The gain or loss arising from the revaluation of assets.
rights issue	The issue of new shares by a company to existing shareholders. The 'rights' to buy the new shares are usually fixed at a price below the current market price.
share capital	The nominal value of the shares that have been issued by a company.
share premium	The amount received by a company for its shares that is in excess of their nominal value.
shareholders' funds	The total of the shareholders' interest in a company. It consists of share capital plus reserves and is equal to the *net assets* of the company.
short-term debt	A type of *current liability*. A loan that is repayable within one year from the date of the balance sheet.
solvency	The ability to pay debts as they become due.
statement of total recognized gains and losses	A statement of all the gains and losses (both realized and unrealized) of an accounting period that are attributable to shareholders. Financial Reporting Standard No. 3 requires all companies to publish this statement.
stocks and work in progress	This consists of items purchased for resale and includes raw materials required for production, partially completed products (work in progress) and finished products.
subsidiary	A company that is controlled by another company (a parent company). Control can occur because either more than 50 per cent of the voting rights are owned by another company or because a 'dominant influence' is exercised by another company.

tangible assets	Normally applied to those *fixed assets* that have a physical existence, such as land and buildings, plant and machinery.
total assets	The total of the fixed assets and current assets of a company.
turnover	The sales revenue of an accounting period.
unlisted investments	Investments which are not listed on a stock exchange.
window dressing	Manipulation of financial statements in order to give a misleading or unrepresentative impression.
working capital	An alternative name for *net current assets*, i.e. the current assets less current liabilities of a company.
written down value	The value of assets in the books of a company. This is usually the historical cost less the cumulative amount of depreciation written-off at the balance sheet date.

Appendix D: Glossary of ratios

A glossary of the ratios used in the text is given below. A more detailed explanation of the terms in these ratios can be found in either the glossary of accounting terms (Appendix C) or the appropriate chapters.

Profitability and performance

Return on capital employed (ROCE)

$$\frac{\text{Trading profit before interest, taxation and extraordinary items}}{\text{Average capital employed}} \times 100$$

measures the efficiency with which the long-term capital has been employed.

Return on total assets (ROTA)

$$\frac{\text{Trading profit before interest, taxation and extraordinary items}}{\text{Average total assets for the period}} \times 100$$

measures the efficiency of the overall trading return on the business as a whole.

Return on net total assets

$$\frac{\text{Trading profit before interest, taxation and extraordinary items}}{\text{Average net total assets for the period}} \times 100$$

measures the efficiency of the trading return on the net assets of the business.

Return on equity (ROE)

$$\frac{\text{Profit after interest and preference dividends but before tax and extraordinary items}}{\text{Average ordinary share capital, reserves and retained profit for the period}} \times 100$$

measures the company's efficiency in earning profits on behalf of its ordinary shareholders.

Earnings per share (EPS)

$$\frac{\text{Profit after interest, taxation and preference dividends but before extraordinary items}}{\text{Average number of ordinary shares outstanding in the year}} \times 100$$

measures the return per share of earnings available to shareholders. (Alternative methods of computation are given in the text.)

Price-earnings ratio (PE ratio)

$$\frac{\text{Market price per share}}{\text{Earnings per share}}$$

reflects the stock market's expectations of the future earnings of the company. The higher the number, the greater the expectations.

Return on sales (ROS)

$$\frac{\text{Trading profit before interest, taxation and extraordinary items}}{\text{Total sales}} \times 100$$

measures the profit margin on sales, i.e. on a company's trading activity.

Asset turnover

$$\frac{\text{Total sales}}{\text{Average (net) total assets}}$$

The asset figure can be either total or net total assets depending on which other profitability ratios are being calculated. The ratio measures the performance of the company in generating sales from the assets at its disposal.

Quality of profit

$$\frac{\text{Net cash inflow from operations}}{\text{Operating profit}} \times 100$$

Operating profit is net profit before interest, exceptional items and tax. This gives an indication of the amount of operating profit received in cash terms during the year.

Quality of sales

$$\frac{\text{Cash from customers}}{\text{Sales}} \times 100$$

gives the proportion of sales received in cash during the year.

Cash return on capital employed

$$\frac{\text{Net cash inflow from operations}}{\text{Average capital employed}} \times 100$$

Net cash inflow includes dividends from related undertakings during the year. This ratio measures the cash return generated by the long-term capital employed in the business (cash equivalent to ROCE).

Cash return on total assets

$$\frac{\text{Net cash inflow from operations and investments}}{\text{Average total assets for the period}} \times 100$$

measures the cash return from trading and investment by the business as a whole.

Efficiency and effectiveness

Debtor turnover

$$\frac{\text{Sales}}{\text{Trade debtors}}$$

The year-end debtors are taken. The ratio gives the number of times the debtors are turned over in the year, measuring efficiency of collection.

Average collection period

$$\frac{\text{Trade debtors}}{\text{Sales}} \times 365$$

is the average time it takes to collect the cash from the debtors.

Creditor turnover

$$\frac{\text{Purchases}}{\text{Trade creditors}}$$

gives the number of times the trade creditors are turned over in the year.

Creditor payment period

$$\frac{\text{Trade creditors}}{\text{Purchases}} \times 365$$

gives the average length of time the company is taking before it pays its creditors.

Stock turnover

$$\frac{\text{Cost of sales for the period}}{\text{Stock at the end of the period}}$$

gives the frequency with which the stock is turned over during the year.

Stock-turnover period

$$\frac{\text{Stock at the end of the period}}{\text{Cost of sales for the period}} \times 365$$

reveals the average period that items are held in stock.

Employee efficiency

$$\frac{\text{Wages for the period}}{\text{Sales for the period}} \times 100$$

gives the proportion of sales paid out in employee costs.

Sales per employee

$$\frac{\text{Sales for the period}}{\text{Average number of employees}}$$

measures the amount of sales generated per employee.

Return per employee

$$\frac{\text{Operating profit}}{\text{Average number of employees}}$$

gives the profitability of the company per employee.

Value added per employee

$$\frac{\text{Value added}}{\text{Average number of employees}}$$

provides the average value added by each employee.

Capital employed per employee

$$\frac{\text{Capital employed}}{\text{Average number of employees}}$$

states the average amount of assets employed in relation to the employees used by the company.

Specific costs to sales ratios

(a) $$\frac{\text{Administration costs}}{\text{Sales}} \times 100$$

(b) $$\frac{\text{Research and development costs}}{\text{Sales}} \times 100$$

(c) $$\frac{\text{Manufacturing costs}}{\text{Sales}} \times 100$$

Each of these, and similar ratios for other costs, are primary measures of the impact of these different costs on profits.

Liquidity and stability

Current ratio (working-capital ratio)

$$\frac{\text{Current assets}}{\text{Current liabilities}}$$

measures the amount of liquid and near liquid resources available to meet short-term creditors.

Quick ratio (acid test ratio)

$$\frac{\text{Current assets minus stocks}}{\text{Current liabilities}}$$

i.e.

$$\frac{\text{Net monetary assets}}{\text{Current liabilities}}$$

This ratio concentrates on more readily realizable, or liquid, assets available to meet short-term creditors.

Cash interest cover

$$\frac{\text{Net cash inflow from operations and interest received}}{\text{Interest paid}}$$

measures the sufficiency of cash from operations from which the interest can be paid.

Cash dividend cover

$$\frac{\substack{\text{Net cash inflow from operations and interest received} \\ \text{Dividends received from related undertakings} \\ -\text{Interest paid} - \text{Tax paid} - \text{Dividend paid to preference shareholders}}}{\text{Dividend paid to equity shareholders}}$$

measures availability of net cash from operations after payment of financing and tax charges for payment of ordinary dividends.

Cash debt coverage

$$\frac{\substack{\text{Net cash inflow from operations} - \text{Tax paid} \\ -\text{ Interest and dividends paid} + \text{Interest and dividends received}}}{\text{Loans maturing within next year}} \times 100$$

This ratio states the percentage of loans to be repaid in the next year that can be met out of the net cash inflow from operating activities.

Defensive interval

$$\frac{\text{Quick assets (net monetary assets)}}{\text{Average daily operating cash outflows}}$$

shows how many days a company could survive at its present level of operating activity if no inflow of cash was received from sales or other sources.

Capital structure, investment and financial risk

Long-term debt to equity ratio

$$\frac{\text{Long-term loans + Preference shares}}{\text{Ordinary shareholders' funds}} \times 100$$

measures the ratio of long-term borrowing to equity.

Long-term debt to total long-term finance ratio

$$\frac{\text{Long-term loans + Preference shares}}{\substack{\text{Long-term loans + Preference shares and} \\ \text{ordinary shareholders' funds}}} \times 100$$

provides an alternative way of considering what is sometimes called the debt to equity ratio. It shows the amount of long-term debt finance as a percentage of total long-term finance.

Total debt to total assets ratio

$$\frac{\text{Long-term loans + Short-term loans}}{\text{Total assets}}$$

provides a measure of asset coverage for all outstanding loans.

Interest cover
Traditional

$$\frac{\text{Profit before interest and tax and extraordinary items}}{\text{Gross interest payable}}$$

calculates the number of times the interest payable is covered by profits available for such payments.

Dividend cover

$$\frac{\text{Profit available for paying ordinary dividends}}{\text{Ordinary dividends (net)}}$$

gives an indication of the extent to which profits cover dividends. (It is the reciprocal of the payout ratio.)

Fixed assets to total assets ratio

$$\frac{\text{Fixed assets}}{\text{Total assets}} \times 100$$

gives the proportion of total assets that consist of fixed assets.

Long-term funds to total assets ratio

$$\frac{\text{Long-term liabilities + Preference shares and ordinary shareholders' funds}}{\text{Total assets}} \times 100$$

measures the proportion of total assets funded by long-term funds.

Total owing to total assets ratio

$$\frac{\text{Short- and long-term creditors}}{\text{Total assets}} \times 100$$

provides the proportion of total assets financed by third-party funds.

Capital gearing

$$\frac{\text{Profit before interest, tax and extraordinary items}}{\text{Profit before tax and extraordinary items}}$$

highlights the effects on profits brought about by the interest paid on borrowings.

Capital expenditure to turnover

$$\frac{\text{Capital expenditure for the year}}{\text{Sales}} \times 100$$

gives an indication of the level of capital expenditure incurred to sustain the particular level of sales.

Capital expenditure to depreciation

$$\frac{\text{Capital expenditure for the year}}{\text{Annual depreciation expense}}$$

gives an indication of the replacement rate of new for old assets.

Capital expenditure to tangible fixed assets ratio

$$\frac{\text{Capital expenditure for the year}}{\text{Gross book value of tangible fixed assets}} \times 100$$

is a better ratio for giving an indication of the replacement rate of new for old assets.

Capital acquisitions ratio

$$\frac{\begin{array}{c}\text{Net cash inflow from operations}\\ -\text{ Net interest paid} - \text{Dividends paid} - \text{Tax paid}\end{array}}{\text{Net cash outflow on investment}} \times 100$$

indicates the proportion of investment expenditure on both new and replacement assets financed by internally generated funds.

Leased assets to tangible fixed assets

$$\frac{\text{Net book value of leased assets}}{\text{Net tangible fixed assets}} \times 100$$

indicates the proportion of tangible fixed assets which are leased rather than owned by the company.

Further reading

Altman, E.I. (1968) 'Financial ratios, discriminant analysis and the prediction of corporate bankruptcy', *Journal of Finance*, September.

Altman, E.I., Haldeman, R.G. and Narayanan, P. (1977) 'Zeta analysis: a new model to identify bankruptcy risk of corporations', *Journal of Banking and Finance*, June.

Anderson, O.D. (1976) *Time Series Analysis and Forecasting*, London: Butterworth.

Argenti, J. (1976) *Corporate Collapse*, New York: McGraw-Hill.

Bartley, J.W. and Boardman, C.M. (1990) 'The relevance of inflation adjusted accounting data to the prediction of corporate takeovers', *Journal of Business Finance & Accounting* 17 (1), Spring.

Beaver, W.H. (1966) 'Financial ratios as predictors of failure', *Empirical Research in Accounting*, supplement to *Journal of Accounting Research*.

Beaver, W.H. (1981) *Financial Reporting: An Accounting Revolution*, Englewood Cliffs, NJ: Prentice Hall.

Belkaoui, A. (1983) *Industrial Bonds and the Rating Process*, Westport, CT: Quorum Books.

Bernstein, L.A. (1978) *The Analysis of Financial Statements*, Homewood, IL: Dow-Jones/Irwin.

Blake, J. (1987) *Company Reports and Accounts: Their Significance and Uses*, London: Pitman.

Cadbury Report (1992) *Report of the Committee on the Financial Aspects of Corporate Governance*, London: Gee & Co.

Ellis, J. and Williams, D. (1993) *Corporate Strategy and Financial Analysis*, London: Pitman.

Ernst & Young (1997) *UK GAAP*, London: Macmillan.

Foster, G. (1986) *Financial Statement Analysis*, 2nd edn, Englewood Cliffs, NJ: Prentice Hall.

Gibson, C.H. and Boyes, P.A. (1979) *Financial Statement Analysis*, Boston, MA: CBI Publishing.

Ingham, H. and Harrington, L.T. (1980) *Interfirm Comparison*, London: Heinemann.

Institute of Chartered Accountants of Scotland (1988) *Making Corporate Reports Valuable*, London: Kogan Page.

Institute of Chartered Accountants of Scotland (1993) *Auditing into the Twenty-first*

Century, a discussion document issued by the Research Committee of the ICAS, Edinburgh.

Johnson, B. and Patient, M. (1985) *Accounting Provisions of the Companies Act 1985*, London: Farringdon Publishing.

Journal of Business Finance & Accounting (1990) 'Special issue on financial statement analysis', 17 (1), Spring.

Keasey, K. and Watson, R. (1987) 'Non-financial symptoms and the prediction of small company failure: a test of Argentis Hypothesis', *Journal of Business Finance and Accounting* 14 (3).

Lee, T.A. (ed.) (1981) *Developments in Financial Reporting*, Oxford: Allan.

Lee, T.A. (1982) *Company Financial Reporting: Issues and Analysis*, 2nd edn, Wokingham: Van Nostrand Reinhold.

Lee, T.A. and Tweedie, D.P. (1977) *The Private Shareholder and the Corporate Report*, London: Institute of Chartered Accountants in England and Wales.

Lee, T.A. and Tweedie, D.P. (1981) *The Institutional Investor and Financial Information*, London: Institute of Chartered Accountants in England and Wales.

Lev, B. (1974) *Financial Statement Analysis: A New Approach*, Englewood Cliffs, NJ: Prentice Hall.

Lewis, R. and Pendrill, D. (1996) *Advanced Financial Accounting*, 5th edn, London: Pitman.

McLeay, S.J. (1991) 'International financial analysis', in C.W. Nobes and R.H. Parker (eds), *Comparative International Accounting*, Englewood Cliffs, NJ: Prentice Hall.

Mepham, M.J. (1980) *Accounting Models*, Stockport: Polytech.

Palepu, K. (1986) 'Predicting takeover targets: a methodological and empirical analysis', *Journal of Accounting and Economics*, March.

Parker, R.H. (1994) *Understanding Company Financial Statements*, 4th edn, Harmondsworth: Penguin.

Peel, M.J. (1990) *The Liquidation/Merger Alternative: Theory and Evidence*, Avebury: Aldershot.

Peel, M.J. and Peel, D.A. (1987) 'Some further empirical evidence on predicting private company failure', *Accounting and Business Research*, Winter.

Platt, H.D. and Platt, M.B. (1990) 'Developments of a class of stable predictive variables: the case of bankruptcy prediction', *Journal of Business Finance & Accounting* 17 (1), Spring.

Platt, H.D., Platt, M.B. and Pedersen, J.G. (1994) 'Bankruptcy discrimination with real variables', *Journal of Business Finance and Accounting* 21(4), June.

Pratton, C. (1991) *Company Failure*, Financial and Auditing Group, London: ICAEW.

Rappaport, A. (1986) *Creating Shareholder Value – The New Standard for Business Performance*, New York: The Free Press.

Rege, U.P. (1984) 'Accounting ratios to locate take-over targets', *Journal of Business Finance and Accounting*, Autumn.

Slater, J.D. (1996) *The Zulu Principle*, 3rd edn, London: Orion Books.

Smith, T. (1996) *Accounting for Growth*, 2nd edn, Century Business Books.

Stock Exchange (1979 *et seq.*) *Admission of Securities to Listing*, latest edn, London: Stock Exchange.

Swinson, C. (1990) *A Guide to the Companies Act*, 1989, London: Butterworth.

Taffler, R.J. (1983) 'The Z-score approach to measuring company solvency', *Accountant's Magazine*, March.

Taffler, R.J. (1984) 'Empirical methods for the monitoring of U.K. corporations', *Journal of Banking and Finance*, June.

Taffler, R.J. and Tisshaw, H. (1977) 'Going, going, gone – four factors which predict', *Accountancy*, March.

Tamari, M. (1978) *Financial Ratios: Analysis and Prediction*, London: Elek.

Taylor, P. and Turley, S. (1986) *The Regulation of Accounting*, Oxford: Blackwell.

Tolley's Corporation Tax (annually) Croydon: Tolley.

Ward, T.J. (1994) 'An empirical study of the incremental predictive ability of Beaver's naive operating flow measure using four-state ordinal models of financial distress', *Journal of Business Finance and Accounting* 21(4), June.

Ward, T.J. and Foster, B.P. (1997) 'A note on selecting a response measure for financial distress', *Journal of Business Finance and Accounting* 24(6), July.

Index